I0823597

H. af Klint

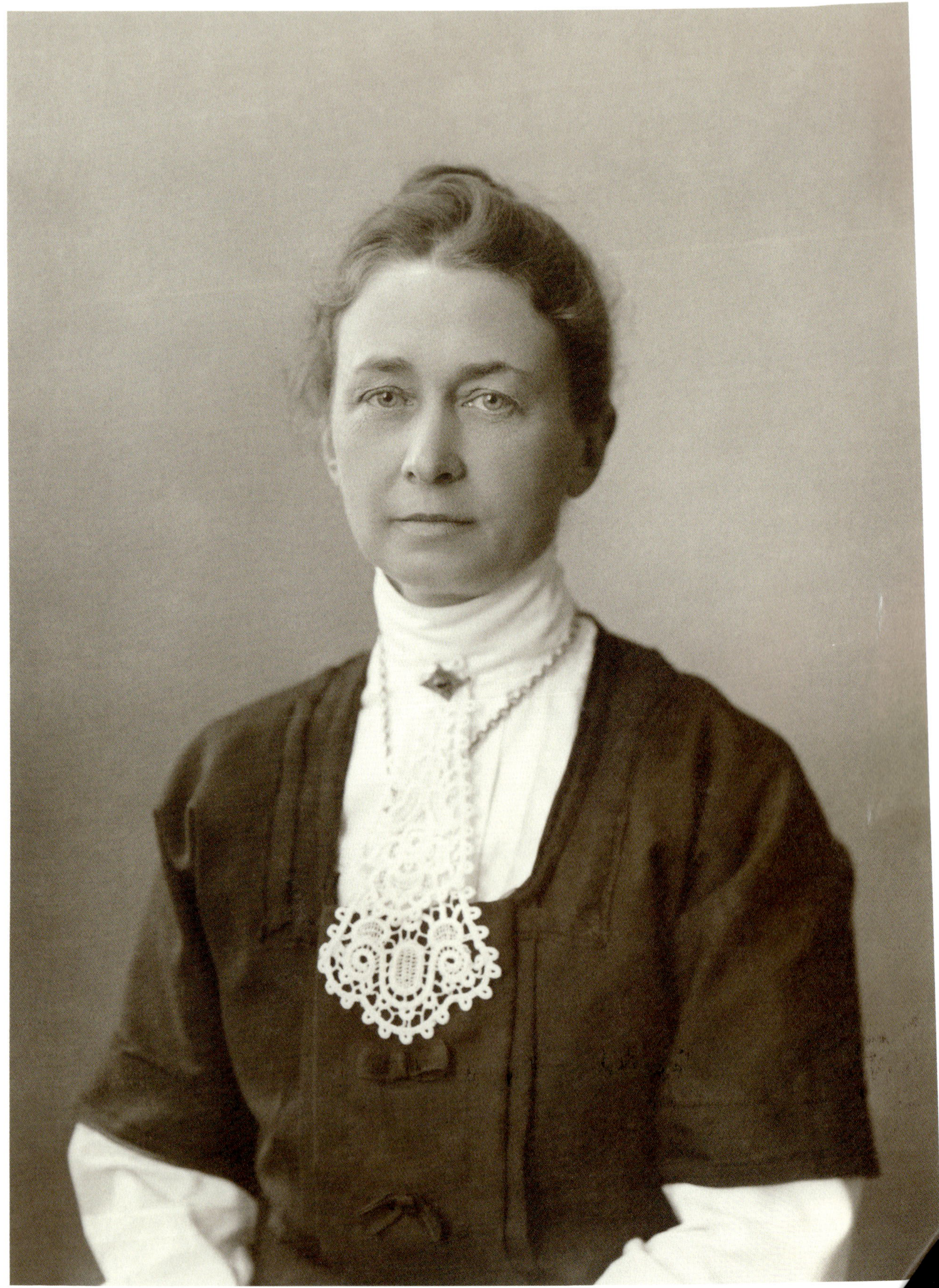

Janis Mink

Hilma af Klint

1862–1944

Art as Spiritual Quest

TASCHEN

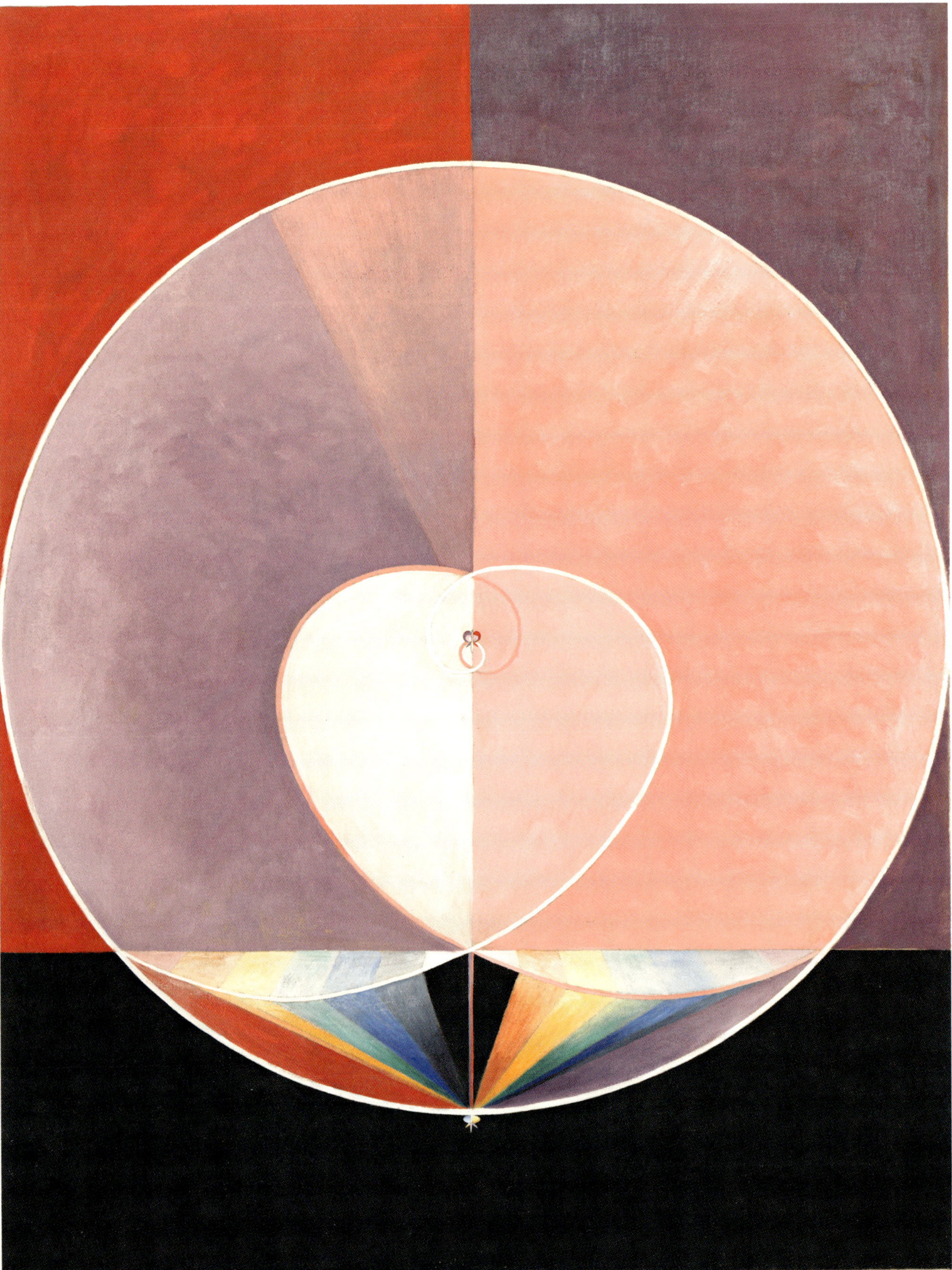

Contents

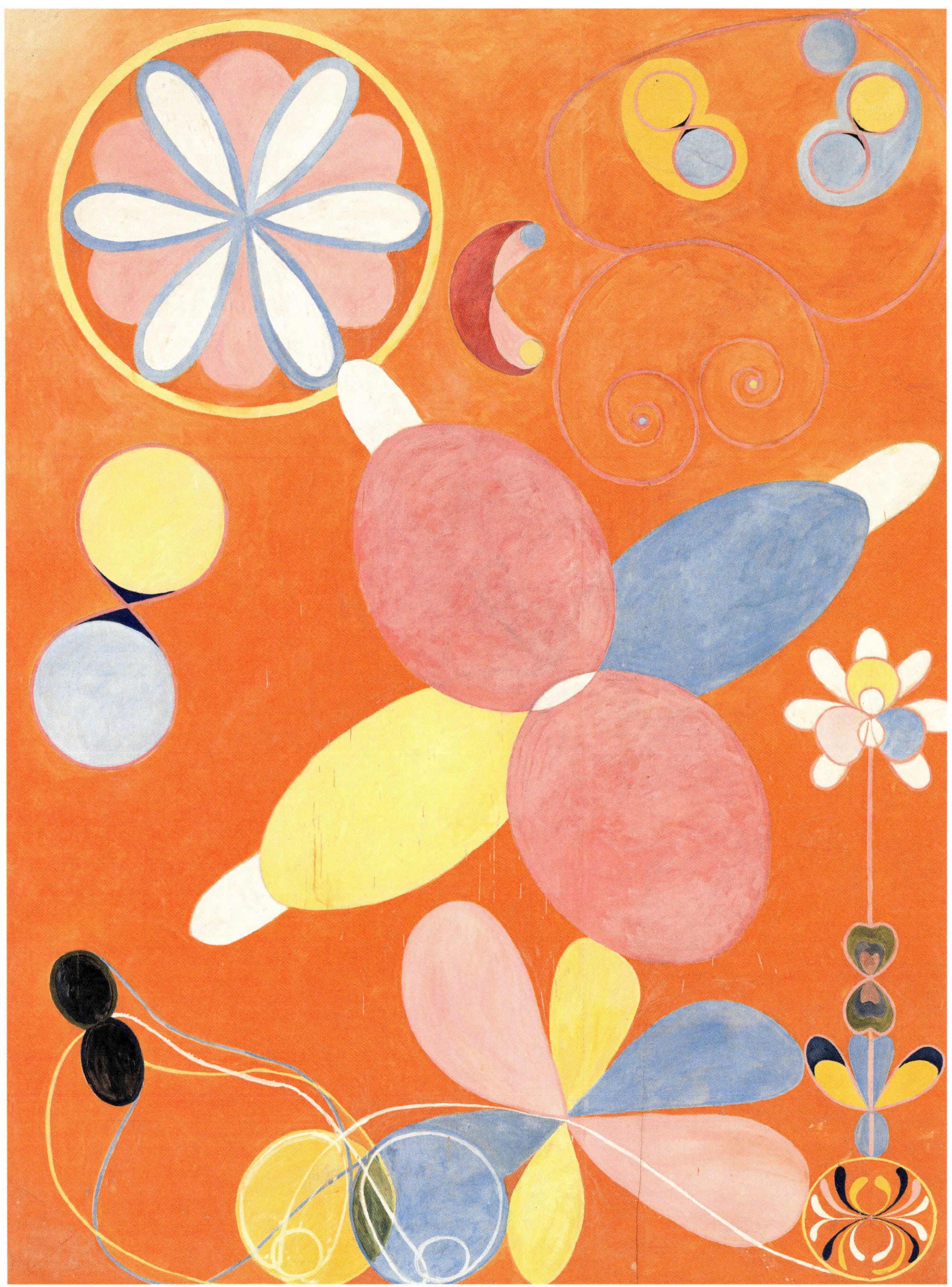

Introduction: Lift Off

When Hilma af Klint (1862–1944) painted her very large picture *The Ten Largest, Group IV: No. 4, Youth* (*Ynglingaåldern*) (p. 6) at the age of 45, she had safely navigated herself past what would have been considered a marriageable age. She lived with her mother and worked as a professional artist painting commissioned portraits, selling landscapes, and sometimes illustrating texts. As drawings from her art academy years showed, she could deftly render human anatomies from both living models and plaster casts. She could also accurately draw botanical ornament and specimens, architectural detail, and household objects. However, the "youth" she pictured in her 1907 painting looked altogether different from the naturalistic and commercial work at which she had been trained to excel. This painting didn't hail from the academy. The large scale of the picture was new. Its vibrant colors made no reference to a seascape or landscape. The painting's forms did not assemble into a recognizable scene or person. No perspective charted depth or believable space.

Instead, *No. 4, Youth* demonstrated a busy, dynamic athleticism. Warmth and energy exude from the work even today. A convergence of geometric shapes kinks over into dance, as if a body abstracted by movement and costume were projected onto a flat screen. Vignettes surround the convergence, telling tales in a sign language that only the initiated understood, but others can intuit. Two rounded shapes repeat as a couple, one blue and one yellow, and approach each other in several different areas of the painting, extending their small dark tips towards each other as if to touch. In the lower right corner, a folkloristic, ornamental plant shape with an inverted, heart-shaped flower touches the point of another heart-headed element bearing down like an arrow from above. The entire lower edge of the painting is occupied by the outlines of two intertwined and reclining figures, whose dark heads meet in a kiss, or a dark eternity. Af Klint only *almost* shows such things—she distills, invents, relates, and subverts in her image of the youthful joy of life.

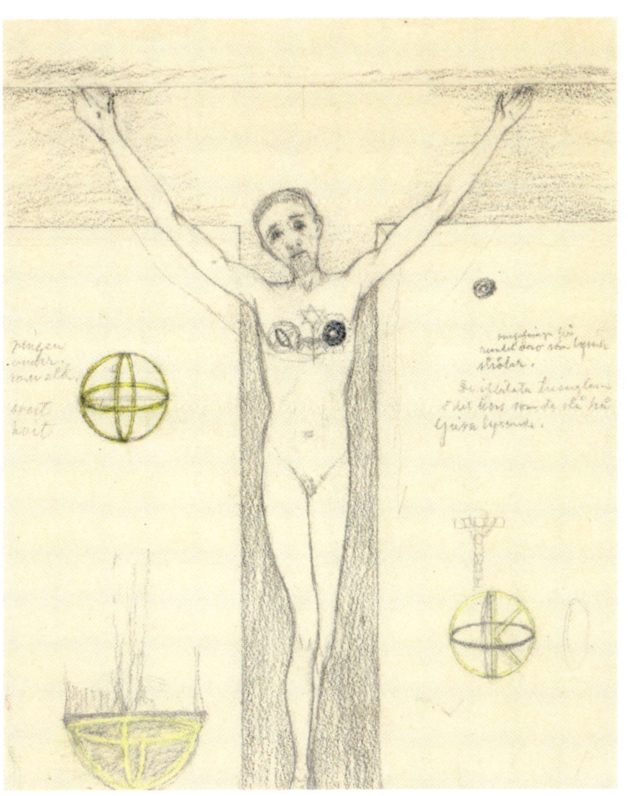

Symbolistic Study (Symbolistisk studie), 1913
Graphite and crayon on paper,
30 x 24 cm (11⅞ x 9½ in.)
Stockholm, Hilma af Klint Foundation,
HaK 1748

The Ten Largest, Group IV: No. 4, Youth (Ynglingaåldern), 1907
Tempera on paper mounted on canvas,
315 x 234 cm (124 x 92¼ in.)
Stockholm, Hilma af Klint Foundation, HaK 105

Today, an audience no longer expecting only naturalistic art can experience a painting like *No. 4, Youth* as a total lift-off, a picturing of that memory of first sensations of sexual touch, the effervescent, even giddy realization of how one and one equals far more than two. This fresh-faced young thing with a wheel or a petaled flower for a head has loosened its stays, and cartwheels into a peachy place: Devachan, the realm of the gods (*The US Series*, p. 9). Ecstasy may be found here.

It hardly seems possible that af Klint, whose family name means "cliff," would jump off one and take such pictorial risks (*Picture Painted 1931*, p. 8). Seemingly bound to the earthly existence of an upper-class woman born in Sweden in 1862, she transcended gender expectations (*Symbolistic Study*, p. 7), bloomed within a collective of like-minded females, and communicated freely with spirit realms and nature. As an artist, she had the confidence to commit paintings that were incomprehensible during her own lifetime to a posterity she was sure would fully appreciate what she did. Society would evolve, be able to understand. After all, even she herself could not completely discern the meaning of the spiritual paintings she let loose upon the world.

Picture Painted 1931 (Bilder från år 1931), 1931
Watercolor on paper, 29 x 23 cm (11½ x 9 in.)
Stockholm, Hilma af Klint Foundation, HaK 780

OPPOSITE ABOVE
The US Series, Group VII: No. 4, 1908
Watercolor and graphite on paper,
26 x 36 cm (10¼ x 14¼ in.)
Stockholm, Hilma af Klint Foundation, HaK 88

OPPOSITE BELOW
The US Series, Group VII: No. 11, 1908
Watercolor and graphite on paper,
26 x 36 cm (10¼ x 14¼ in.)
Stockholm, Hilma af Klint Foundation, HaK 95

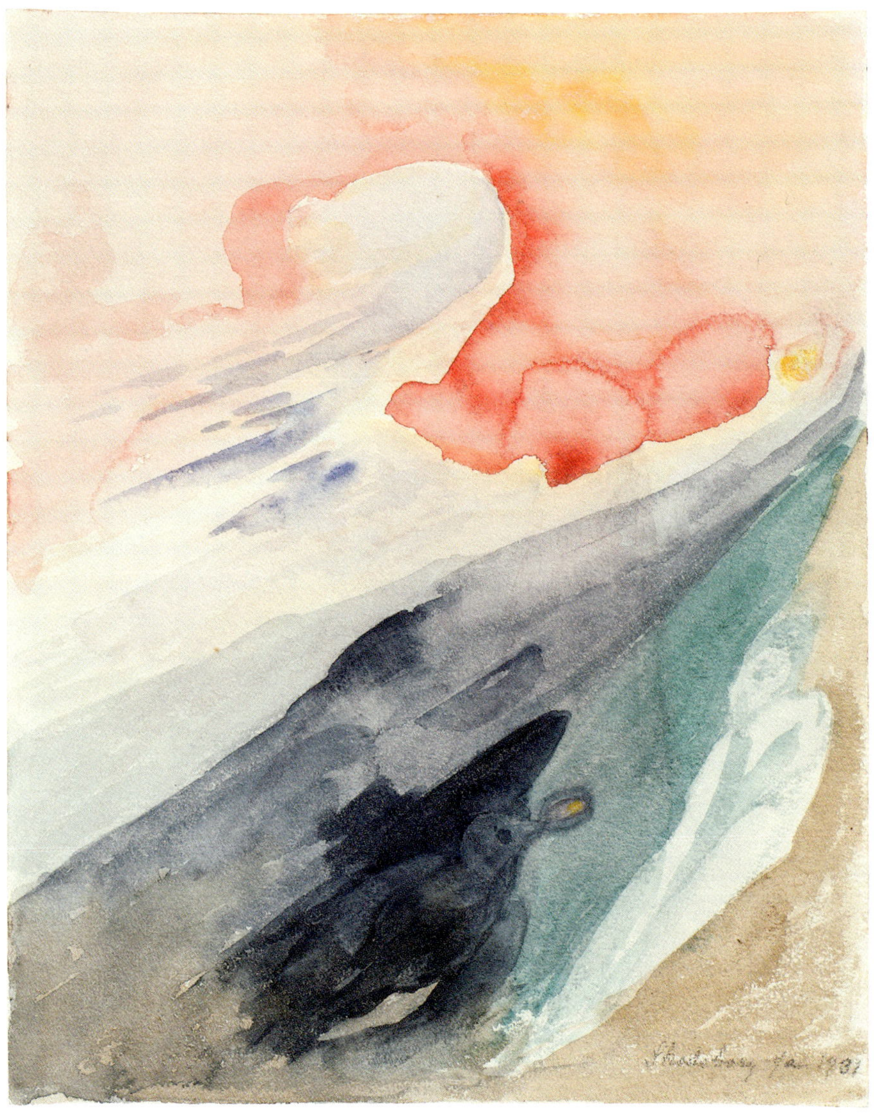

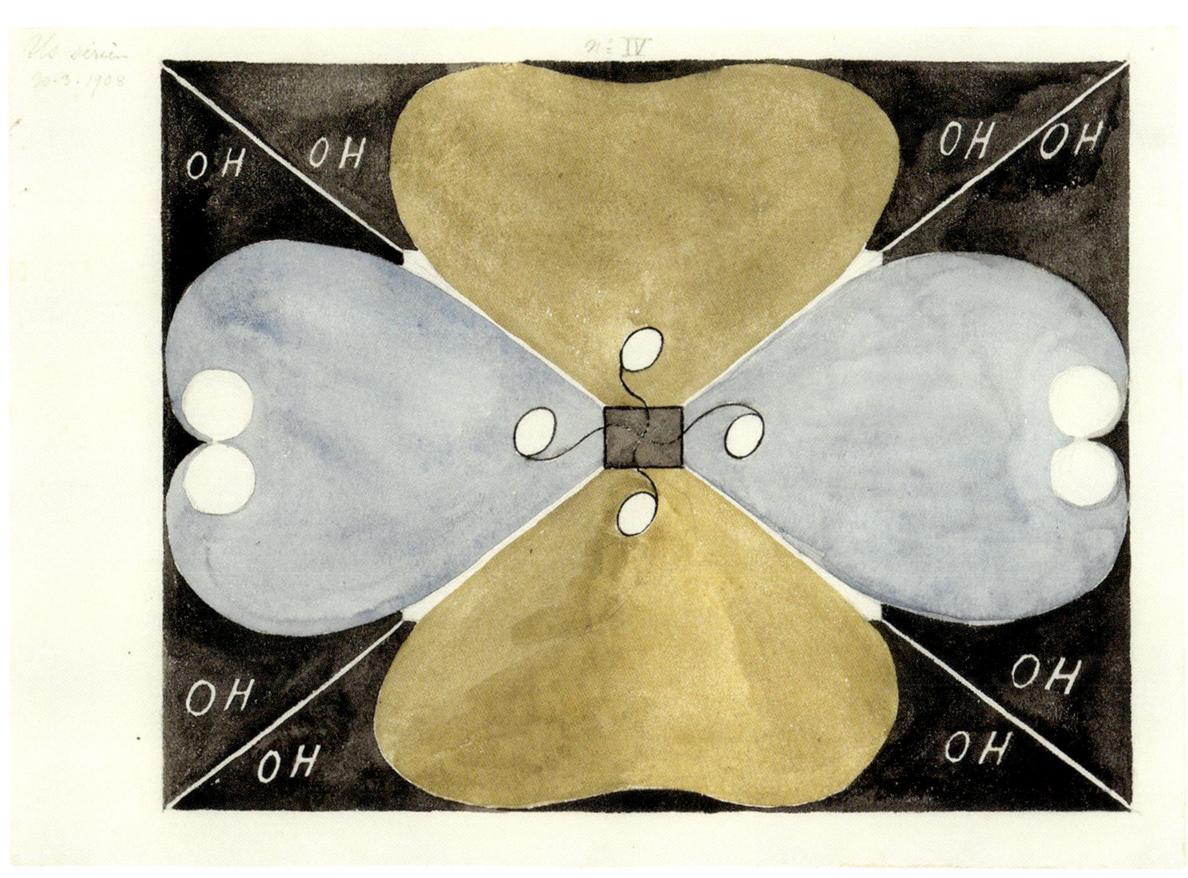
OH
OH
OH
OH
OH
OH
OH
OH

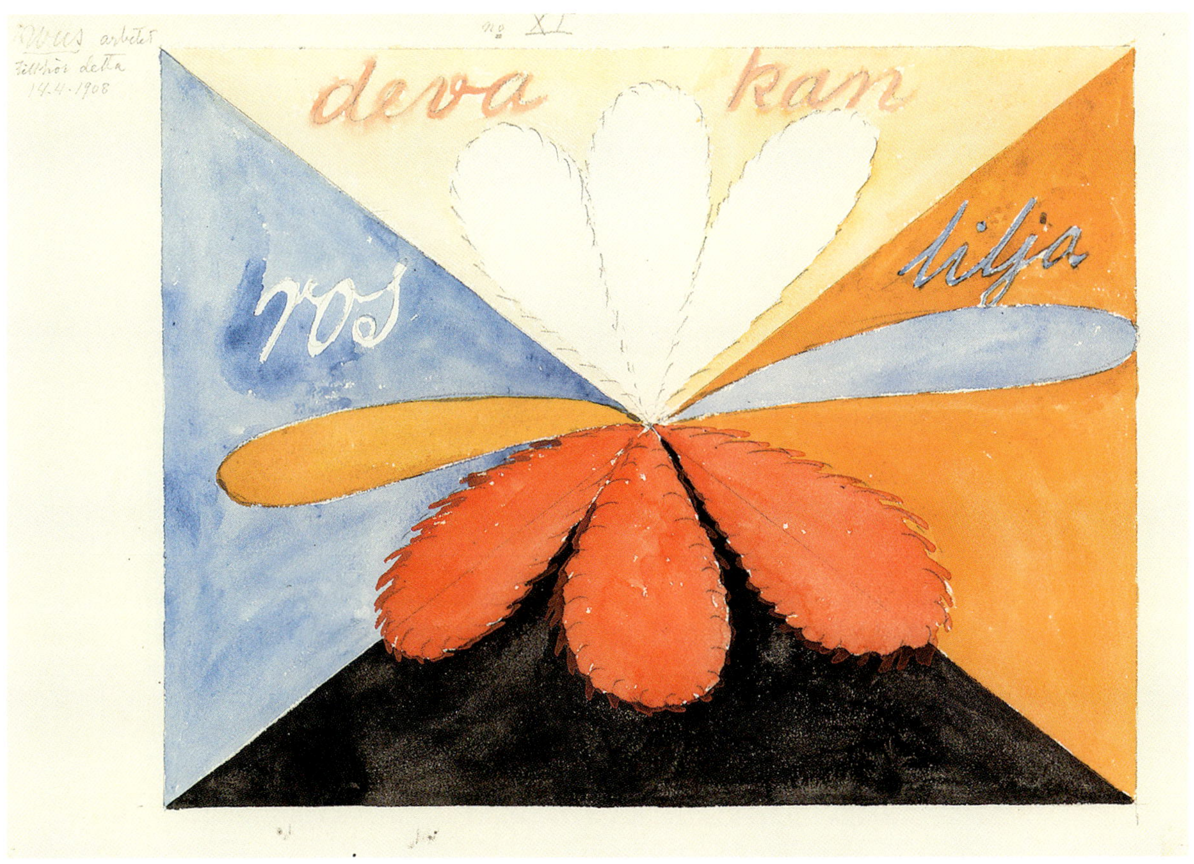
deva
kan
ros
lilja

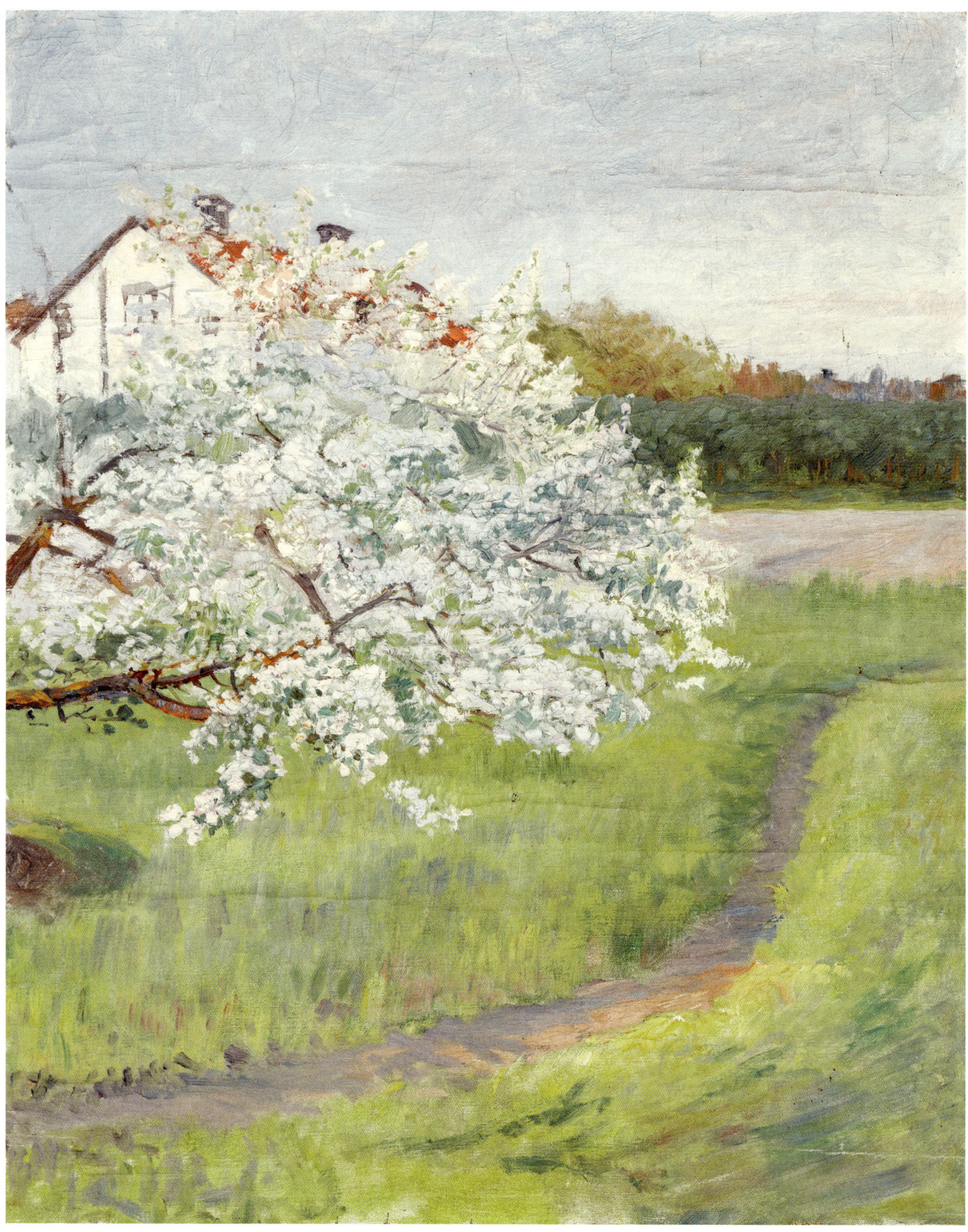

In This Life:
Youth, Studies, and Early Professional Career

While she did not believe it was her first incarnation, the artist Hilma af Klint began her life on earth on October 26, 1862, in Solna, just northwest of Stockholm's center. The af Klint family lived on the waterfront in a large northern Renaissance-style palace that also housed a Swedish military academy for naval officers, which her father, the naval commander Victor af Klint (1822–1898), directed (*Winter Landscape with Boat* and *Cityscape*, pp. 12 and 14). Her mother, Mathilda Sonntag (1832–1920), hailed from Finland as a member of the Swedish upper class there, and was the directing force behind af Klint family life. Hilma came into the world as her mother's fourth child; the family included two other children two years apart, Gustaf, a boy, and Ida, a girl, and a firstborn girl that had died as a toddler. Another girl, Hermina, would be born when Hilma af Klint was eight years old.

The artist's father was not the first af Klint to run the Karlberg Military Academy. Hilma's naval officer great-grandfather, Erik (1732–1812), had been academy director, and some of his male descendants followed him and were appointed to its leadership. Erik had displayed military prowess against Russia, and in 1790 he was knighted and granted the noble signification "af" for the Klint family name by King Gustav III. The family was then allowed to buy property and invested in two estates on the island of Adelsö, one of the islands in Lake Mälaren, just west of Stockholm (*Fruit Tree in Blossom near House*, p. 10).

Erik and his son Gustaf (1771–1840) earned additional renown as cartographers. Commissioned by Sweden's king, father and son surveyed and mapped their country's coastline and its depths. Having discovered a passion, Gustaf, who was Hilma's grandfather, further cultivated this skill. He continued to draw many more maps, including charts of the North and Baltic Seas, the Norwegian coast, and other Swedish water bodies, published as atlases (*The First Modern Atlas of the Baltic Sea*, p. 11). His scientific observations and patient plumbing of the watery depths pitted his intelligence and wherewithal against nature as he sailed away from the social strictures of an urban setting. As an older woman, Hilma af Klint would still receive some royalties from her grandfather's work. Maps and mapping stood for af Klint family accomplishment, but also enterprise and freedom.

Little is documented of the artist's early childhood, except that her first six years were spent in the environs of the military academy. Karlberg Palace is a

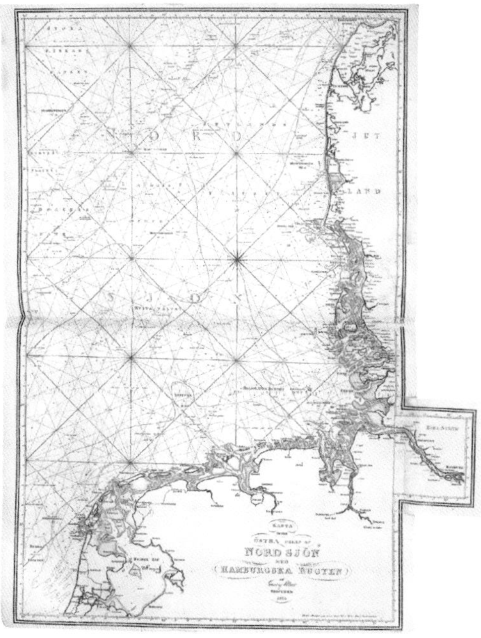

Gustav af Klint, *Hans Maajt Konungen egnas sweriges Sjö Atlas (The First Modern Atlas of the Baltic Sea)*, c. 1830
Double-page engraved sea chart of the Swedish coast, entire book 71 x 56 cm (28 x 22 in.)

Fruit Tree in Blossom near House (Blommande fruktträd vid hus), n/d
Oil on canvas, 54 x 43 cm (21⅜ x 17 in.)
Stockholm, Hilma af Klint Foundation, HaK 1461

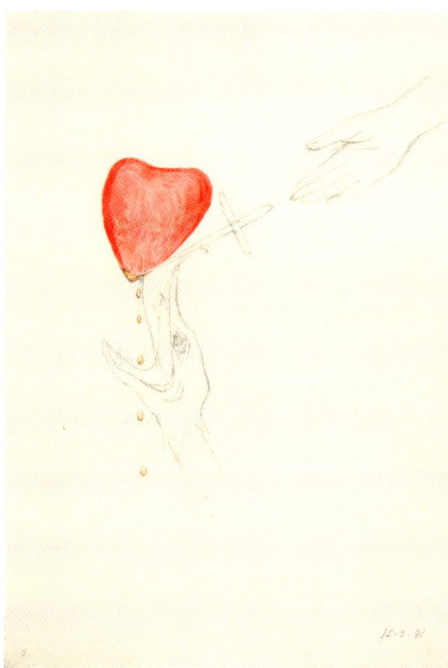

March 14, 1941
Watercolor and graphite on paper,
49 x 33.5 cm (19⅜ x 13¼ in.)
Stockholm, Hilma af Klint Foundation, HaK 1023

spacious and imposing structure built as an aristocratic residence in 1630, and at times in its history the palace served as a Swedish royal residence. Although the building changed over centuries, the palace's lakefront location, its grounds, and distinct architectural details spoke of a noble past. Stockholm's growth and a railroad encroached upon some of the estate by the time Hilma af Klint was a child; however, its grounds still featured a small temple dedicated to the goddess Diana, as well as the grave marker of Pompe, a Swedish king's dog.

When af Klint was six years old, the family moved to a nearby well-to-do neighborhood to reside separately from the academy. Nautical tradition, discipline, aristocratic heritage, and the routine of the military academy retained a presence in the children's daily life, except in summer, when af Klint's father sailed out with his cadets, and the rest of the family moved to Adelsö. There were two family estates on the island. Young Hilma lived in a cottage at Tofta Manor, which had been purchased by her grandfather (*The Home at Tofta*, p. 18). Another estate, Hanmora, housed cousins. The extended family members and guests who summered at these estates saw each other often.[1] During the warmer, lengthened summer days in Sweden—some June days lasting more than 18 hours—nature erased time. Adelsö's flowering meadows and grassy fields beckoned summer after summer. Wavelets lapped at the island's tree-lined shores (*Seascape with Sunset*, p. 15). The artist's experiences in nature fundamentally shaped her preference for a simple lifestyle and gave her an understanding of the countryside's plant and animal life (*Reeds at Sunset*, p. 19).

Hilma af Klint did not love her schooling, which emphasized religious topics. The Lutheran af Klints went to church on Sundays in a country where Lutheranism was the state religion. On religious holidays they usually visited the Stockholm Cathedral on Stadsholmen, where a huge equestrian statue of Saint George overcoming the dragon by medieval German sculptor Bernt Notke dominated the interior. Saint George saves a princess from a dragon, a symbol of sin and the powers of darkness. The sculpture was covered in gold leaf, and made a deep impression on af Klint. She may have pictured herself in the role of the saint, who was shown with soft, resolute features. Saint George

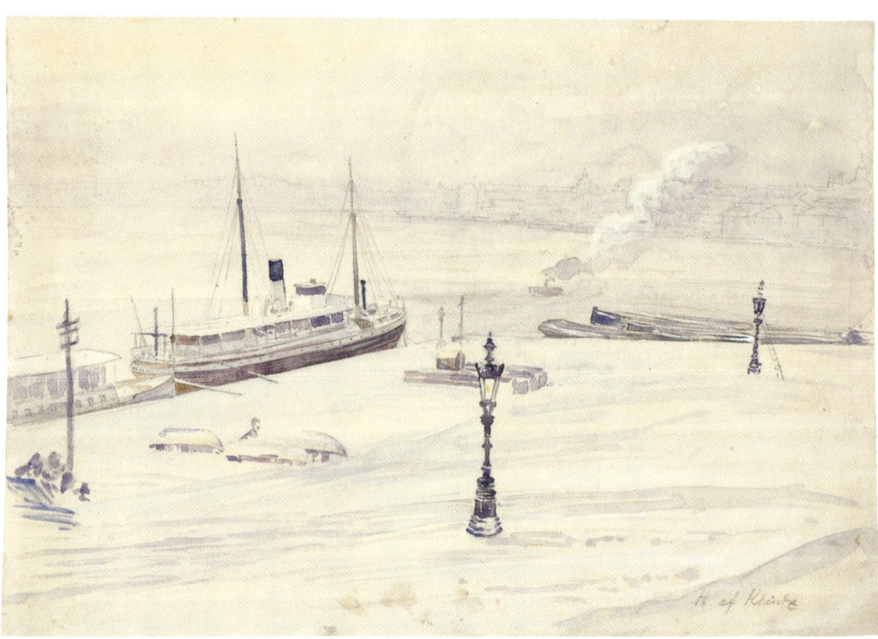

Winter Landscape with Boat (Vinterlandskap med båt), n/d
Watercolor and graphite on paper,
25 x 35.5 cm (9⅞ x 14 in.)
Stockholm, Hilma af Klint Foundation, HaK 1212

later appeared as an alter ego in some of her paintings, and the dragon rearing up from the ground with open jaws returned in some of the last drawings she made in her life (*March 14, 1941*, p. 12).

Despite their religiosity, the family was open-minded. Biographer Julia Voss relates that the af Klints rejected dogmatism and gave their girls plenty of social and religious freedom. "The[y] also considered instruction in the natural sciences an essential part of any education. Mathematics and physics were as much a part of the seafaring life as the masts and sails of a ship."[2] Sailors, unable to see or control the wind, must be able to spontaneously read its force to move forward. Hilma would come to be attracted to invisible forces, to spiritual concepts outside of the Christian faith, while Ida would become a feminist, fighting for women's suffrage.

Through social circles, the teenage Hilma af Klint experienced her first séances, gatherings held in total contradiction to the Christian faith. The practice was surprisingly widespread. Spiritualism was founded in 1848 by the American Fox sisters, and spread through literate, upper-class European society. Spiritualists believed that it was possible to contact the spirits of the dead, who could advise those left behind. The willingness of a percentage of the elite to embrace Spiritualism signaled the waning power of the state church, as well as its inadequacy in resolving the incompatibility of modern scientific discoveries with its teachings. Prominent spiritualists were often women. They tended to align with progressive social causes, like the abolition of slavery, birth control, and women's suffrage. Af Klint probably attended her first spiritualist gathering with Bertha Valerius (1824–1885), an unmarried Swedish portrait painter, professional photographer, and spiritualist prominent in Stockholm at the time, who founded a group of the like-minded called Cloverleaf.

Careers were not the norm for the upper-class Swedish female; women who pursued additional education or professional studies were thought to be acquiring a hobby. Yet after finishing her schooling in 1879, af Klint matriculated at the Technical School (*Tekniska Skolan*) and began art studies, with a concentration in classical portraiture. In the all-female classes, she met the slightly older Anna Cassel (1860–1937), with whom she would collaborate and become intimate. A work af Klint made in 1932, over 50 years after they met, features a series of portraits of Anna (*From 1936. Persian Era. Egyptian Era. During the Middle Ages! 1700s*, p. 13). They depict her friend's face in a cross of bright light, each corner of the image anchored by one of Anna's past incarnations, sometimes as a man and sometimes as a woman.

In their student days, the friends shared an interest in the occult as well as their ambition to become artists. Af Klint, eager to learn quickly and excel, signed up for additional portraiture classes at Kerstin Cardon's art school while attending the Technical School. Cardon, another unmarried woman artist, supported herself through teaching and painting high society portraits. Such portraits were commissioned and then paid for; they were not created for the open market. Her focus on portraiture showed that af Klint aspired to independence as a professional artist who could make a living.

In 1880 Hilma af Klint lost her younger sister Hermina, suddenly and unexpectedly. It has been widely suggested that her sister's death fueled Hilma's interest in mediumship and séance. The oldest document in the Hilma af Klint Foundation's archive today is a 170-page notebook given to af Klint by Valerius that covers séances held from 1879 to 1882.[3] According to the notebook, remarkably illustrious historic personalities took up contact with Stockholm from the

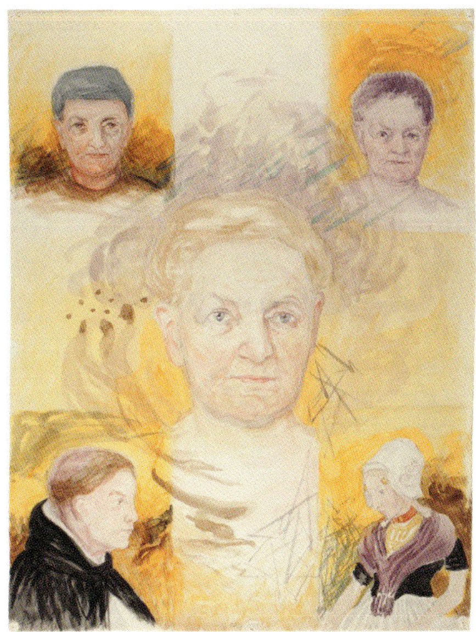

From 1936. Persian Era. Egyptian Era. During the Middle Ages! 1700s
Watercolor on paper, 54.5 x 41 cm (21½ x 16¼ in.)
Stockholm, Hilma af Klint Foundation, HaK 896

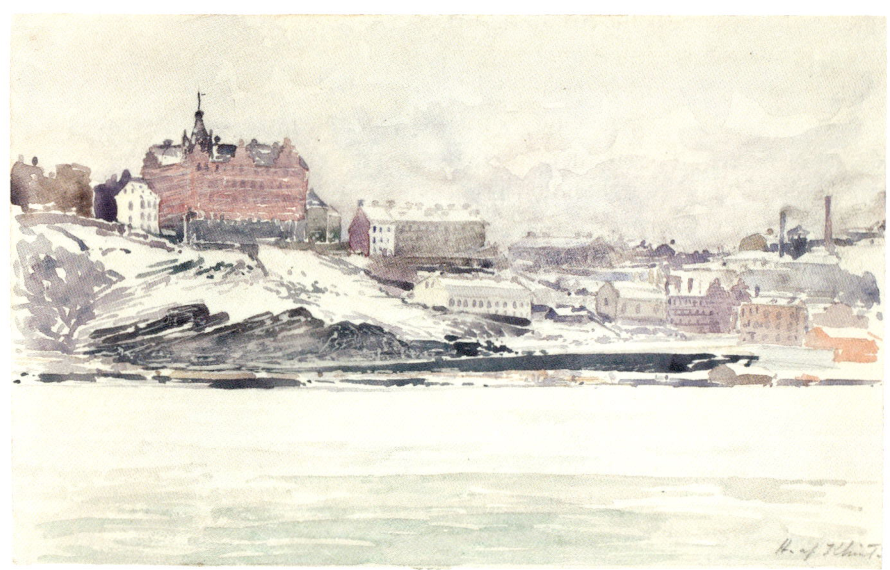

Cityscape (Stadslandskap), n/d
Watercolor and graphite on paper,
16 x 25.5 cm (6⅜ x 10 in.)
Stockholm, Hilma af Klint Foundation,
HaK 1217

spirit realm, including Swedish botanist Carl Linnaeus and French philosopher Voltaire. Less famous spirits documented in the notebook complained about the way the state church defended its dogmatic approach to God's truth. The spirits spoke of delightful heavenly dwellings that awaited.[4] Valerius further solidified her standing in 1886 when she published a book called *Messages from the Unseen World* (*Meddelanden från den osynliga verlden*).

As af Klint approached adulthood and educated herself, she consorted with many upper-class women and some men who were interested in an extended worldview. Discoveries and theories in both the natural and human sciences affirmed the existence of unknown subtleties and invisible worlds, and transformed how space, time, and material were understood. During the 19th century, technology made it increasingly possible to send communications through space, and to communicate with distant beings. How different was a telegraph or a telephone call from a message received from a spirit realm during a séance? It was conceivable that electromagnetism might even explain the nature of such spirit messages. Charles Darwin's theory of evolution (published 1859) had shaken the biblical creation story, and Christianity was already threatened when, in 1882, the year Hilma af Klint turned twenty, Friedrich Nietzsche announced that God is dead, and that spiritless Sunday worshipping had killed him.[5] It was now up to humanity to reorient itself in a world without God's rules, and to invent a new moral system. While af Klint never renounced Christianity—she taught Sunday school as a young adult—her behavior indicates that she continually amended her faith to reflect her evolving world view.

Book 2, July 11, 1898
Graphite on paper, 31 x 26 cm (12¼ x 10¼ in.)
Stockholm, Hilma af Klint Foundation,
HaK 1515

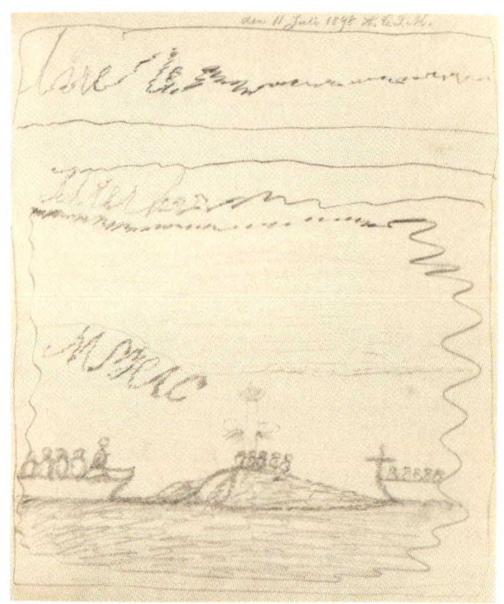

The Royal Academy of Fine Arts in Stockholm had been accepting female students since 1864, though in a department segregated from the men. Af Klint entered the academy in 1882 and graduated with honors in 1887. She then took a studio in a building at Hamngatan 5, which she shared with two other female artists. Located in a central district of Stockholm, the neighborhood was an arts hub with a cinema nearby. Blanch's Art Salon was located near her studio building. A gallery run by the Art Society was in the same building, too, below her studio. It informed visitors about the era's stylistic tendencies, such as Impressionism and Symbolism. Blanch's Café had electric lights and international newspapers. The café populated the ground floor of af Klint's building, until its space was absorbed by the Art Society, which morphed into the Swedish General Art Association (*Sveriges Allmänna Konstförening*).[6] Af Klint worked right at the pulse of Stockholm's art scene and had a clear view of society's interaction with it. She was likely informed about European art developments of the time—for example, she probably saw an exhibition of Edvard Munch's paintings at Blanch's Art Salon in 1894—though did not commit to trends or write about other artists. She never joined with artists who formed an opposition to academic art and broke from stylistic conventions, though she did later become the secretary of the new Association of Swedish Women Artists (founded 1910).

As a graduate, Af Klint had made an auspicious landing. She was just 25 years old and was recognized as a professional artist.[7] Her family supported her career choice. She had like-minded friends. She had her own studio. The money sufficed. Af Klint's early work was reviewed positively because she excelled at conventional painting. She intended to sell her work to the middle and upper classes, and understood their expectations for art. The size of her canvases and the subject matter she chose make this clear. The idea of working as an avant-gardist, of making art for art's sake, exploring media, or effecting an about-face change in subject matter for her commercial audience did not occur to her. Such notions were not appropriate to the product she was trained to produce. For the most part, her early work belongs to her era and was calculated to sell.

Seascape with Sunset (Sjölandskap med solnedgång), n/d
Oil on canvas, 38.5 x 56.5 cm (15¼ x 22¼ in.)
Stockholm, Hilma af Klint Foundation, HaK 1290

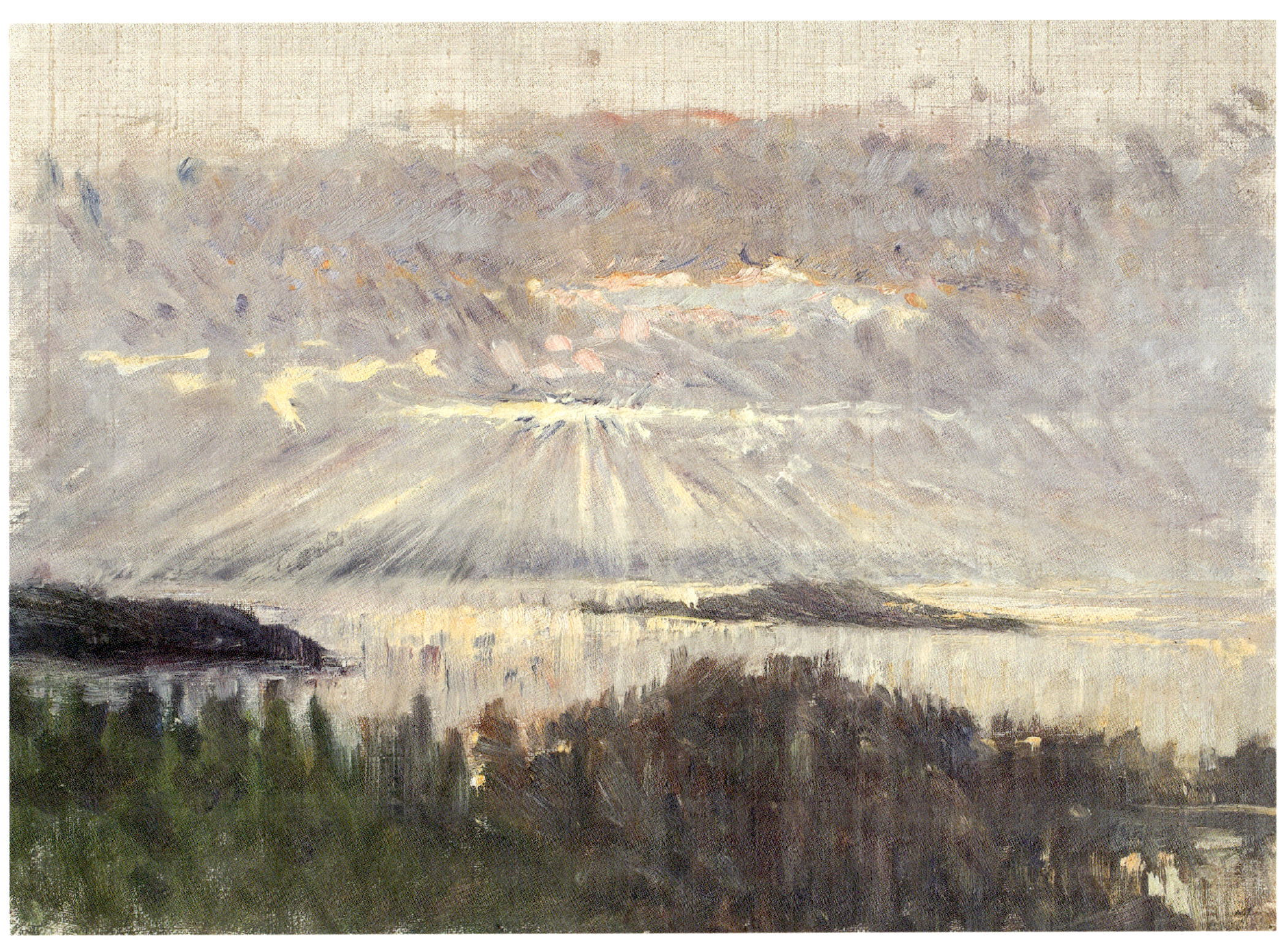

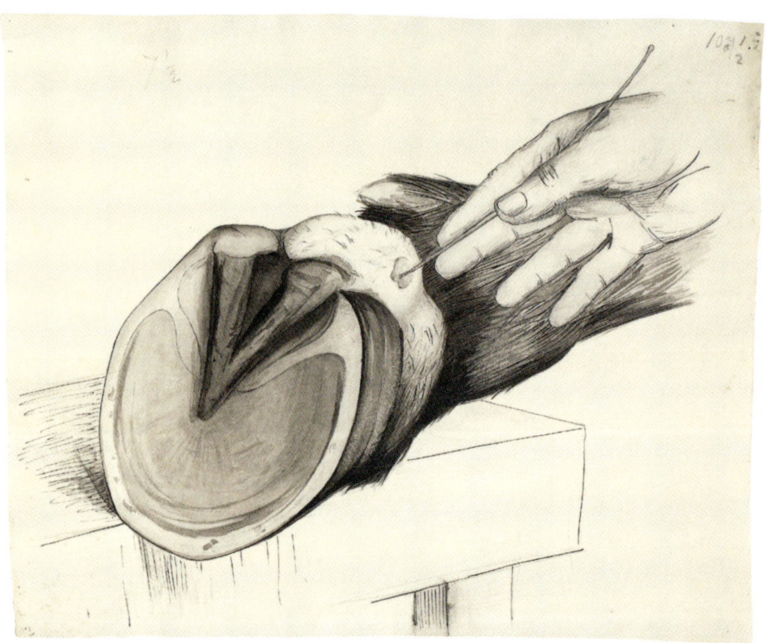

Study, Horse's Hoof (Studie, hästhov), 1900–01
Graphite on paper, 35 x 42 cm (13⅞ x 16⅝ in.)
Stockholm, Hilma af Klint Foundation,
HaK 1300

At times she favored some of Claude Monet's (1840–1926) Impressionist motifs, as is reflected in her *Woman with Veil* (p. 17) that echoes his touching painting of his veiled wife Camille on her deathbed (*Camille Monet on her Deathbed*, p. 17). The elevated view, indistinct forms, and colors of *Winter View of Kungsträdgården* (1890) recall Monet's wintry, tree-lined *Boulevard des Capucines* (1873–74), which he painted from inside Félix Nadar's upstairs photography studio. Monet knew the innovative painting would hang in that studio, and be seen in the First Impressionist Exhibition held in spring 1874. Af Klint's studio also overlooked a socially significant street: she had a view of the allée adjacent to the *Kungsträdgården*, or King's Garden. She could see the comings and goings of artists to Blanch's Art Salon, the premier address for independent art exhibitions.[8] To the right in af Klint's *Winter View of Kungsträdgården*, a small figure steps into the road carrying gold-framed oil paintings. The figure hoists both elbows to lift the works above the snow lining the thoroughfare. This local scene reflects af Klint's attention to Stockholm's artists working and exhibiting for the open market while hoping to become known and attract commissions.

Af Klint's teachers at the academy had recognized her as a gifted illustrator. She could draw in a fashionable style that recalled art nouveau and arts and crafts watercolors, like those of Carl Larsson, who used an outline drawing style to show familial, folksy, and rural subject matter. Yet as Hilma af Klint worked as a freelance and commissioned artist, her own and Stockholm's spiritualist life continued to develop. In 1890 Huldine Beamish (1859–1931), who, with Valerius, was a founding member of Cloverleaf, chartered a splinter spiritualist group in Stockholm that became well known, even to the King of Sweden, the Russian author Leo Tolstoy, and some followers in England. Beamish named her group the Edelweiss Society, after the distinctive white, star-shaped mountain flower whose rarity and closeness to heaven made it a symbol for purity, love, and dedication. She wore white, and her followers wore the white flower as a badge or jewelry.

Beamish reported visions and paranormal events. Her spiritual salon met for séances in a room with an altar, much like in a temple, decorated with a palm frond from Jerusalem. Her group recorded messages from beyond the material world, both as text and drawing. Especially of interest for af Klint, during séances Beamish made mediumistic drawings of the kind now called automatic drawings. Beamish's drawings combined symbolic elements with lines and geometric shapes suggesting plant forms, movement, and evolution. Beamish included reincarnation in her spiritual beliefs, recognizing her own past life in no lesser figure than Saint Catherine of Siena (1347–1380).

In 1891 af Klint channeled spiritual messages herself for the first time. In 1896 she briefly joined the Edelweiss Society, only to leave after a probable personality clash. During an Edelweiss séance, though, the spiritualist subgroup The Five (De Fem) was founded—its members were af Klint, Sigrid Hedman (1855–1922), Anna Cassel, and two sisters, Cornelia Cederberg (1854–1933) and

Mathilda Nilsson (1844–1923). Cederberg had also studied at the art academy and was a trained artist.

The Five worked together for 10 years, holding spiritualist meetings as they had learned to do. They wore gowns over their clothes, met in a room with an altar, and began each meeting with prayer, a meditation, a Christian sermon, and a New Testament reading.[9] A writing tool attached to a small wooden disc with wheels, called a psychograph and guided unconsciously by those touching it while seated around a table, helped them record messages, or they worked through a trance medium chosen from the group, often Sigrid Hedman. They documented their esoteric research in notebooks with automatic writing and drawings, as Beamish had done. Any one of the participants might be doing the drawing. In the beginning, small "seascapes" with the initials of the women suggest they were "all in one boat" (*Book 2*, p. 14). Words and names appeared. Dots, lines, and vegetal and floral shapes showed up. The mark-making could include energetic vibrations, pencil stabs, swirls, spirals, and concentric or ranging forms. They could be faint or forceful. The intended abandonment of personal control did not eliminate the individuality of the woman gripping the pencil, whose "hand" flowed into the drawings, too. It is not always possible to discern

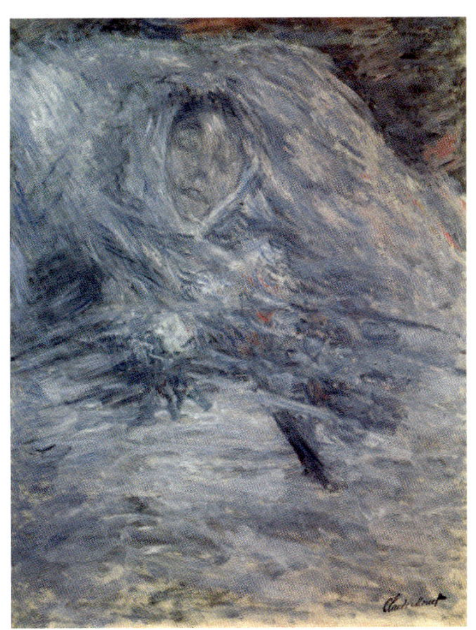

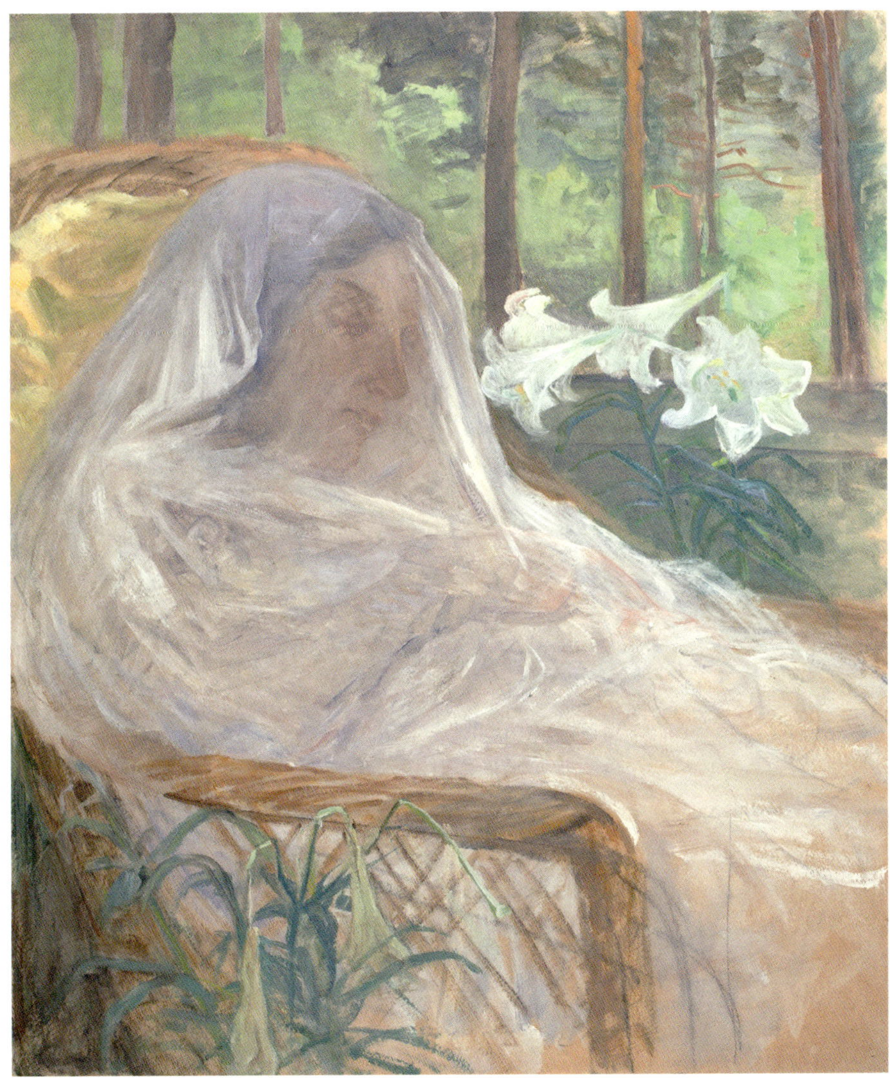

ABOVE
Claude Monet, *Camille Monet on her Deathbed*, 1879
Oil on canvas, 90 x 68 cm (35½ x 26⅞ in.)
Paris, Musée d'Orsay

Woman with Veil (Kvinna med slöja), n/d
Oil and crayon on paper,
77 x 63.5 cm (30⅜ x 25 in.)
Stockholm, Hilma af Klint Foundation,
HaK 1440

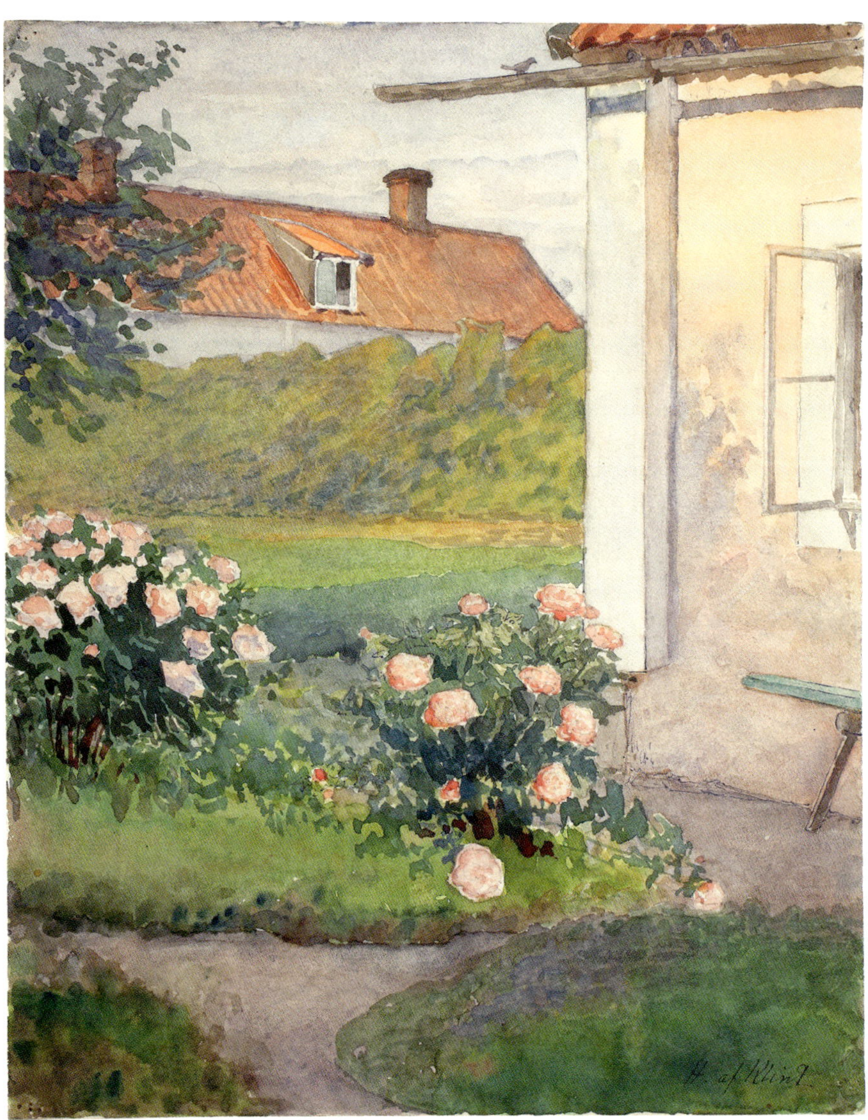

The Home at Tofta (Hemmet på Tofta), n/d
Watercolor, ink, and graphite on paper,
29 x 23 cm (11½ x 9 in.)
Stockholm, Hilma af Klint Foundation,
HaK 1216

who did a particular drawing, nor the orientation of some of the drawings. Some appear completely abstract and position themselves on the paper as if descended from on high. Drawings with diagonally crossing lines and central forms (often flowers) may suggest the physical formation of the women seated around the table as they sought a trancelike state. These automatic pencil drawings included motifs that would be reused in later work because they were considered valuable input from the Higher Masters who had presented themselves. The spirits had only male names and returned multiple times: Gregor, Georg, Clemens, Ananda, and Amaliel. The women considered themselves merely tools of the spirits, whose messages they channeled and tried to understand.

From 1900 to 1901 af Klint and Cassel accepted commissioned work to illustrate a textbook about horse surgery for John Vennerholm (1858–1931), a progressive professor from the Veterinary Institute in Stockholm. Vennerholm honored sentience in animals. He wanted to improve the health outcomes of work animals and get them more humane treatment, such as encouraging the use of anesthesia for animals undergoing surgery to manage their pain, which was not customary at the time. The commission—a job one would hardly expect to be

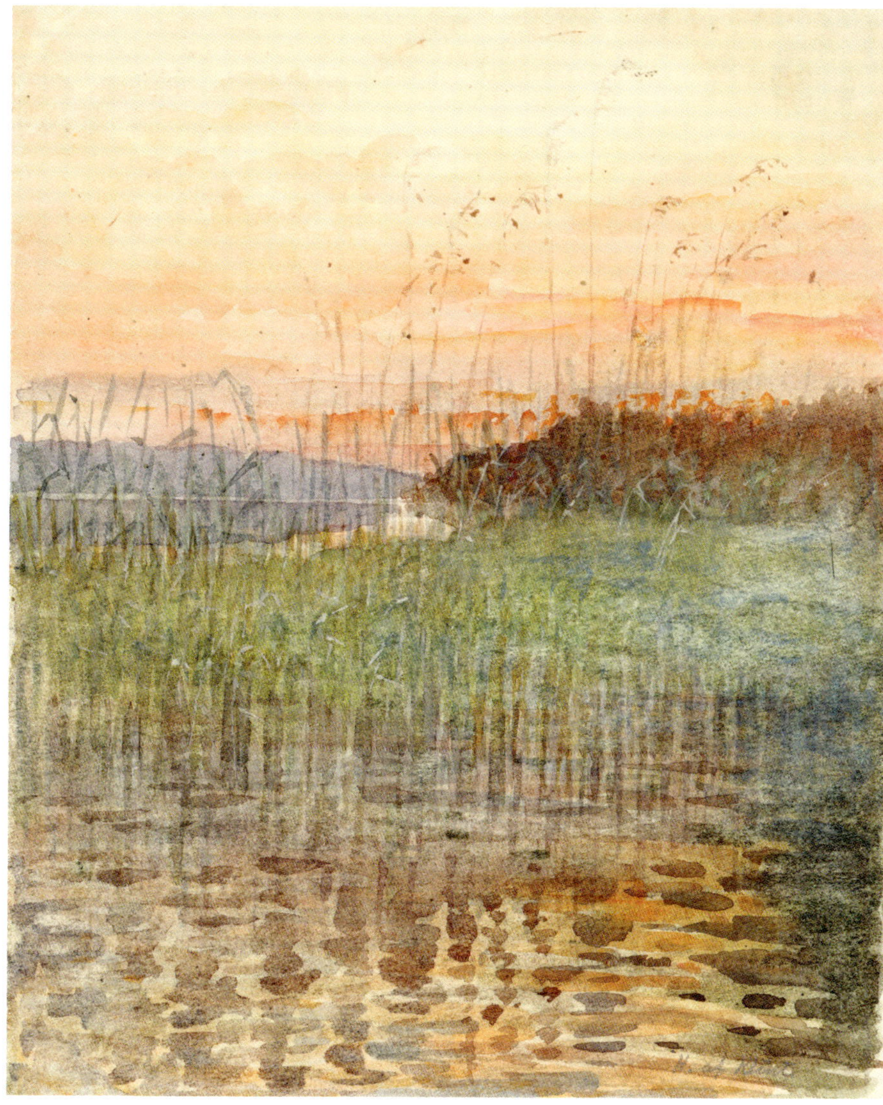

Reeds at Sunset (Vass i solnedgång), n/d
Watercolor on paper, 24.5 x 19 cm (9¾ x 7½ in.)
Stockholm, Hilma af Klint Foundation,
HaK 1721

handed to two almost middle-aged women of an elevated social class—immersed them in a completely male work environment.[10] Af Klint and Cassel faced brutal conditions, often worked outdoors in an open courtyard in both cold and heat, and saw great suffering. Diseased or decaying animal anatomies challenged the clarity of the technical drawings they were supposed to deliver, yet their academic training ensured visual continuity in the book. Dissections and surgeries educated both af Klint and Cassel about animal anatomy and exposed them routinely to anatomical parts that, in humans, had posed decency problems in art school. Drawing the horses honed their skills in the depiction of interior organs (*Study, Horse's Hoof*, p. 16). A copy of the finished publication remained in af Klint's library during her lifetime.[11] It was their first shared commission.

It may have been around this time, as she witnessed the callous treatment of sentient creatures on such scale, that af Klint decided to forgo eating meat. This decision was supported by her spiritualist leanings. She believed vegetarianism purified the body and mind and made a person more fit for the higher vibrational frequencies of esoteric communication. A plant-based diet was thought to enhance clairvoyance and it aligned with principles of compassion and nonviolence.

Nature in all its forms was fundamental to af Klint's worldview, and to her early subject matter. The art nouveau style that reigned in Europe around 1900 used organic shapes and sinuous lines. Af Klint drew a few embroidery designs with highly stylized flowers that conformed to contemporary fashion. Many of her mediumistic drawings flow with an art nouveau line. In contrast, her numerous undated botanical studies show the precise observation of a scientific researcher. Delicately graceful as finished images, the botanicals depict both cultivars and wildflowers. The growth habit of the plants, the behavior of the buds, flowers, seeds, and stems, and the disposition of the leaves express each plant's uniqueness. The actual flower usually occupies a small fraction of the paper. As is customary in botanical illustration, much of the drawing sheet is a white, neutral void. The bloom often turns away in profile, lifting into the outer reaches of the empty sheet.

One early study of a rose's stem singles out the contradiction of soft, upward-growing green leaves among punishing, reddened, downward-pointed red thorns (*Rose*, p. 20). For context, on the same sheet af Klint positions the thorny stem above a small, quick sketch of the entire bush. Sometimes, instead of only one plant being featured in all its forms, the artist invites a discrete number of wildflowers to form a select company on a page. Did she choose them because they grew near each other at the same time? Do they express a particular location? Was she interested in the colors or healing properties associated with the flowers? Although she illustrated children's books, af Klint did not personify flowers as elves or fairies, as did the Swedish illustrator Elsa Beskow and the German illustrator Sibylle von Olfers. The flowers express their own essence. Trees form the subject of multiple studies in charcoal. While these realistic drawings are not dated, in format and style they parallel Cassel's tree drawings from 1910 onward.[12] The two friends seem to have sketched outdoors together on Adelsö and elsewhere.

Rose (Ros), n/d
watercolor, ink, and graphite on paper, 35.5 x 17 cm (14 x 6¾ in.)
Stockholm, Hilma af Klint Foundation, HaK 1344

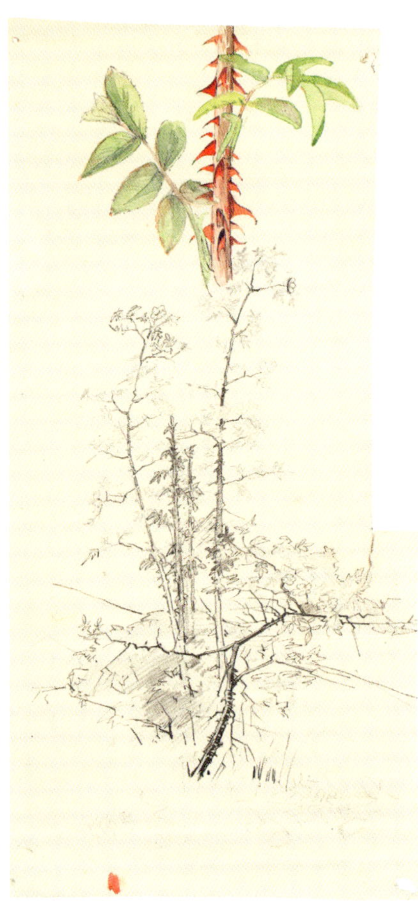

It was from Cassel's sisters that af Klint learned about the Theosophists, a group the pair joined as paying members in 1904. Theosophy, an esoteric movement which had grown from Spiritualism, was founded in 1875 by Helena Blavatsky (1831–1891) and Henry Steel Olcott. The movement's name came from the Greek "theos," meaning "god," and "sophia," for "wisdom." Disaffected with American Spiritualism's wayward path, in 1877 Blavatsky published her influential *Isis Unveiled*, a book that professed to harness ancient esoteric knowledge for contemporary use. Theosophy succeeded in attracting many of Spiritualism's followers. Åke Fant, the first scholar to write extensively about Hilma af Klint, believed Lutheranism's decline and the readiness to turn to Spiritualism gradually crystallized into the acceptance of the new religion of Theosophy, which saw itself as a nondenominational, universal belief system subsuming all world religions. Blavatsky had absorbed aspects of several Eastern religions, including the concepts of karma and reincarnation and the practice of yoga.[13]

Af Klint's open-minded parents had not hindered their daughter's development and seem to have accepted—perhaps even facilitated—her exposure to intellectual freethinkers within their own social circles. A tradition of familial support and noninterference played a large role in af Klint's ability to become and remain an artist. As an unmarried daughter, she became a companion for her mother. This caretaking arrangement also offered a safe space for the artist's same-sex relationships, which, had they been openly acknowledged, would not have been tolerated. Af Klint's personal world remained invisible to all but her closest associates, and probably even her immediate family.

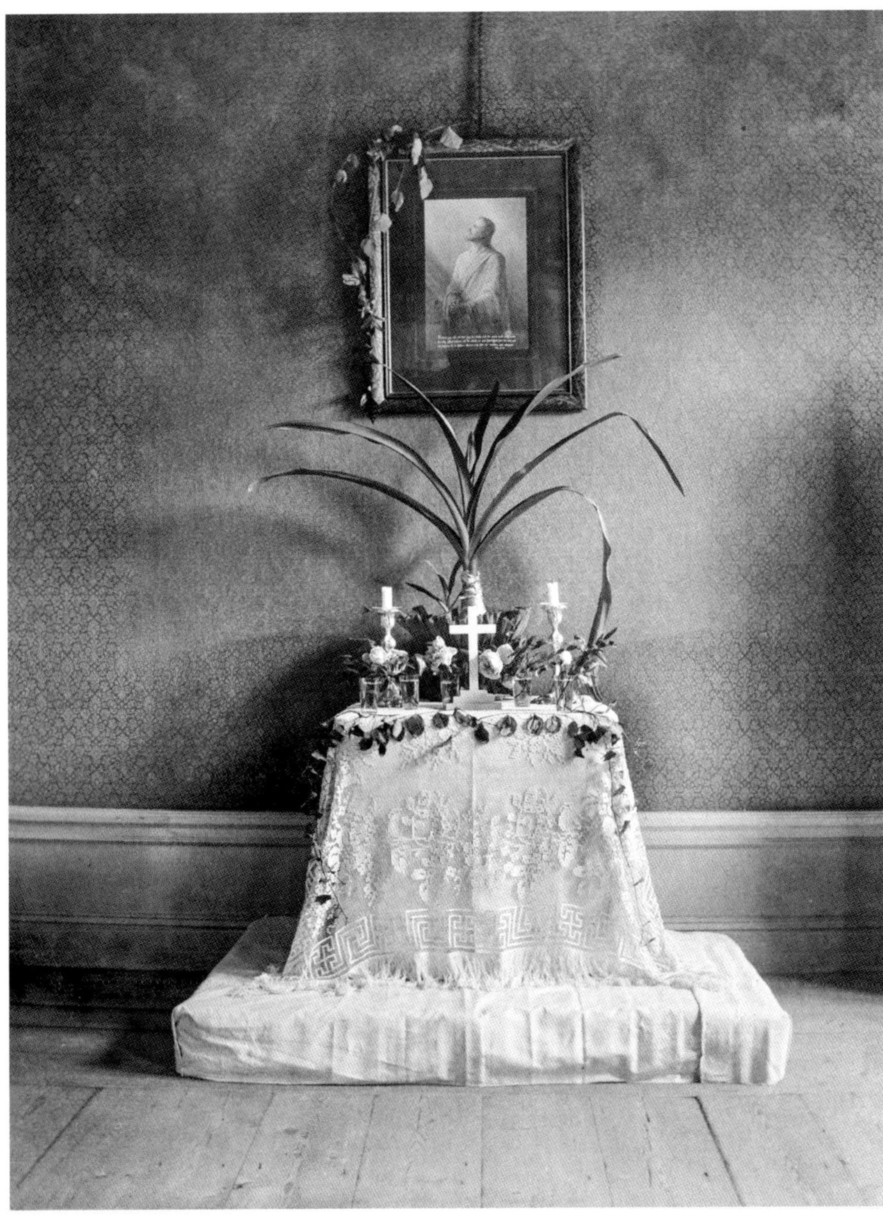

Photograph of room with an altar decorated with a palm frond from Jerusalem. Location of af Klint's séances with The Five.

Af Klint's esoteric research and her art did not merge naturally at first. Holding everything together were the friendships and romantic alliances among the participating women. The exclusively female, esoteric practice they agreed to maintain over time lead to shifting personality dominances and intimacies. In 1904 af Klint felt herself in touch with the Higher Master Ananda, who told her she would one day make astral paintings that would proclaim a new philosophy of life. In 1906 the commission arrived from the Higher Master Amaliel. In 1907 af Klint received a message that she would become the leader of The Five. While this led to the dissolution of the group, a new group grew over time to admit thirteen women, with varying degrees of individual participation. Cassel remained to collaborate with af Klint. Together they began the spirit-commissioned series of paintings that came to be known as "The Paintings for the Temple."

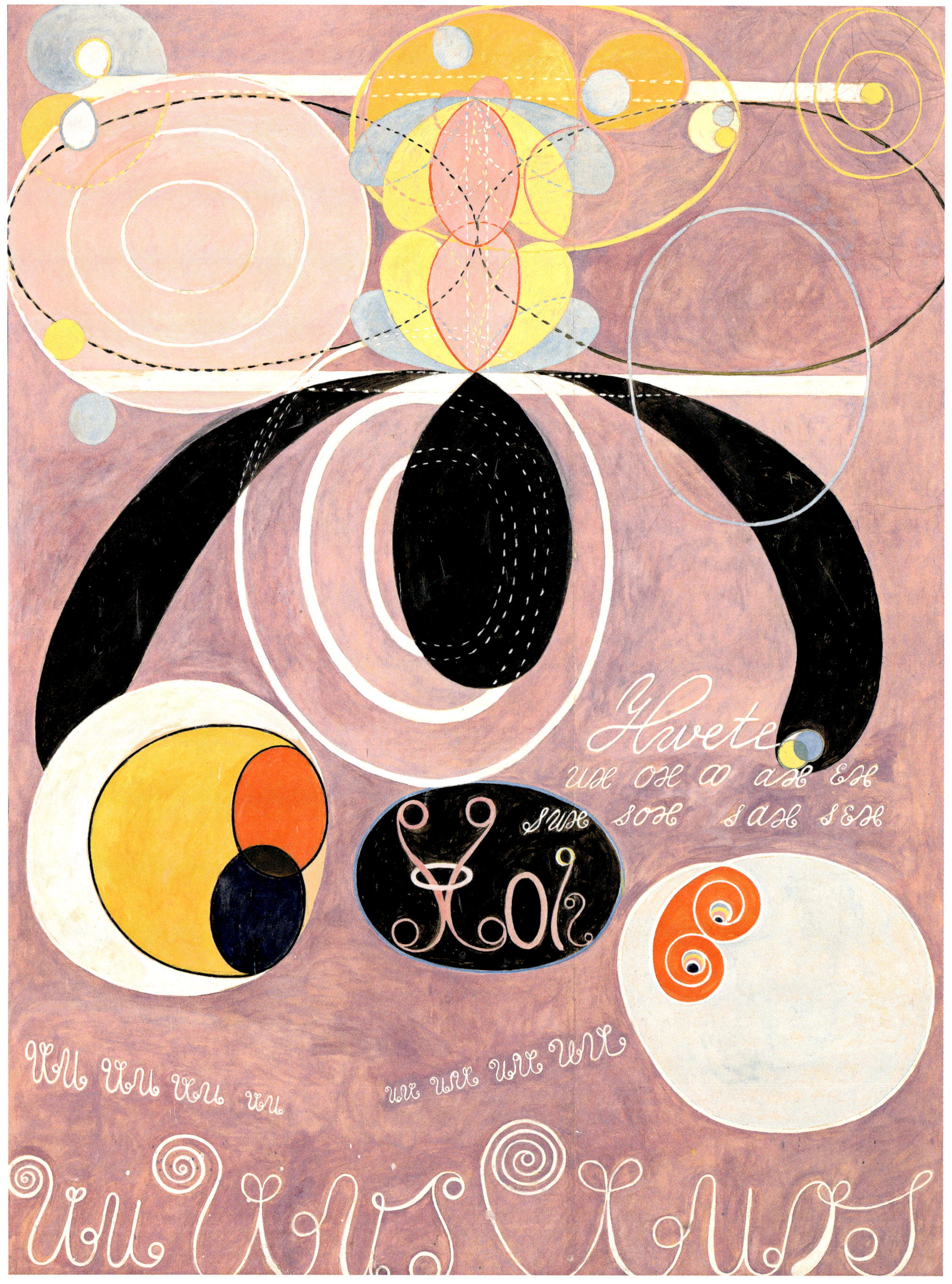
Hwete

Commissioned: “The Paintings for the Temple,” 1906–08

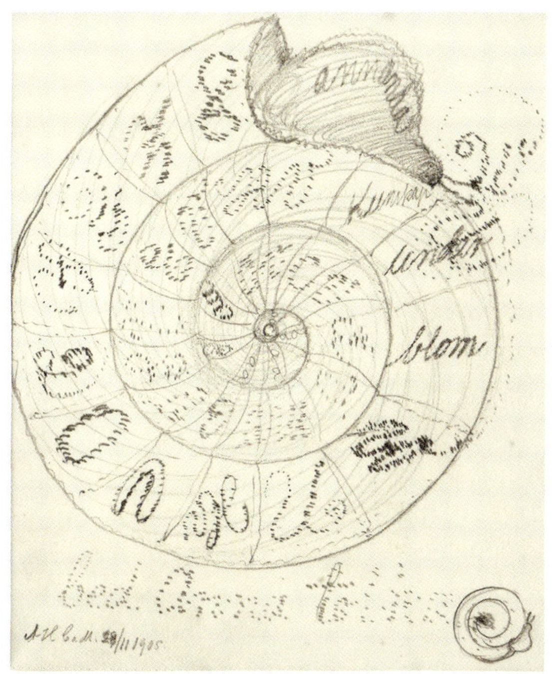

Drawing from Book 13,
January 24, 1905–January 10, 1906
Graphite on paper, 31 x 26 cm (12¼ x 10¼ in.)
Stockholm, Hilma af Klint Foundation,
HaK 1526, S13

If the automatic drawings of The Five were an unchaining from what Anna Cassel, Cornelia Cederberg, and Hilma af Klint had learned at the art academy and an exploration of unknown spiritual planes, then “The Paintings for the Temple” were a blossoming of that process. Art for a nonexistent temple: From the beginning, this was a leap of faith. Yet Amaliel’s commission would grow into a sequence of distinct series, each with its own theme, format, and numbered order. These 193 paintings, executed from 1906 to 1915, were regarded by af Klint as her major life accomplishment. This chapter and the next introduce this sprawling, complex visual thought temple through careful (if speculative) looking at individual paintings and present the context of Klint’s influences and experiences during the many years of its making.

When af Klint received the message that she should be the leader of an astral painting initiative, the collective of The Five fractured, yet the group’s notebooks full of automatic drawings stood waiting as a rich trove of forms and patterns. Af Klint’s mediumistic experiences during her years with Spiritualist groups and The Five informed her working method. As she wrote on the first day of 1906, “Amaliel presented me with a task, and I immediately said Yes. The expectation was that I would dedicate a year to this task. In the end it became the greatest work of my life.”[14] Af Klint began the project together with Cassel, Cederberg, and Magdalena Augusta “Gusten” Andersson, and others assisted, including af Klint’s studio mates, who had initially been shocked by what she was doing.

Art historian Hedvig Martin explains that Cassel and af Klint’s initial goal was to create images from the “Akashic Records.”[15] Founder of the Theosophical Society and theoretician of Theosophy Helena Blavatsky had adopted the Sanskrit term *akasha* for a type of life force or universal soul. The mythic Akashic Records were supernatural documents thought to contain the story and experience of this life force, back to every life form’s origin, but also into its future. Cassel and af Klint hoped to access images from the records, to capture *akasha* in legible form.

Blavatsky, channeling Hinduism and Buddhism instead of the Bible, had also explained the origin of the cosmos in detail. In her book *The Secret Doctrine*,

The Ten Largest, Group IV: No. 6, Adulthood (Mannaåldern), 1907
Tempera on paper mounted on canvas,
315 x 234 cm (124 x 92¼ in.)
Stockholm, Hilma af Klint Foundation, HaK 107

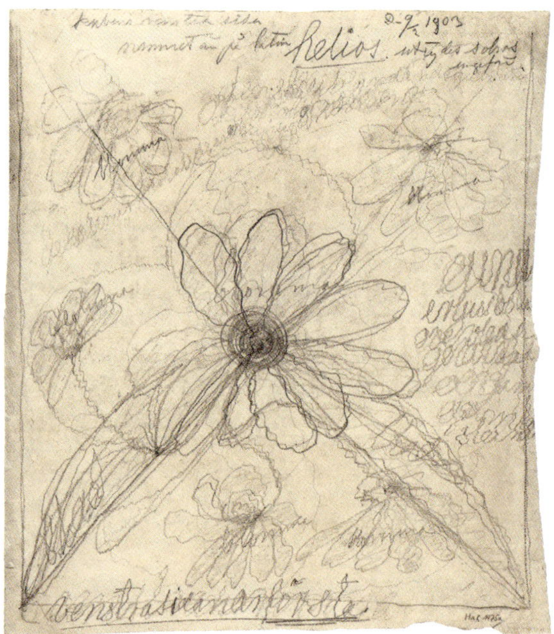

February 9, 1903
Graphite on paper, 47 x 41 cm (18⅝ x 16¼ in.)
Stockholm, Hilma af Klint Foundation, HaK 1475

"Automatic" drawing done during a meeting of The Five (De Fem).

first published in 1888, she brings in seven stanzas she identifies from the ancient Tibetan *Book of Dzyan.* A short sampling of the text conjures mythic images of vibration, darkness, a germ, slumbering waters, and eggs:

2. THE VIBRATION SWEEPS ALONG, TOUCHING WITH ITS SWIFT WING (SIMULTANEOUSLY) THE WHOLE UNIVERSE, AND THE GERM THAT DWELLETH IN DARKNESS: THE DARKNESS THAT BREATHES (MOVES) OVER THE SLUMBERING WATERS OF LIFE. …

3. 'DARKNESS' RADIATES LIGHT, AND LIGHT DROPS ONE SOLITARY RAY INTO THE WATERS, INTO THE MOTHER DEEP, THE RAY SHOOTS THROUGH THE VIRGIN EGG; THE RAY CAUSES THE ETERNAL EGG TO THRILL, AND DROP THE NON-ETERNAL (PERIODICAL) GERM WHICH CONDENSES INTO THE WORLD EGG.

The Secret Doctrine expounds a world of arcane and expressive processes and ideas which opened af Klint's mind as a liberating force. In one section, Blavatsky talks about the hidden deities or "architects" who fashioned the cosmos out of chaos. They are male-female, both spirit and matter, both good and evil, and thus embody unity.[16] She doubles down on androgyny and places the fluidity of gender at the heart of creation and spirituality. This would have made sense to af Klint, who was born female but identified with maleness.

The spirit Amaliel had warned af Klint that there would be trials ahead in her project. The Higher Master would work through the human artist, who was only the instrument of their will. Theoretically at least, the human instrument could even be absolved of responsibility for the paintings' content. Led by af Klint, the collective of female artists appeared unafraid to take truly daring steps.

Between October 1906 and September 1907, Cassel and af Klint made over 120 sketches for the first series of "Paintings for the Temple." These resulted in only 26 small, finished works, named "The WU/Rose Series, Group 1" or "Primordial Chaos." They resembled expressive drawings or diagrams. The existence of preliminary sketches contradicts af Klint's reports that her hand felt guided by an exterior force while painting. However, they constitute an outpouring of ideas that is commensurate with how the work would go forward: as a series of conceptual families from which ideas could fan out, evolve, reiterate.

Primordial Chaos, The WU/Rose Series, Group I: No. 1, 1906–07
Oil on canvas, 53 x 37 cm (20⅞ x 14⅝ in.)
Stockholm, Hilma af Klint Foundation, HaK 01

Primordial Chaos, The WU/Rose Series, Group I: No. 2, 1906–07
Oil on canvas, 53 x 36.5 cm (20⅞ x 14⅜ in.)
Stockholm, Hilma af Klint Foundation, HaK 02

Primordial Chaos, The WU/Rose Series, Group I: No. 4, 1906–07
Oil on canvas, 53 x 37 cm (20⅞ x 14⅝ in.)
Stockholm, Hilma af Klint Foundation, HaK 04

Primordial Chaos, The WU/Rose Series, Group I: No. 9, 1906–07
Oil on canvas, 51.5 x 37 cm (20⅜ x 14⅝ in.)
Stockholm, Hilma af Klint Foundation, HaK 09

"The WU/Rose Series, Group 1" or "Primordial Chaos" (1906–07)

The small size of the first series of "Paintings for the Temple"—all approximately 53 x 37 centimeters, or 20.8 x 14.5 inches—belies how audaciously the works depicted the origin of the universe. *No. 1* (p. 25) presents a low, dark horizon line, with further dark lines suggesting a storm whose wind and pelting rain obfuscates an unfurling embryonic form. In *No. 2* (p. 25), diagonal streaks, heated by orange and yellow, shoot through an indistinct atmosphere. Defined mainly by blues, white, and the bare canvas, the image separates into lighter and darker vectors. A swan-like shape materializes, carrying a spiral shell. A seascape assembles. Two small companion stars—are they af Klint and Cassel?—link in the center of the painting, connecting in an exchange of energy.

No. 9 (p. 25) in the series includes the words "vestal" and "asket" (*vestal och asket*), and the letter "y," with the words for man or lord and service

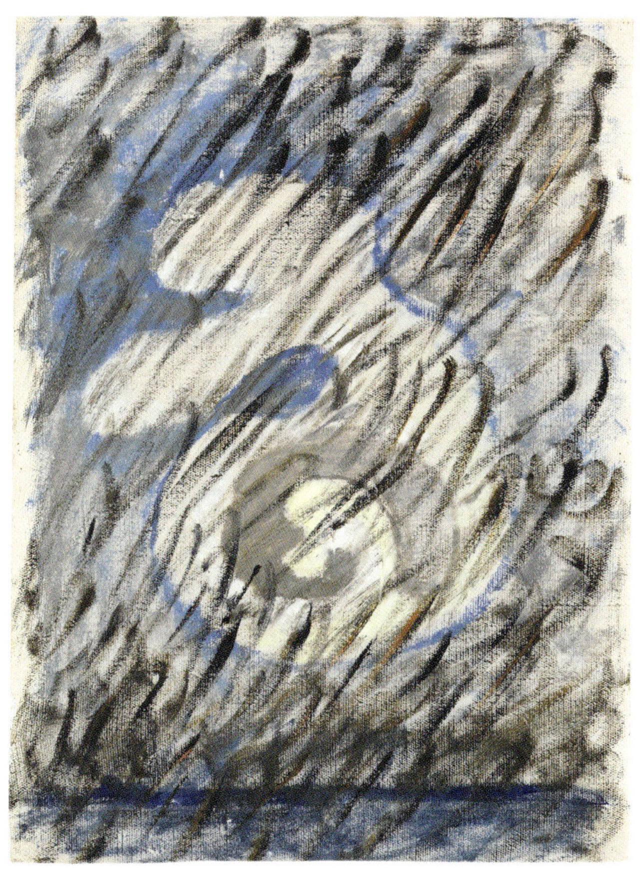

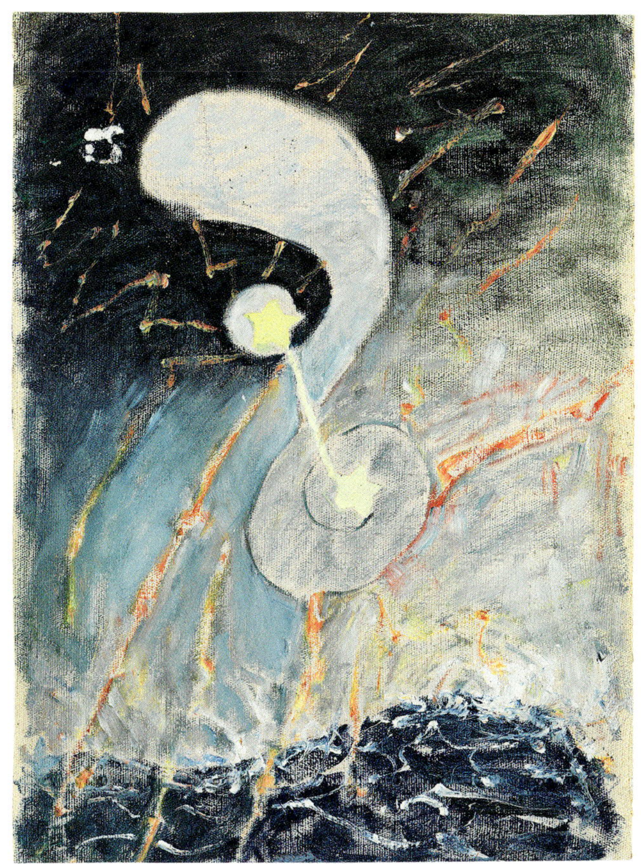

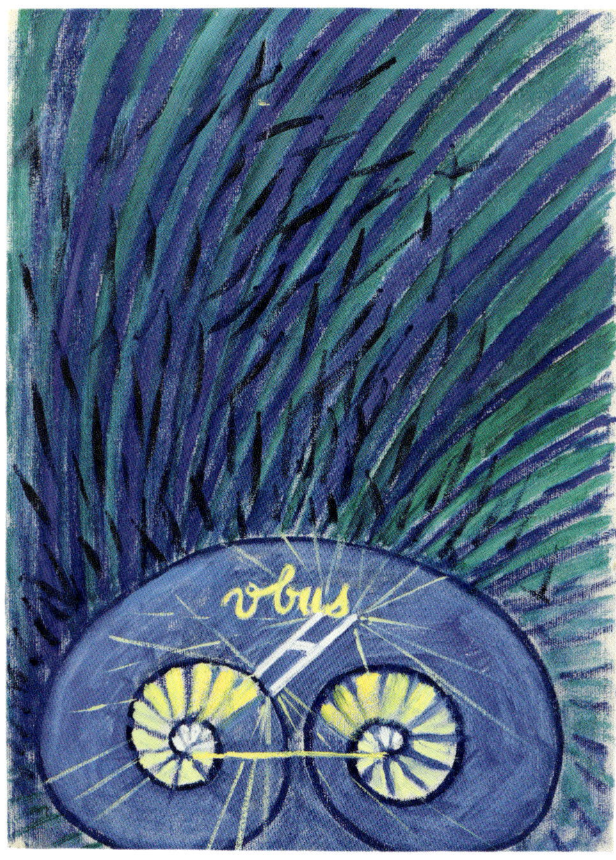
vbus

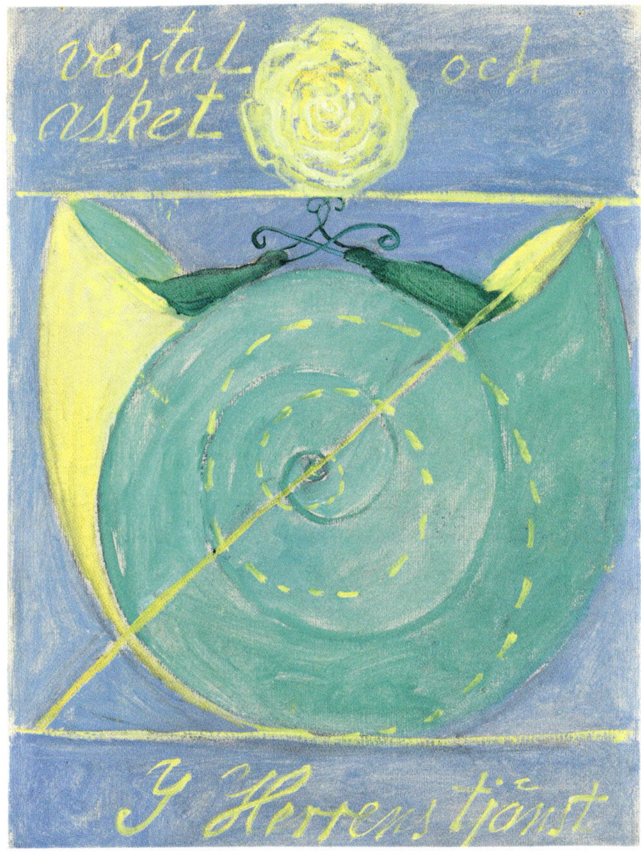
vestal
och
asket
Herrens tjänst

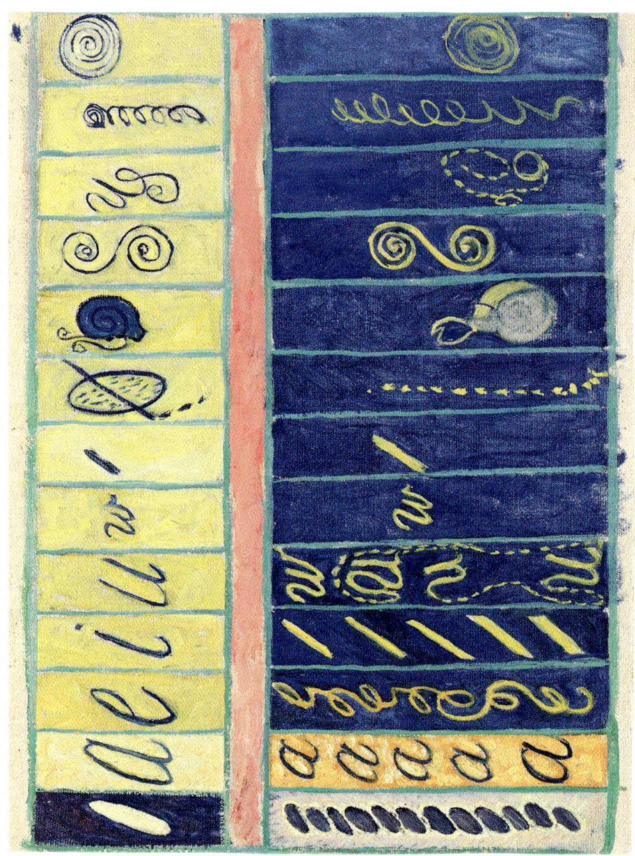

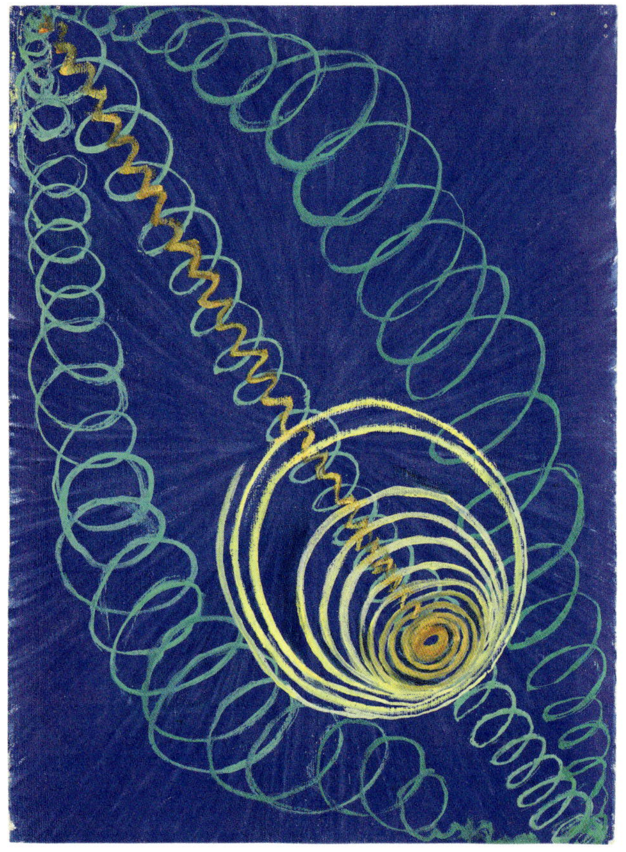

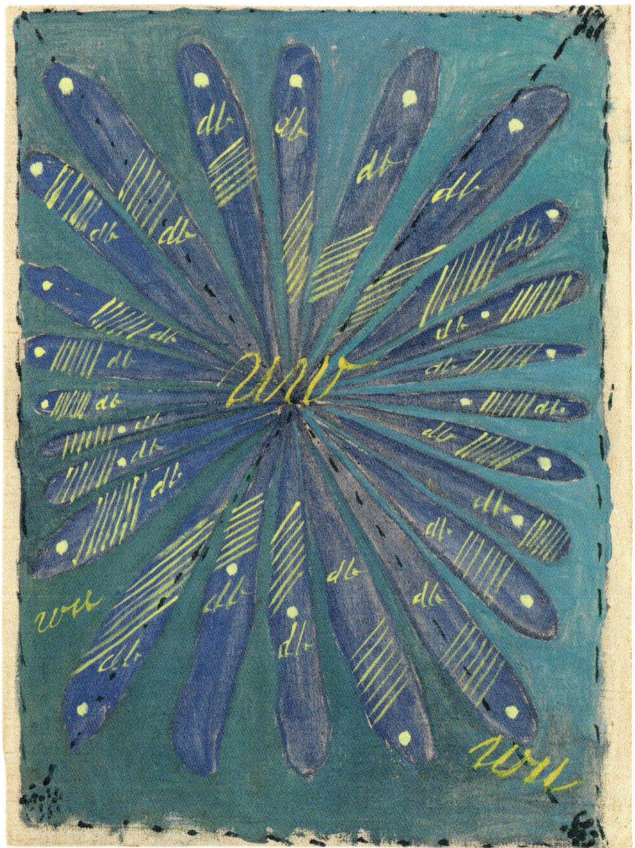

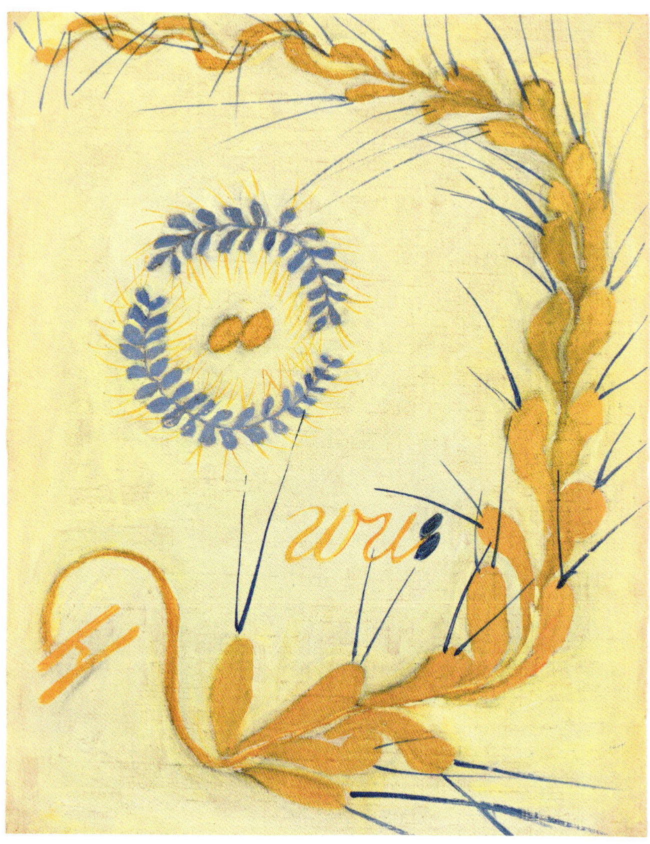

(*Herrenstjänst*). "Vestal" refers to the virgin priestesses who took care of the fire in the temple of Vesta and stands for Cassel. The "asket," or ascetic, represents af Klint, understood by the artists as a male counterpart to the vestal. The names suggest chastity and religious service. The painting features a green snail shell that overlays a yellow snail shell reversed behind it, so that the shell openings face each other. They center in a somewhat diagonally bisected rectangle, with a yellow diagonal line passing through both snails' spirals. The snail carries with it several associations. Af Klint's father's research ship had been named *The Snail* for its slow work taking magnetic and meteorological measurements.[17] Since most land snails are hermaphroditic, carrying both male and female reproductive organs, the creature also embodies the unification of the sexes, a nonbinary state of gender.

The limited use of only blue, yellow, and green unifies the canvases in the first series, which otherwise vary widely in style and genre. Some look like cartoonish spacescapes, while others resemble diagrams or book illustrations (*Nos. 4, 10, 16,* and *26*, pp. 25–26). In the quick application of pure bright color and outlining of forms, Klint and Cassel's work shares expressive qualities with Fauvism, a new painting movement then flourishing in France. Af Klint's biographer, Julia Voss, notes that the unnatural yellow of the series evokes the glow of radioluminescence.[18] The science of radioactivity was young at the time. In 1903 Pierre and Marie Curie had been awarded the Nobel Prize in Physics for their discovery of radium and polonium.

Blue and yellow also had symbolic significance for af Klint: In her work, blue often represented female, while yellow stood for male. The two emerging green snails thus contain both male and female aspects in a single gender. In an intimate gesture, they reach for each other and raise and intertwine one of their feelers in support of the yellow rose above, as if each snail's sense organ were one of the flower's sepals in a melding of plant and animal. Their remaining feeler umbrellas their partner. Both snails and roses had featured in automatic drawings of The Five, and *No. 9* demonstrates how The Five's notebooks fed into the first works done for Amaliel's commission (pp. 23–24).

These first paintings both show and disguise erotic and emotional content. In a notebook of 1906, af Klint wrote, "We stood at the portal of the prison gate, calm united power kept Hilma and Anna in calm united love."[19] As closeted lesbians, both women lived out part of their emotional lives in their paintings. The first series closes with *No. 26*, painted with a light background reminiscent of a ripe wheat field. An enlarged stalk of labial kernels contorts itself to conform to the rectangular format; yellow kernels sprout blue hairs. Yellows predominate, with a yellow capital "H" and cursive "wu" floating afield. A kind of blue victory wreath positions itself as a nest for two yellow ovals: eggs, testes, or simply two souls resting together. A color switch happens in the depicted nest: There the kernels are blue and sprout yellow hairs.

This synthesis of writing and organic, abstract, and symbolic forms is not like anything else that was happening in the visual arts at the time. Theosophist literature filtered into the paintings with its illustrations, charts, and diagrams. Cloudlike ovoids feature in the book *Man Visible and Invisible* by theosophist Charles W. Leadbeater (1954–1934). Here, color plates illustrate how man is enveloped by an egg-shaped colored aura, or astral body, perceptible only to clairvoyant sight. The book's frontispiece also featured a full-page grid of 25 colored squares arranged as a chart (p. 27, 1903). Using the chart, a clairvoyant could decode the meaning of a person's aura by its color. Full-page illustrations

Primordial Chaos, The WU/Rose Series, Group I: No. 10, 1906–07
Oil on canvas, 51.5 x 37 cm (20⅜ x 14⅝ in.)
Stockholm, Hilma af Klint Foundation, HaK 10

Primordial Chaos, The WU/Rose Series, Group I: No. 16, 1906–07
Oil on canvas, 53 x 37 cm (20⅞ x 14⅝ in.)
Stockholm, Hilma af Klint Foundation, HaK 16

Primordial Chaos, The WU/Rose Series, Group I: No. 25, 1906–07
Oil on canvas, 52.5 x 37.5 cm (20¾ x 14⅞ in.)
Stockholm, Hilma af Klint Foundation, HaK 25

Primordial Chaos, The WU/Rose Series, Group I: No. 26, 1906–07
Oil on canvas, 52.5 x 37.5 cm (20¾ x 14⅞ in.)
Stockholm, Hilma af Klint Foundation, HaK 26

Charles W. Leadbeater, *Key to the Meanings of Colours*, frontispiece from *Man Visible and Invisible*, 1903

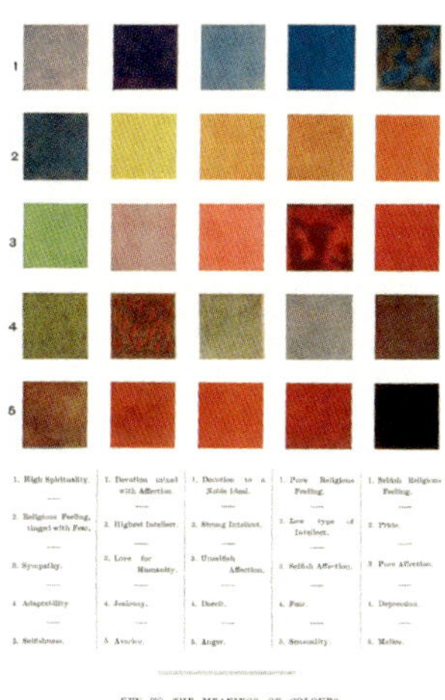

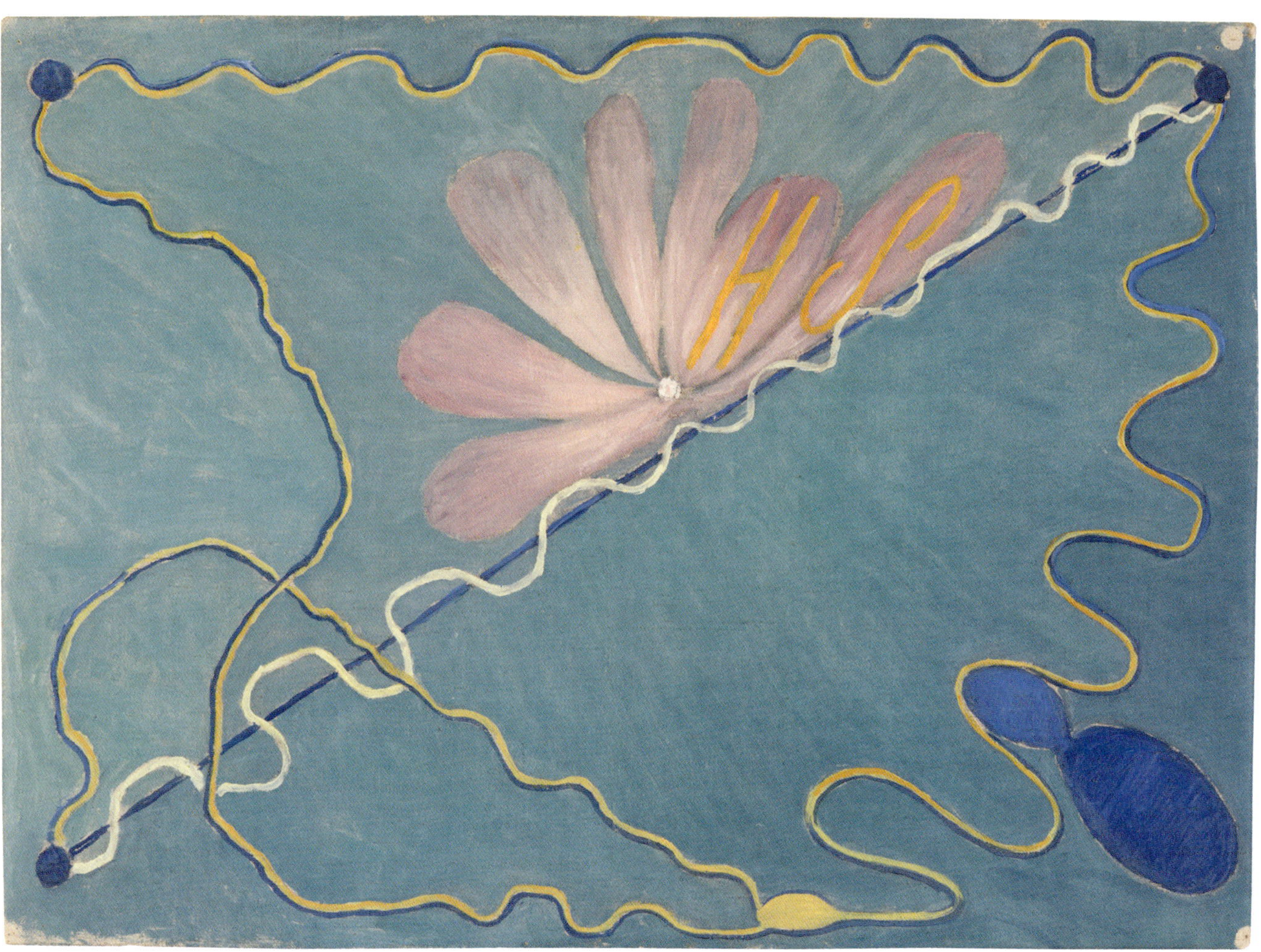

in the book show widely ranging examples. Pastel transparency, rainbow iridescent, and pulsing or patterned auras exist, each indicative of an individual's soul's state of being.

Leadbeater's chart was republished as the frontispiece to *Thought-Forms: A Record of Clairvoyant Investigation* (1905), written with theosophist Annie Besant (1947–1933). The book explained that human thought shaped real vibrations in the world. Under certain circumstances, thought-forms could affect situations and manifest themselves to receptive clairvoyant beings even at a great distance from where they were generated. According to Leadbeater and Besant, thought-forms are encoded with spiritual, intellectual, psychological, and emotional significance through their color and shape, and an adept clairvoyant can see and read them. The book had enormous influence on visual artists in the early 20th century, because it meant that invisible worlds waited to be painted and made visible. Af Klint and Cassel both knew *Man Visible and Invisible* and *Thought-Forms* and were familiar with their shared frontispiece illustration on the meaning of colors.

Af Klint entitled the first series of temple paintings on canvas "The WU/Rose Series, Group 1." To explain what he saw, the art historian Åke Fant attached a second title, "Primordial Chaos," to the series, based on Blavatsky's writing about the origins of the cosmos in *The Secret Doctrine*. Cassel and af Klint's original title, though, leads with the adjacent letters W and U and the idea of a rose. The

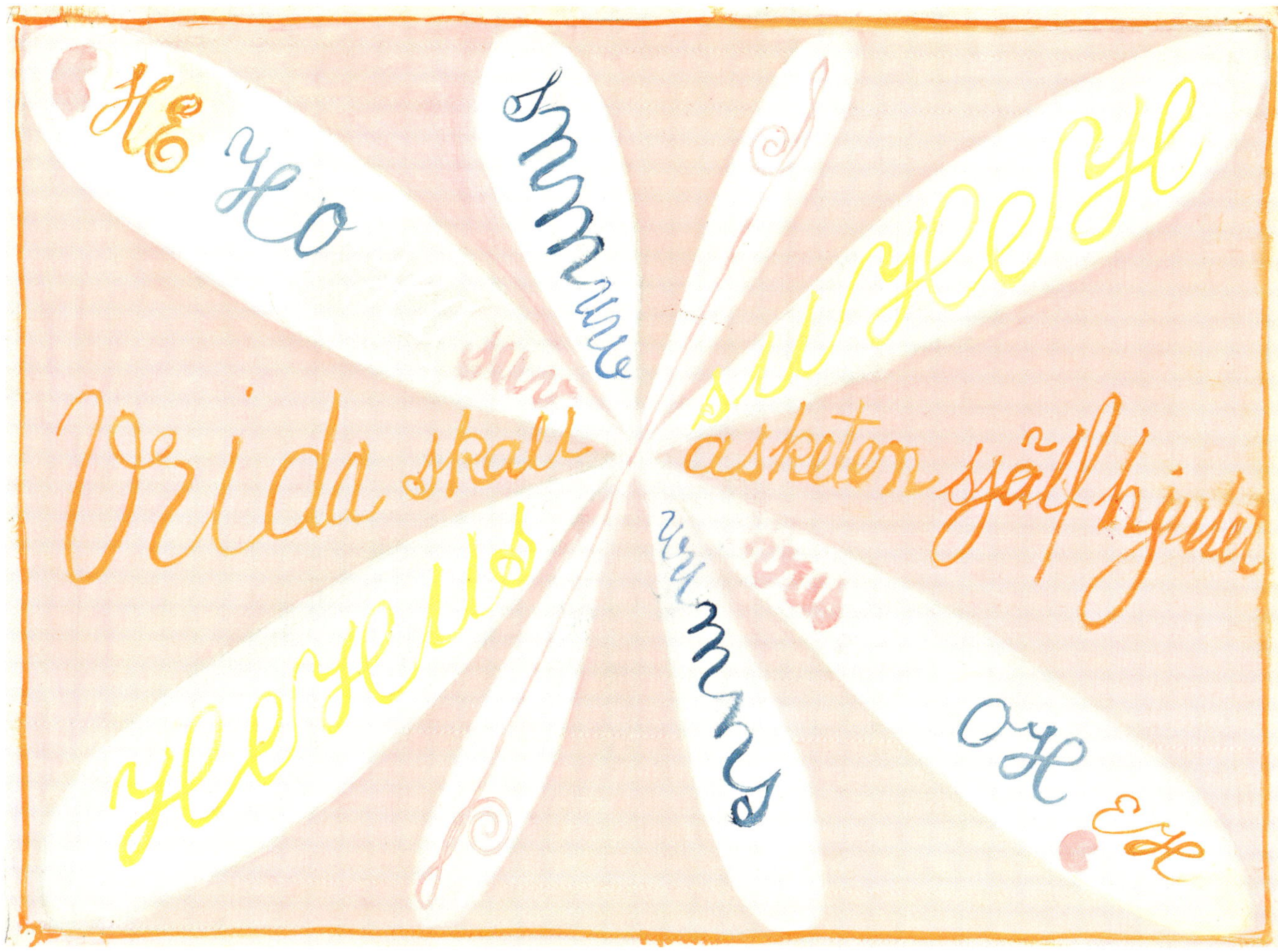

The Eros Series, The WU/Rose Series, Group II: No. 1, 1907
Oil on canvas, 58 x 78 cm (22⅞ x 30¾ in.)
Stockholm, Hilma af Klint Foundation, HaK 27

The Eros Series, The WU/Rose Series, Group II: No. 5, 1907
Oil on canvas, 58 x 79 cm (22⅞ x 31⅛ in.)
Stockholm, Hilma af Klint Foundation, HaK 31

Higher Masters had messaged af Klint about including letters in the paintings.[20] But what did the letters and the flower mean? Aware that this question would arise, af Klint later assembled a handwritten, alphabetized, explanatory glossary of all the letters and terms included in her paintings, of which there would be many.[21] The glossary helps decipher the works, although the meanings are not consistent or singular. Af Klint's phrases, letters, and symbols developed connotations over time, and may even have been self-referential within her oeuvre, to tie works together.

The glossary sheds light on af Klint's title for her first series. "W" has nine entries and "U" has four. The two combined letters "WU" are listed 15 times. Among the meanings for "WU" are "the color pink" and "the chain of evolution that takes place during the struggle inside and outside of humanity, also faith in development." "WU" can also mean "pink rose and white lily" and "the mystic name of the temple." The meaning of "WU" hovers but does not alight. Mystery remains as particles of meaning assemble, continue to vibrate, and dissolve.

"Eros is the fusion of all colors and announces, among other things, understanding in love."

HILMA AF KLINT, NOTEBOOK, HAK 556, MARCH 26, 1907

"The Eros Series—The WU/Rose Series, Group II" (1907)

A pure pastel pink stands at the center of Leadbeater's color key (p. 27), indicating "unselfish affection." The same color mostly defines the second series of "The Paintings for the Temple," the "Eros Series" (pp. 28–29): a group of eight oil on canvas works that also share the subheading "The WU/Rose Series,

BELOW
Johann Wolfgang von Goethe,
Plate Ft I, *Theory of Colours*, 1810
Etching, aquatint, colored, 29.2 x 22.5 cm (11½ x 8⅞ in.); inv. no. GFz 139
Weimar SWKK, Goethe-Nationalmuseum

OPPOSITE
The Large Figure Paintings, The WU/Rose Series, Group III: No. 1, 1907
Oil on canvas, 148 x 108 cm (58⅜ x 42⅝ in.)
Stockholm, Hilma af Klint Foundation, HaK 38

Group II." Their size increased from the first series (all works were now about 58 x 79 centimeters, or 22 x 31 inches) and the format shifted to horizontal. Floral shapes, flagellating spermatozoids, hearts, words, and letters appear on monochrome backgrounds (*Eros No. 1*, p. 28).

Eros No. 2 features the intersection and layering of Vestal and Asket, with the blue form on top, made clear by broken yellow lines. Such interlocked, recumbent shapes recur in a few of af Klint's compositions as a variation on a Venn diagram; here it features three wavelengths with "vs" written inside them. The glossary deciphers "vs" as "the workday's victory, life's culmination" and "the archetype, perfect harmony." In *Eros No. 3*, the word "Innocence" proclaims itself around a heartfelt, eternal union between "a" and "H" in a composition resembling a decorated envelope sealed by a snail. Several works in this series are subdivided like the flap side of envelopes, and the visual theme of crossing diagonal lines would continue in af Klint's art.

According to Leadbeater's color key, the pastel colors of the series—light blue, pink, and yellow—reference devotion, affection, and intellect. In *Eros No. 4* and *Eros No. 5* (p. 29), the clover and flowers stretch and distort their leaves and petals to expand and more fully occupy the canvas out to its edges and into its corners. The flattened vegetal emblems are overwritten with letters and Swedish words.

"Group II" concludes with *Eros No. 8*, a pale pink and white painting of a pod shape manned by a developing fetal form. The haloed letters "vs" appear again at each tip of the pod. In the empty corners not spanned by the pod, the silhouette of a hook (upper left) and an eyelet (lower right) float in space. A cryptic notebook entry of The Five from September 1907 said, "The eyelet was hooked into by the hook."[22] The hook and eyelet shapes have been filled in but are recognizable in their silhouette. They would become part of af Klint's established iconography.

"The Large Figure Paintings—The WU/Rose Series, Group III" (1907)

The next 10 canvases in "Paintings for the Temple" return to a more figurative approach. Slightly varied in size, they would have exceeded the height, if not the arm span of the petite artist, with the final work reaching 169 x 144.5 centimeters (approximately 67 x 57 inches). In "The Large Figure Paintings," or "The WU/Rose Series, Group III," male and female characters interact and pose in dark, theatrical space. At first glance they appear to reflect Christian motifs—an annunciation, a crucifixion, a pieta—but in fact they embody an ongoing education in Theosophical and Rosicrucian thought.

Two governing forces compete in the painting *The Large Figure Paintings, No. 1* (p. 31). A blond androgyne, posed as an angelic astral being, is backed by a set of swan's wings. The swan's head may be shown in sequential time-lapse positions, or the swan might have two heads, or there may be two swans. The angel's right arm reaches back for a swan's beak, while the bird's webbed foot reaches through to rest on the angel's thigh. These two are intimate. As the angel's legs descend, they develop creaturely fetlocks and weave into the shallow depth of a blue spiral. The spiral, af Klint's symbol for evolution, looks here like part of a machine. The angel grabs its control knob with a fist, while a brown, wooly, satyr-like being grabs the knob from the other side. The two compete for control, resulting in the spiral's constant movement.

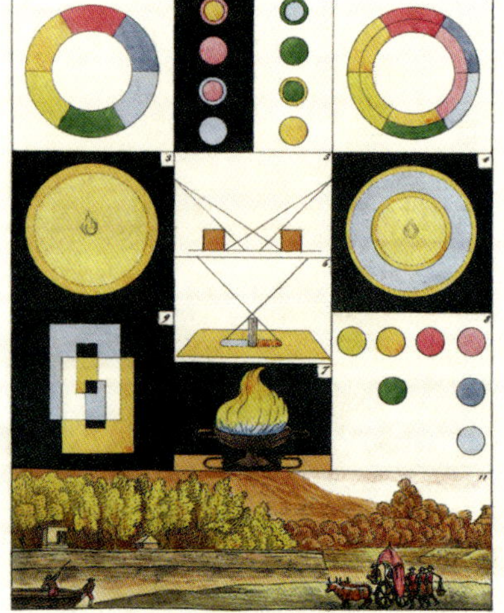

The golden angel may represent Ormuzd (or Ahura Mazda) who, according to Persian mythology, was the twin of Ahriman (or Angra Mainyu), the world's

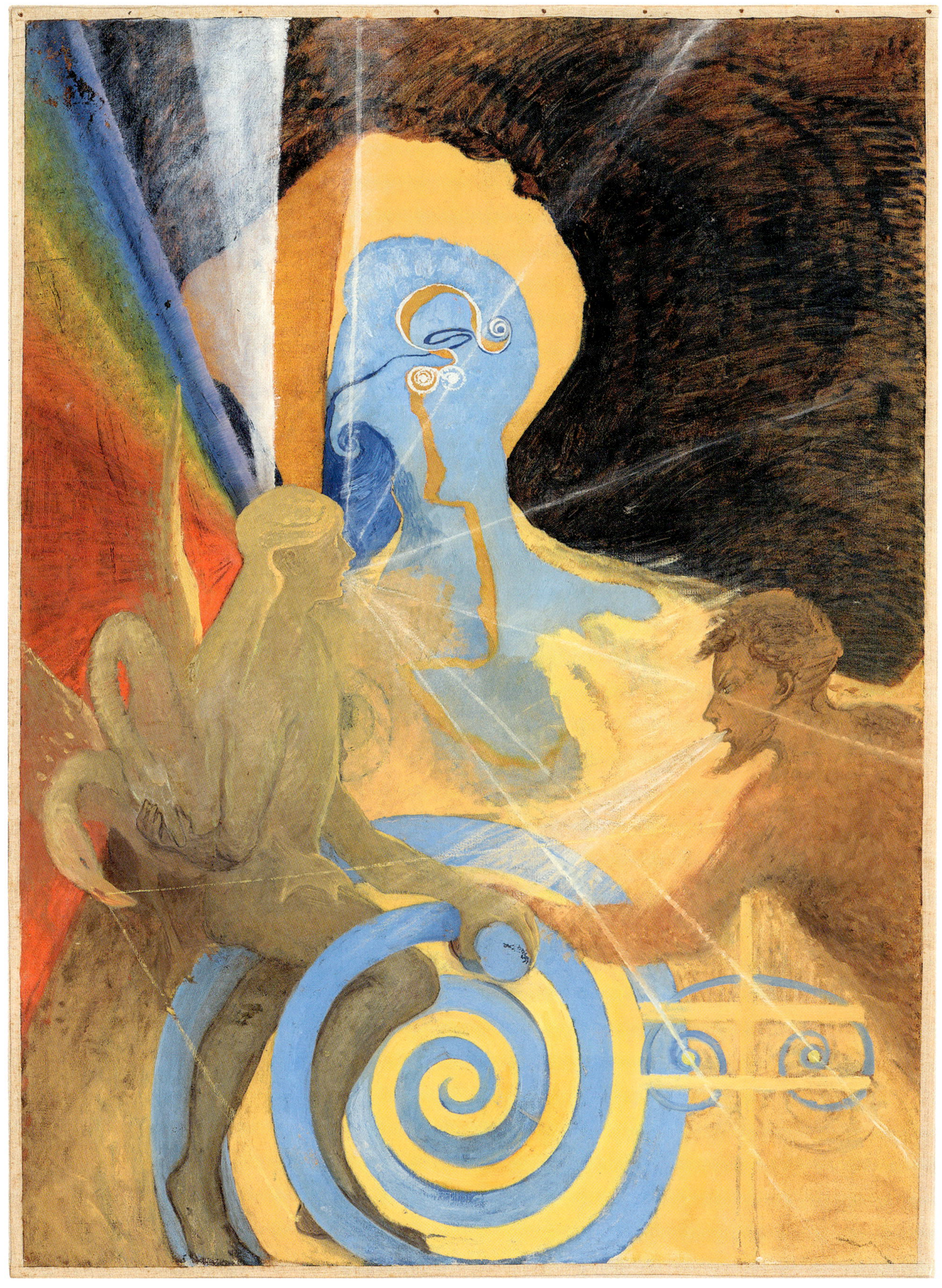

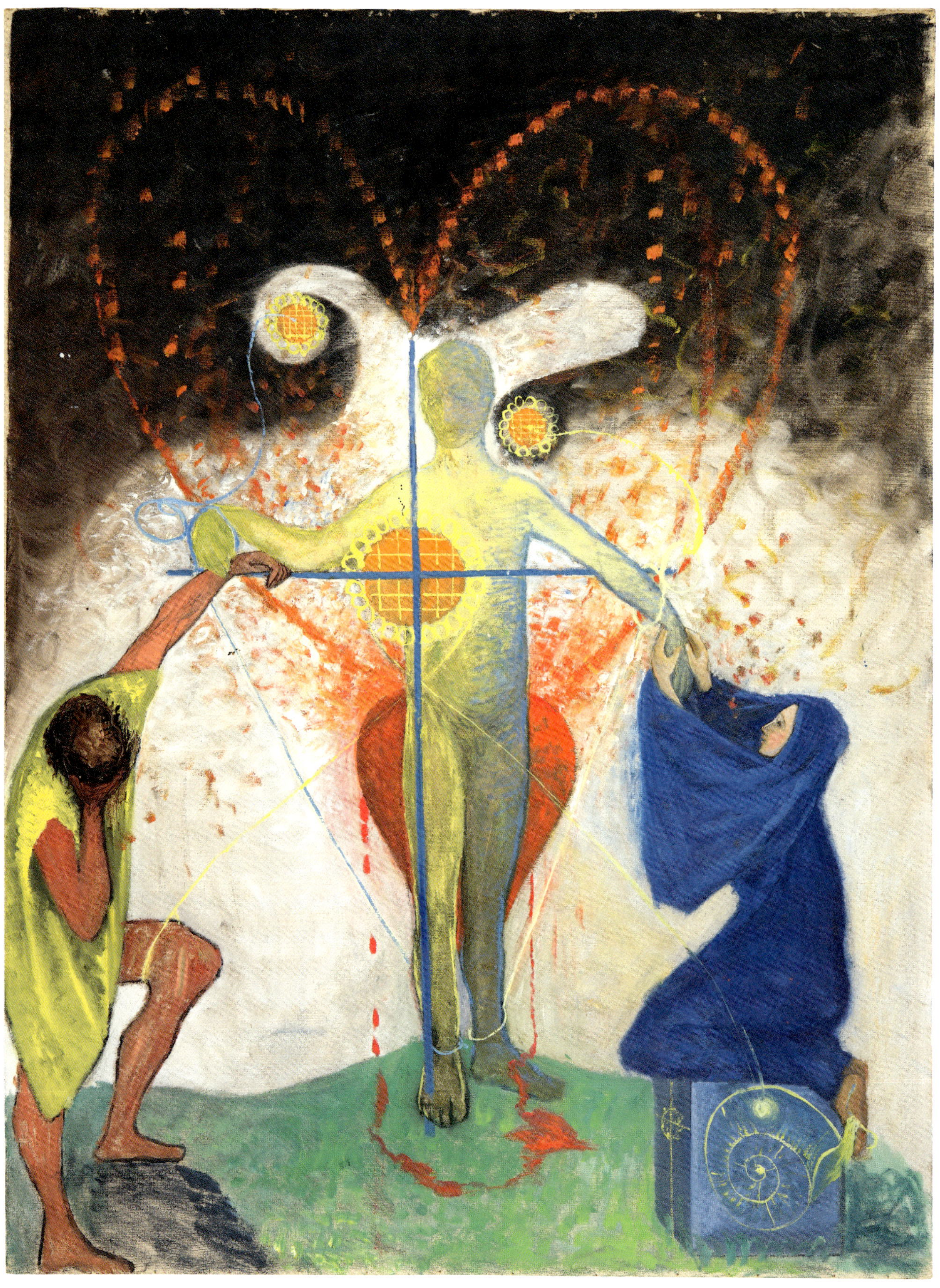

corrupting force. Blavatsky wrote about such figures as "The Sons of Boundless Time" and "the respective representatives of good and evil, of light and darkness, of the spiritual and the material elements in man, and also in the universe and everything contained in it."[23] Af Klint shows Ormuzd as the wisdom-filled astral body of the sun, and thus as light, backed by all the refracting colors of the rainbow and fortified by swans. Message rays transmit from the speaking mouth, which might have been a nod to rapidly developing radio technology at the time.[24] Ahriman opposes the light as a negative counter-creator and blows a funnel of blue fumes onto the control knob. His threat amplifies through his aura, shaped like a rearing blue ectoplasm, silhouetted against the golden aura and surrounding darkness.

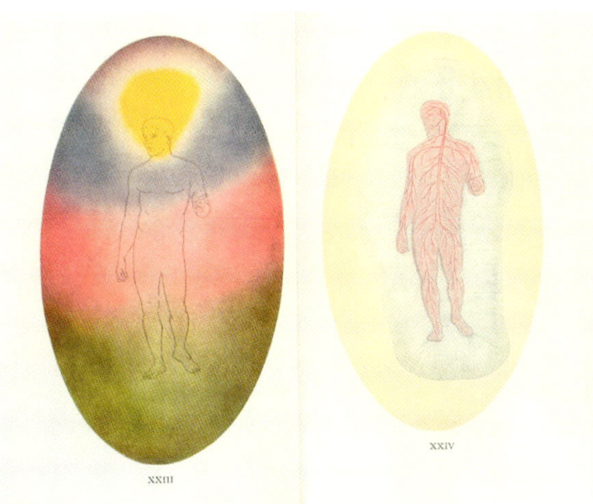

Charles W. Leadbeater, Plate 23, *The Astral Body of the Developed Man* and Plate 24, *The Normal Health-Aura* from *Man Visible and Invisible* (1903), a book dealing with how emotions and consciousness manifest in the human aura.

OPPOSITE
The Large Figure Paintings, The WU/Rose Series, Group III: No. 2, The Key to All Work to Date (Nyckeln till hittillsvarande arbete), 1907
Oil on canvas, 150 x 118 cm (59 x 46½ in.)
Stockholm, Hilma af Klint Foundation, HaK 39

It was around this time—in 1907–08—that af Klint began developing interest in the ideas of Rudolf Steiner (1861–1925), who had edited the scientific writings of Johann Wolfgang von Goethe (1749–1832) and was interested in his *Farbenlehre* (*Theory of Colours*, p. 30). Steiner believed that *Farbenlehre* included a holistic understanding of natural phenomena and implied a new worldview. Af Klint would have been aware that, for Goethe, blue and yellow were the fundamental colors of light.

In another of af Klint's *Large Figure Paintings*, the second in the series, the scene resembles a crucifixion (p. 32). She returned repeatedly to this motif and synthesized it with theosophically inspired imagery. The half-yellow, half-blue outlined figure with a soft face and a faint penis stands glowing behind the cross, which penetrates its foot. The figure evokes the scale, equanimity, and pose of Leadbeater's standing model in *Man Visible and Invisible* (p. 33). A bleeding red heart levitates behind the figure's lower body, while a dripping trail of blood encircles its feet. Spurts or splashes of blood draw the broken outline of a second, much larger heart suspended in space behind the figure's upper body. A crosshatched form repeats in three versions. The two smaller ones each trail a yellow or blue vine that wraps the wrists and ankles of the figure standing behind the cross. The larger crosshatched form affixes itself behind the cross's center. Its yellow filaments tie to the mourning and supplicant figures, male and female, left and right. The blue-cloaked female figure kneels on a light blue cube traced with the yellow spiral of a snail shell. She clasps the standing figure's hand, and, although not fainting, takes a position like the Virgin Mary in scenes of Christ's crucifixion or his deposition from the cross. As he buries his head in one hand, the mourning male figure hangs his other wrist over the crossbar.

Green grass, brightened with yellow, undulates as a living ground. Behind the standing figure, a white aura lifts and dispels darkness. The aura may have released one crosshatched sunflower/bacillus ball and is about to drop the next one, or the opposite may be true, and the round yellow and orange forms are rising. Does the heart reign over suffering and death, or does love equate to suffering? Is af Klint relating resurrection in the Christian sense to reincarnation as understood in Eastern religions? Is the resurrected or reincarnated figure a product of the man and woman, a union of their opposites? These questions, and more, stand unanswered.

PAGE 34
The Large Figure Paintings, The WU/Rose Series, Group III: No. 7a, 1907
Oil on canvas, 159 x 139 cm (62⅝ x 54¾ in.)
Stockholm, Hilma af Klint Foundation, HaK 44

PAGE 35
The Large Figure Paintings, The WU/Rose Series, Group III: No. 8, 1907
Oil on canvas, 159 x 137 cm (62⅝ x 54 in.)
Stockholm, Hilma af Klint Foundation, HaK 46

"The Ten Largest" (1907)

In October 1907, af Klint stopped work on "The Large Figure Paintings" and began the series for which she is arguably the best known: "The Ten Largest."

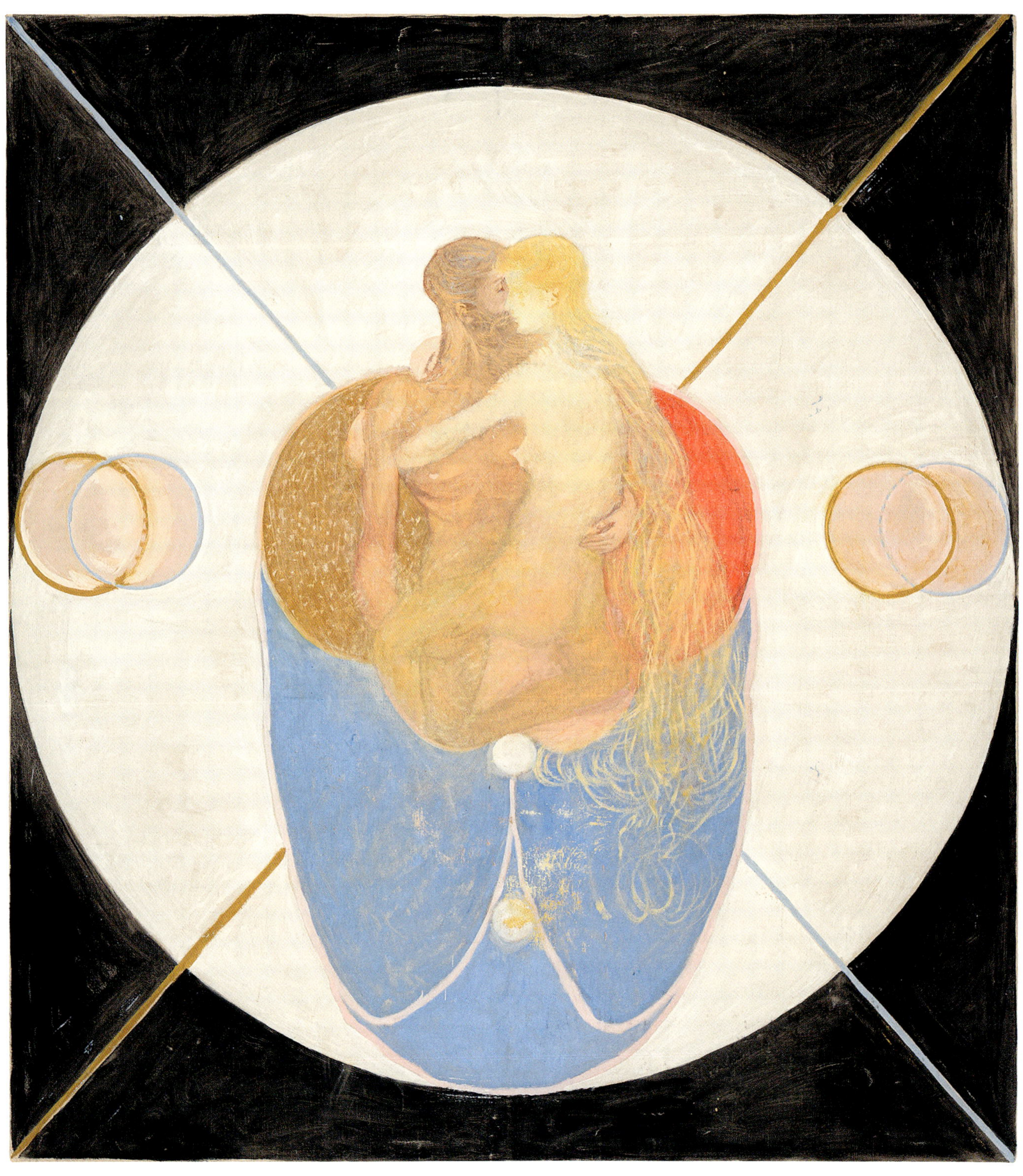

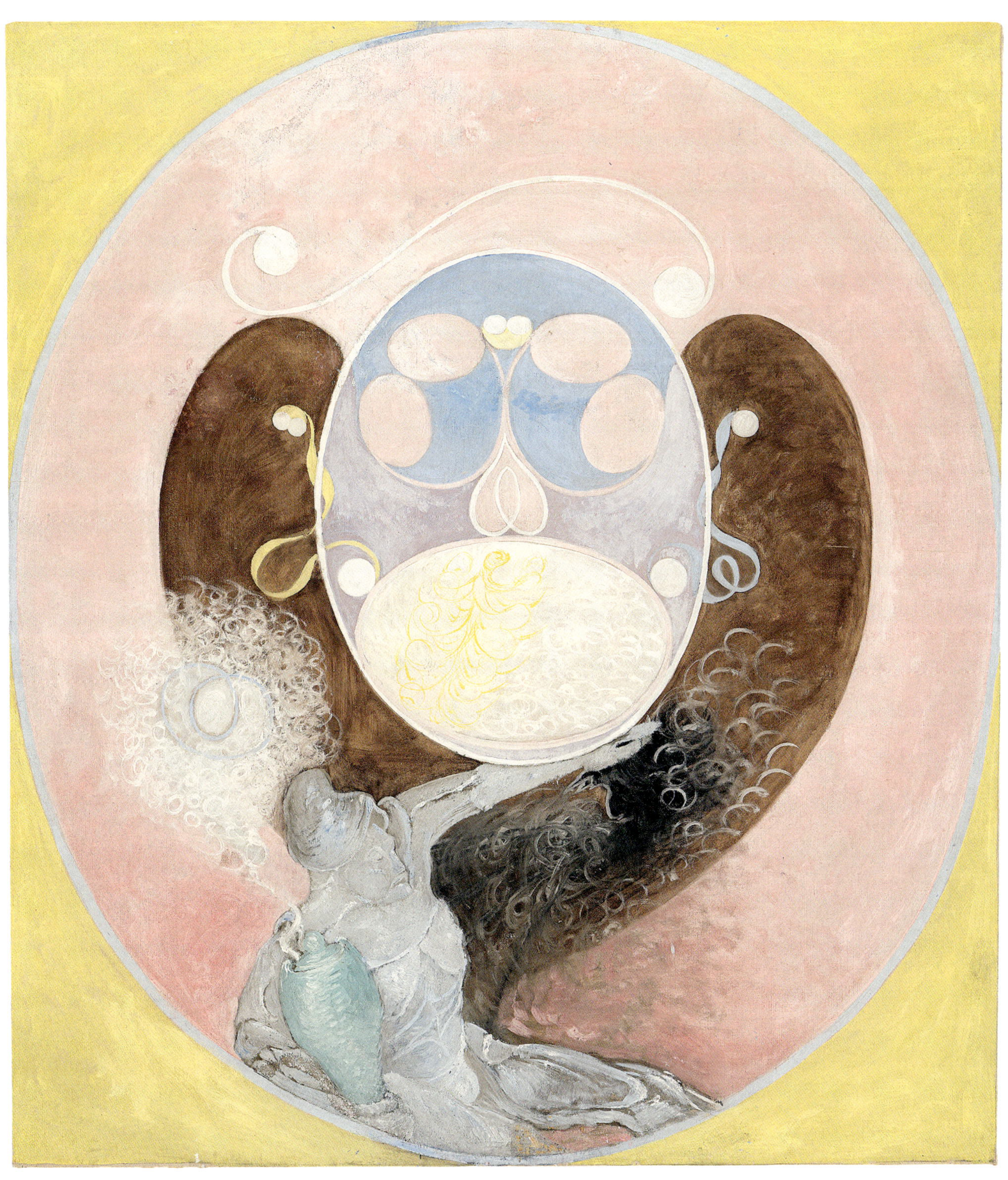

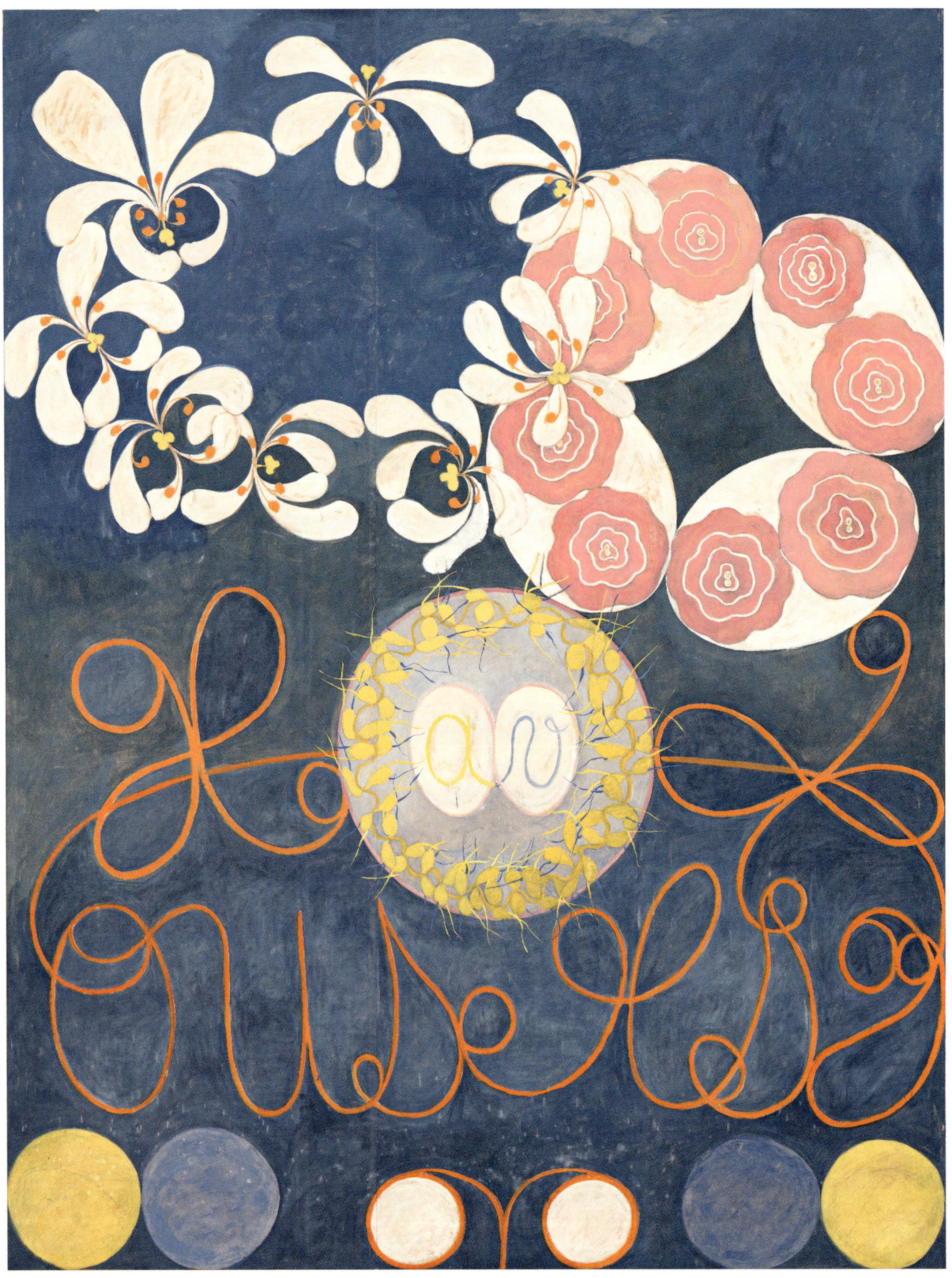
av

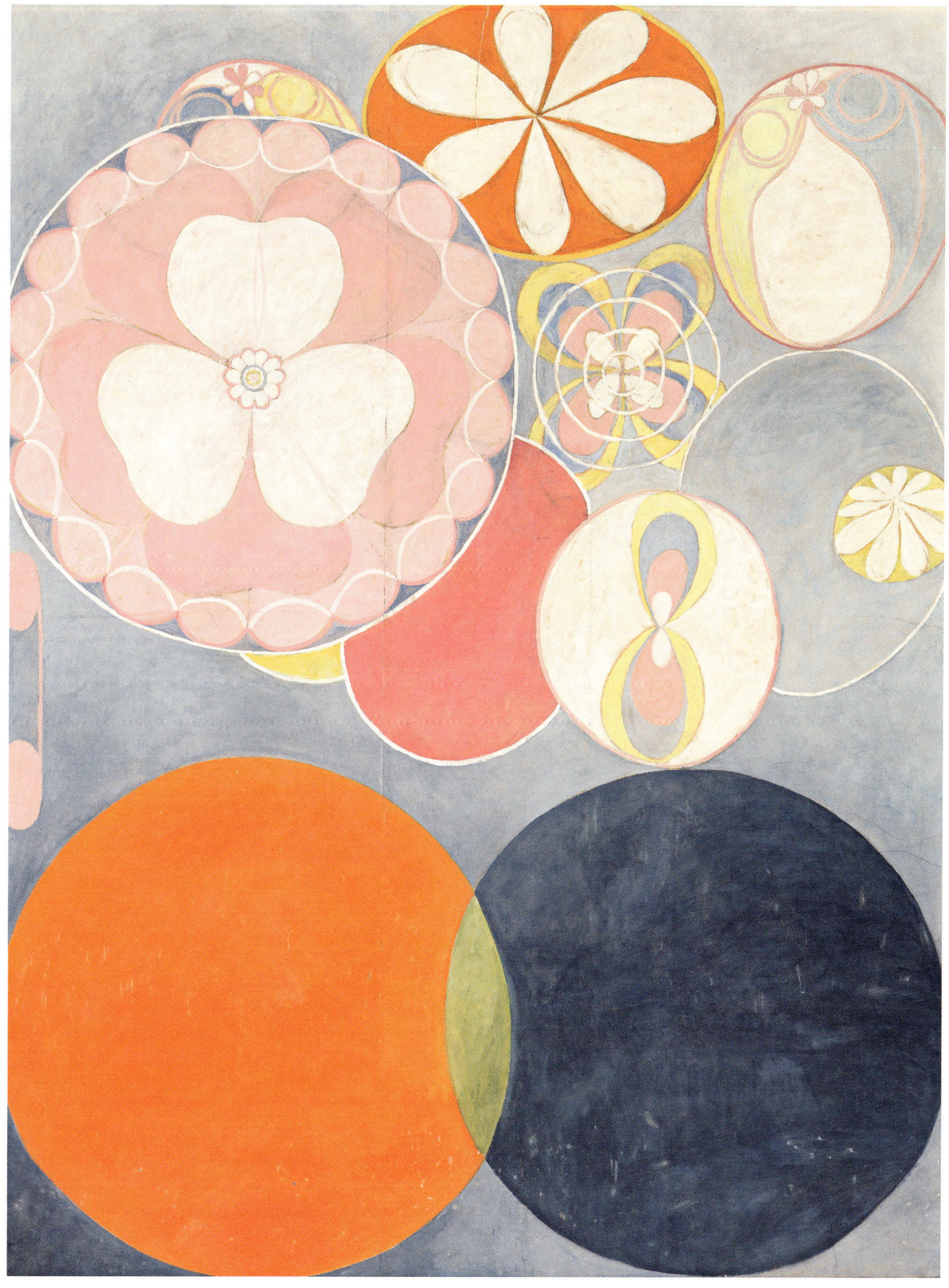

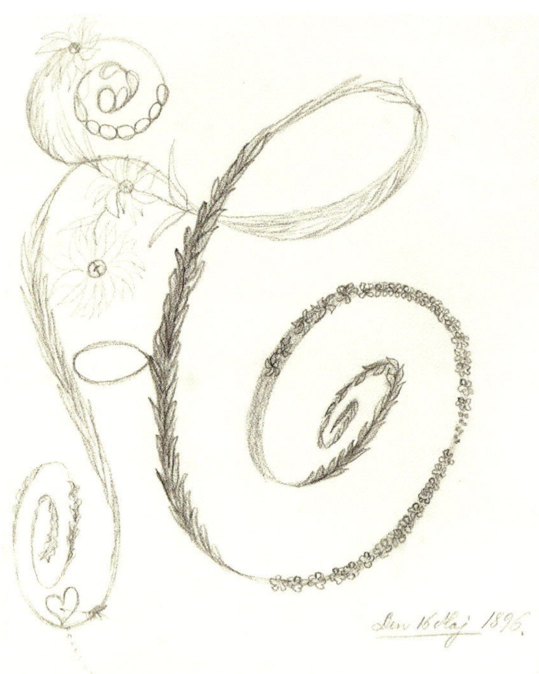

Drawing from Book 3, December 12, 1895–July 14, 1902
Sketchbook 3, 31 x 26 cm (12¼ x 10¼ in.)
Stockholm, Hilma af Klint Foundation, HaK S3-14

PAGE 36
The Ten Largest, Group IV: No. 1, Childhood (Barnaåldern), 1907
Tempera on paper mounted on canvas, 322 x 239 cm (126⅞ x 94 in.)
Stockholm, Hilma af Klint Foundation, HaK 102

PAGE 37
The Ten Largest, Group IV: No. 2, Childhood (Barnaåldern), 1907
Tempera on paper mounted on canvas, 315 x 234 cm (124 x 92¼ in.)
Stockholm, Hilma af Klint Foundation, HaK 103

PAGE 39
The Ten Largest, Group IV: No. 3, Youth (Ynglingaåldern), 1907
Tempera on paper mounted on canvas, 321 x 240 cm (126½ x 94½ in.)
Stockholm, Hilma af Klint Foundation, HaK 104

PAGE 40
The Ten Largest, Group IV: No. 5, Adulthood (Mannaåldern), 1907
Tempera on paper mounted on canvas, 321 x 237 cm (126½ x 93⅜ in.)
Stockholm, Hilma af Klint Foundation, HaK 106

PAGE 41
The Ten Largest, Group IV: No. 7, Adulthood (Mannaåldern), 1907
Tempera on paper mounted on canvas, 315 x 235 cm (124 x 92⅝ in.)
Stockholm, Hilma af Klint Foundation, HaK 108

The spirit Amaliel had been guiding sketches for this new series since August 1907. The paintings were to be twice as big as the previous series—as large as 328 x 240 cm (10.8 x 7.8 feet). The scale of "The Ten Largest" relates to frescoes or altar paintings made for churches and cathedrals like the ones af Klint had visited in Italy in 1903.[25] Because of their size, executing these works required some rethinking of her studio process. Af Klint bought large sheets of architect's paper which she could sketch on and then glue onto canvas. "The Ten Largest" were made not with oil paint, but tempera, a medium that had been most extensively used by medieval and Renaissance artists before 1500, when oil painting overtook it in popularity. Tempera uses egg yolks as the binder, and af Klint made her own paint. The thin, fluid medium required working flat. Placing the large work on the studio floor meant the works had to be stepped on, and traces of footprints have been seen on some of "The Ten Largest." The paper seams are visible. The handmade imperfection of these works is part of their aesthetic, and they recall the automatic drawings of The Five's notebooks (*Drawing from Book 3*, p. 38).

It took just two months to complete "The Ten Largest," which were a collective portrayal of the ages: *Childhood* (pp. 36–37), *Youth* (pp. 6 and 39), *Adulthood* (pp. 22, 40–42), and *Old Age* (pp. 43–44). *Adulthood* comprises four dedicated canvases, while each of the other ages were addressed in two canvases. Each age has its own single background color, shades that come alive with underpainted colors, such as areas of blue under the lavender background, or yellow under orange. The oversized paintings tower over the viewer with flat areas of bright color, abstract symbols, circles, undulating lines, cursive writing, floral and vegetal elements, spiraling snail shells, and ionic volutes that look like breasts. Af Klint scholars have identified labia, ovary, sperm, testicle, and egg shapes among the forms. There are jumps in scale, with microscopic and cellular elements appearing as large as pets, and flowers aspiring to parasol size. Every shape and line floats, undulates, swims, or rotates in its indeterminate pastel realm. The two canvases of *Old Age* come the closest to feeling grounded, their forms stilled and their passions quieted into a companionship of equals.

During the painting of "The Ten Largest," Cassel distanced herself from af Klint, and her feeling of unity with the artist disintegrated. Cederberg stepped in to help with automatic drawing and painting. Several new women had joined members of The Five working with af Klint, including two of her studio mates. Another new participant was Gusten Andersson, who came to the studio to pray, and who, while in a trance, made a drawing of roses and lilies. The wreaths of roses and lilies in the first painting of "The Ten Largest" relate to a coming together: Andersson had a crush on af Klint, and the two flowers embody a relationship that may have replaced Cassel's intense involvement with af Klint.[26] These works speak to release, feeling, color, sex, joy, temperance, and more. Their expanded visual fields and untethered forms activate space in a new way. There is much to read in af Klint's "Paintings for the Temple" that suggests their pictorial space began and ended as a love realm that transcended gender norms and expressed her own relationships within the framework of her ambitions to capture astral images.

After "The Ten Largest," af Klint returned to finish "The Large Figure Paintings" (pp. 31, 32, 34–35). In *No. 6*, she embodied herself as a bearded,

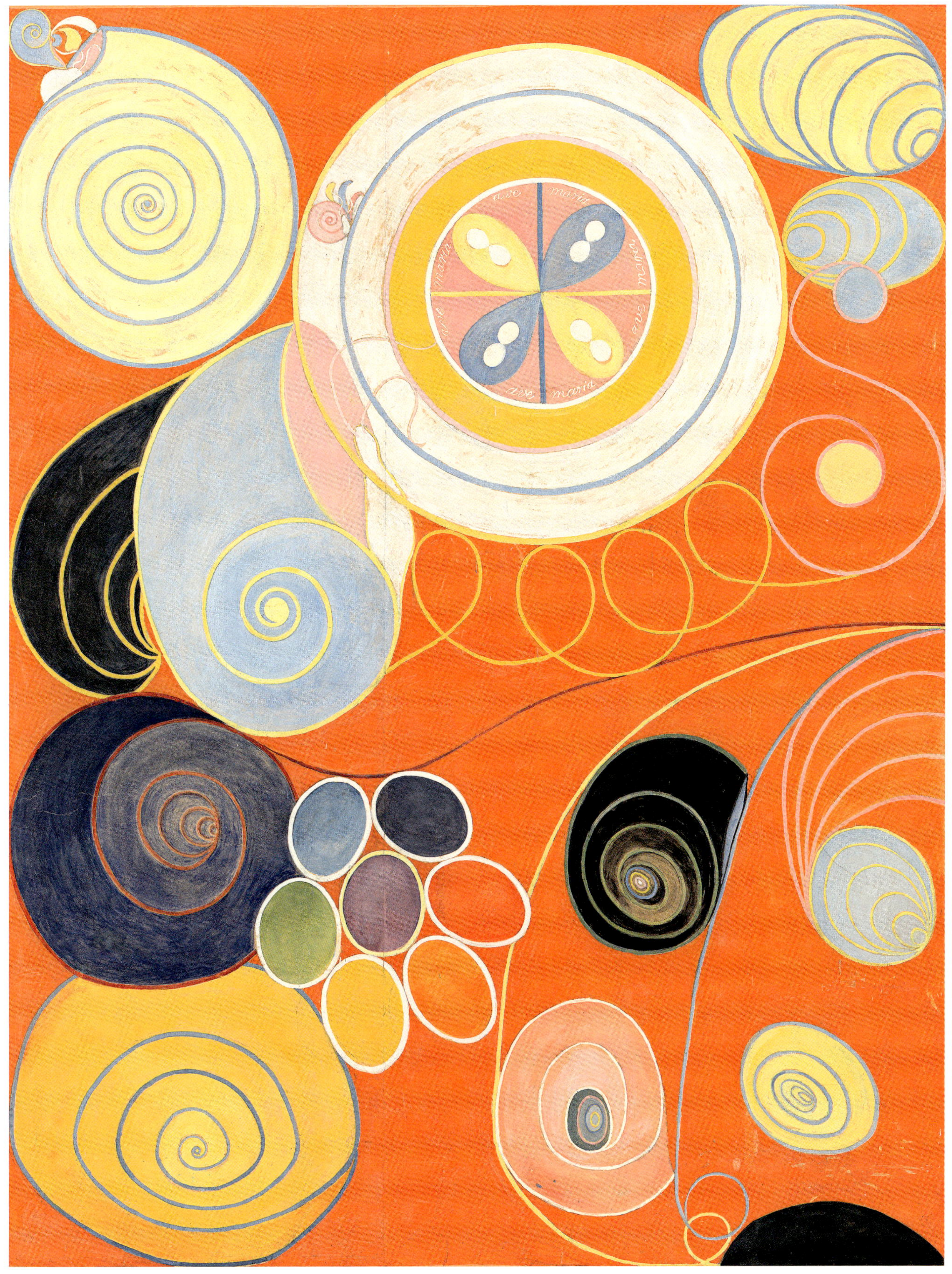
ave maria
ave maria

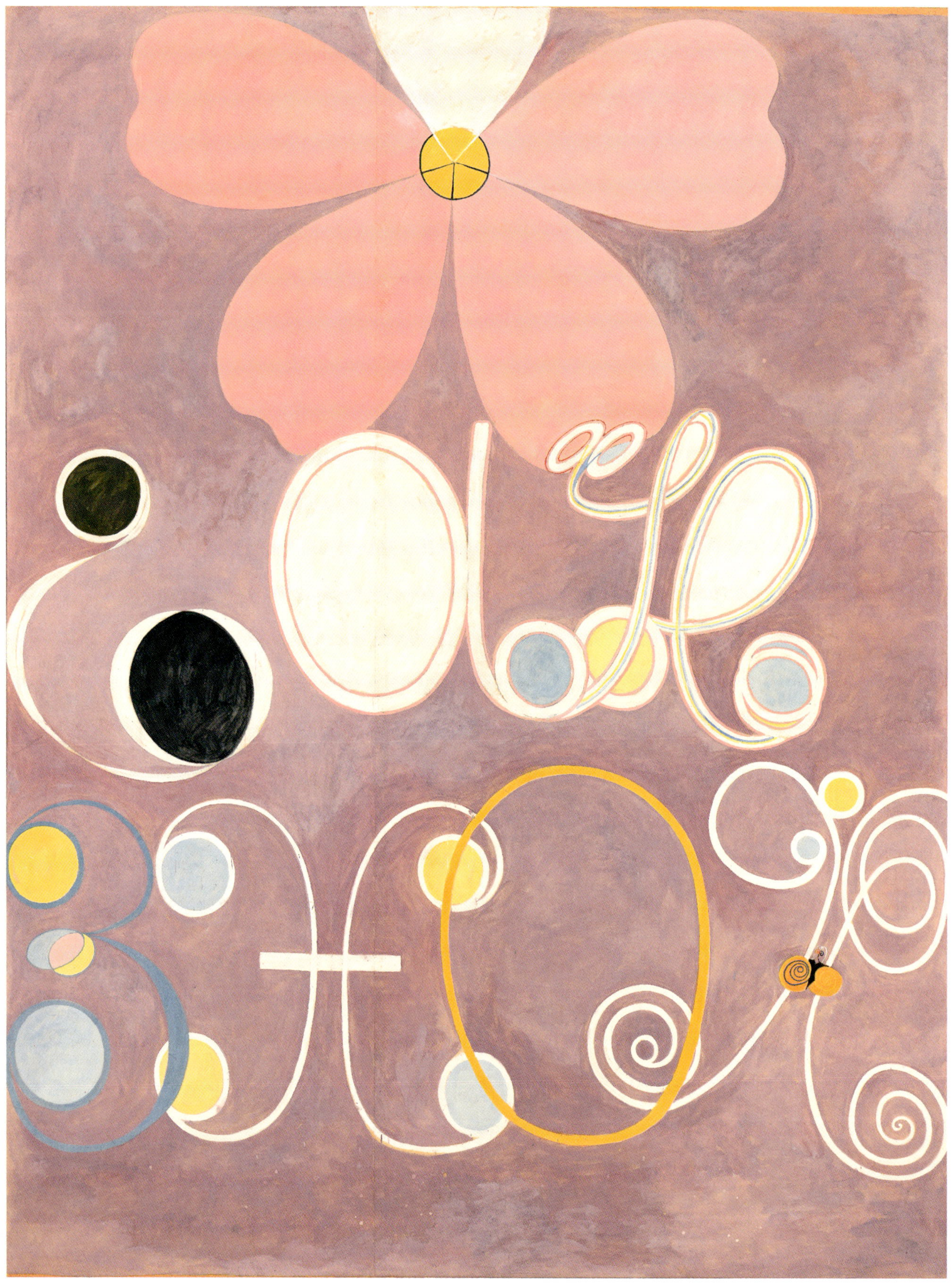

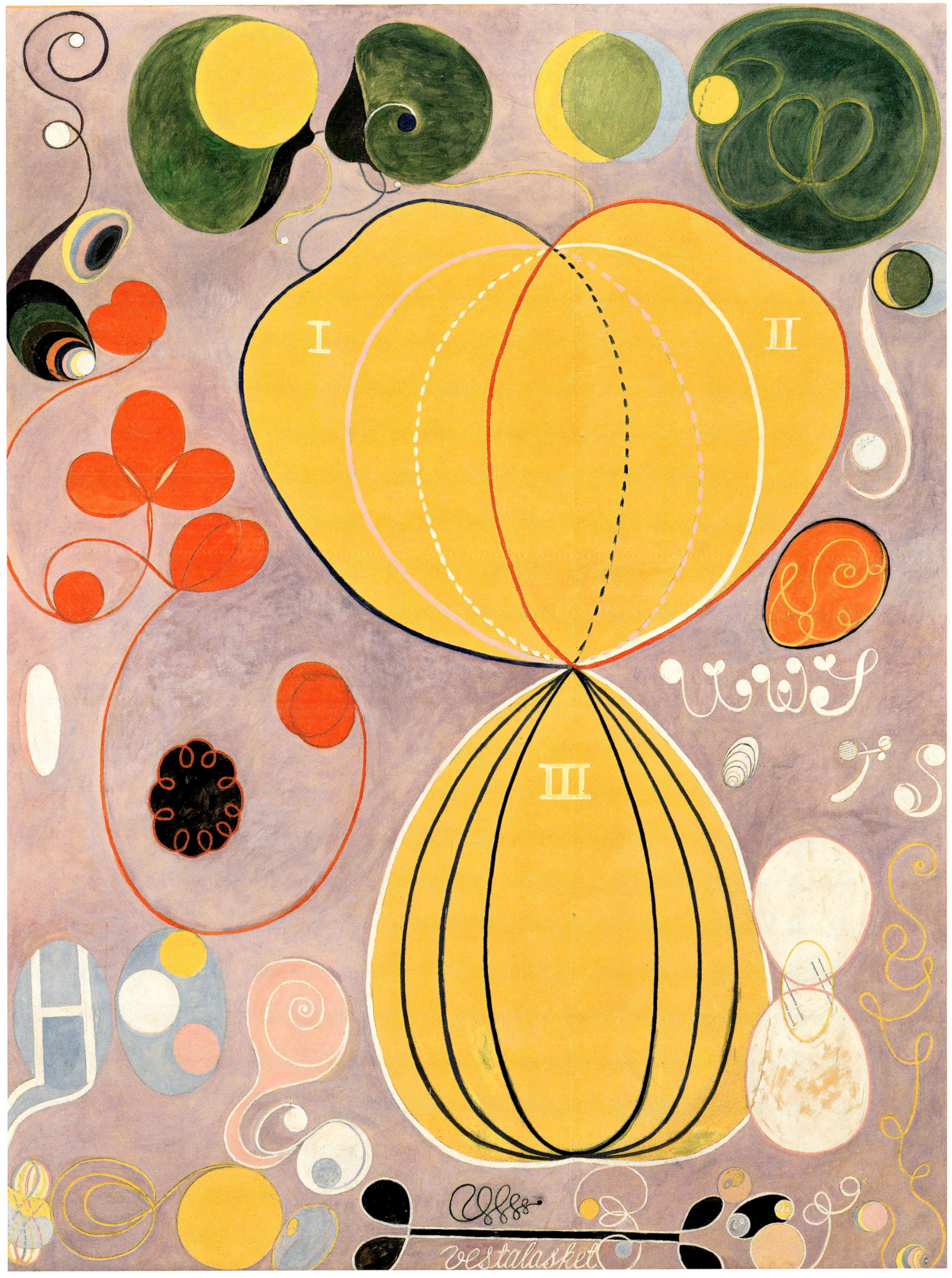
I
II
III
vestalasket

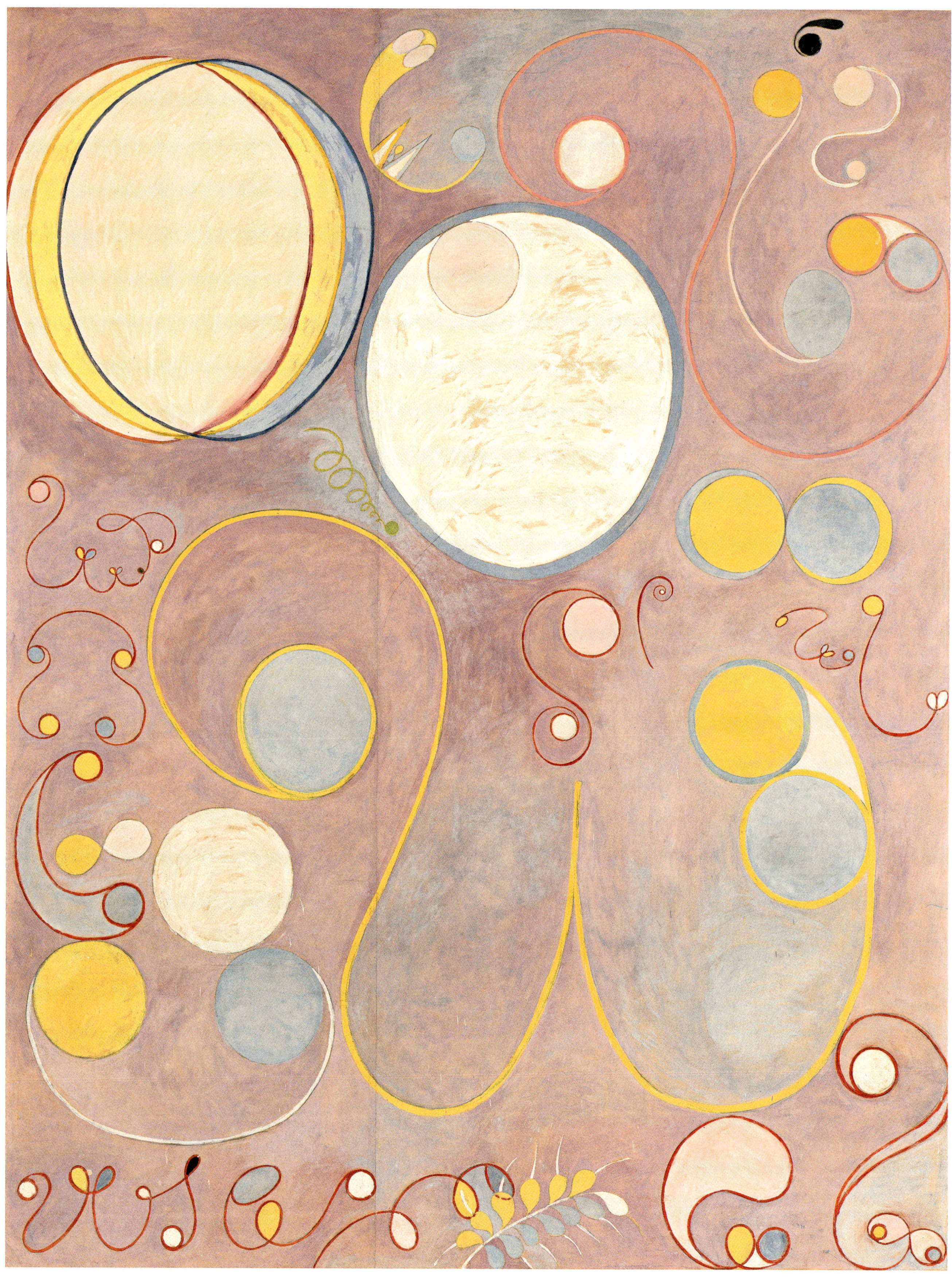

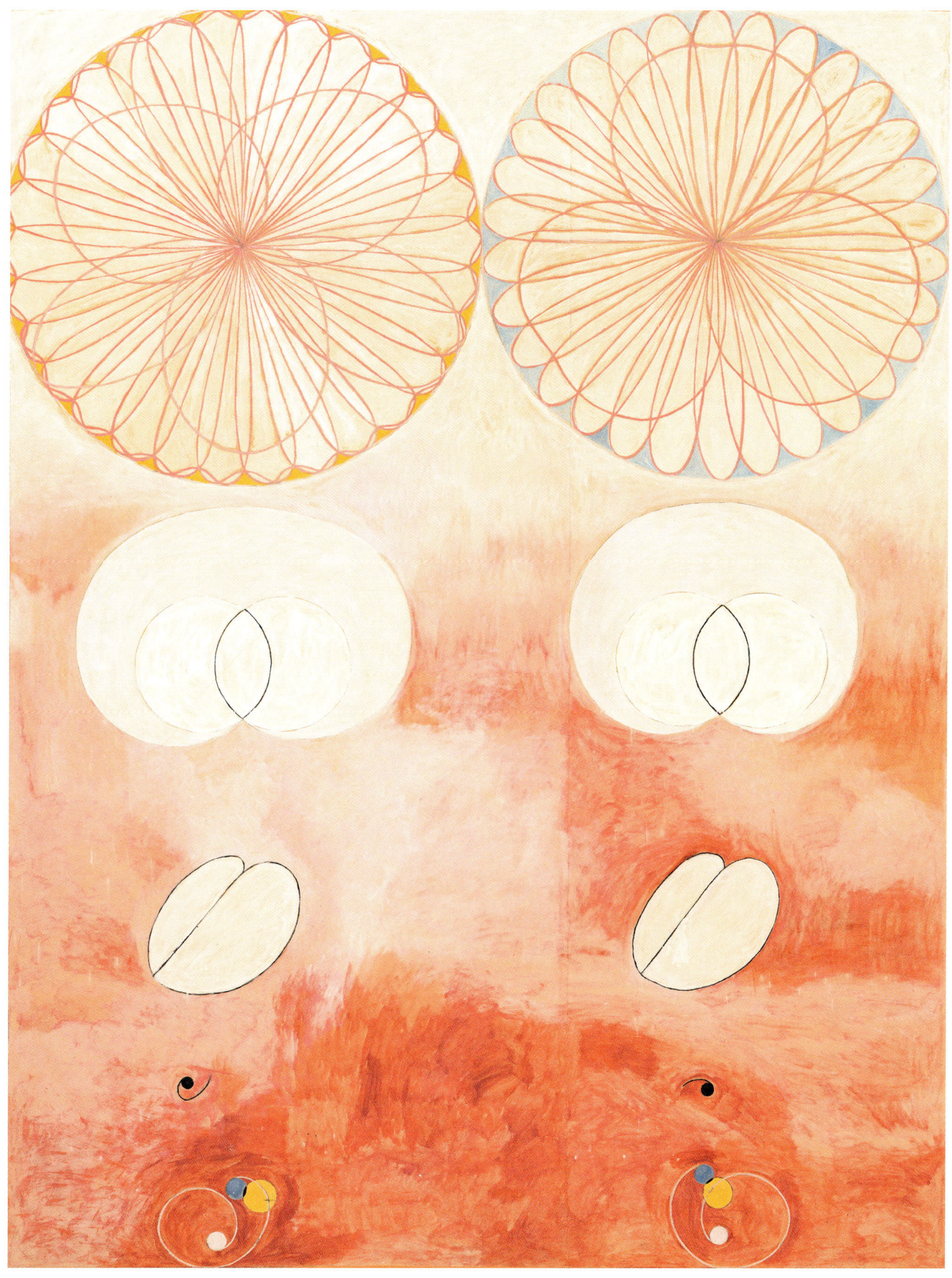

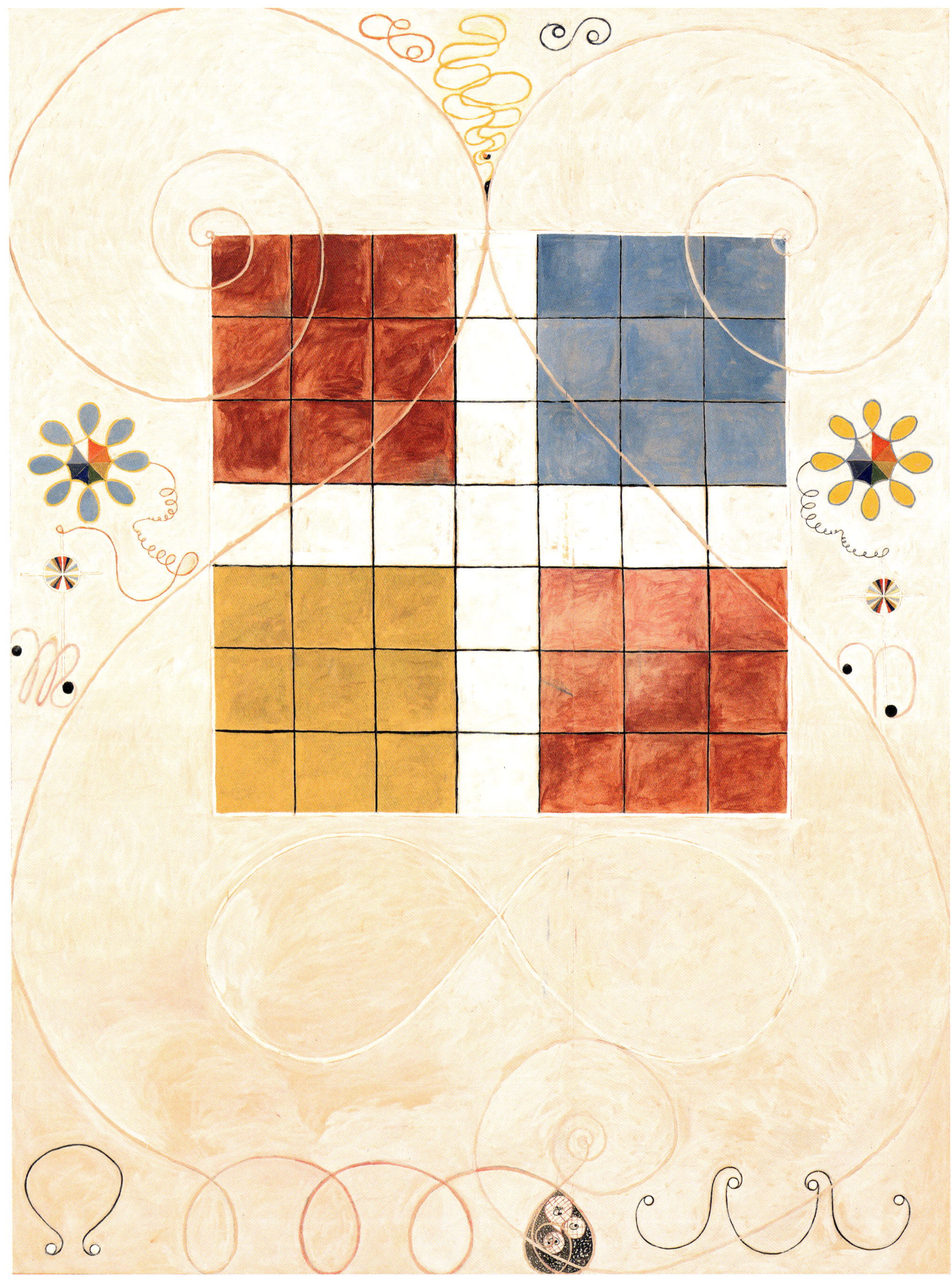

kneeling nude man and Gusten Andersson as a delicate nude maiden with knees held chastely together to one side. The darker-skinned male figure supports the pale female's forearms and thus indirectly also the red cross she holds, which penetrates her chest from behind. Her feet pass strangely under his thigh as she kneels. He frames and controls her, and a sheet of their commingled hair separates their skin from each other. They are as one.

Subdued and praying, the figures look down, while two moonlike circles hover above them. Both are crowned with rose flowers, and seem like storybook characters, perhaps a king and a queen. Their crowns and the red cross allude to the esoteric order of Rosicrucianism, founded in the 17th century, whose symbol was the Rose (or Rosy) Cross. Theosophists recognized a kindred movement in Rosicrucianism, which asserted that its "adepts" possessed secret knowledge that could spiritually transform society. Steiner's 1907 lecture about Rosicrucianism reveals its importance to the mind of the Theosophist:

> Mineral, plant, animal, or man—each is a condensed form of the spirit In this sense, the Rosicrucian theosophy will lead us to understand the spiritual foundations of the world. It does not change us into brooding egotists, but into lovers of life, for it does not despise ordinary life, nor estrange us from our earthly tasks, but it unites us with them.[27]

The allegorical imagery of Rosicrucianism plays itself out in the theater of af Klint's paintings. One of the "manifestos" of Rosicrucianism, *The Chymical Wedding of Christian Rosenkreutz* (1616), is an allegorical romance about the marriage of a couple who live in a castle full of marvels and images of lions. The allegory interprets alchemical processes as symbols of transformation, a kind of mystic marriage, and relates the seven steps of the fictional Rosenkreutz's

PAGE 42
The Ten Largest, Group IV: No. 8, Adulthood (Mannaåldern), 1907
Tempera on paper mounted on canvas,
322 x 239 cm (126⅞ x 94 in.)
Stockholm, Hilma af Klint Foundation, HaK 109

PAGE 43
(The Ten Largest, Group IV: No. 9, Old Age (Ålderdomen), 1907
Tempera on paper mounted on canvas,
320 x 238 cm (126 x 93¾ in.)
Stockholm, Hilma af Klint Foundation, HaK 110

OPPOSITE
The Ten Largest, Group IV: No. 10, Old Age (Ålderdomen), 1907
Tempera on paper mounted on canvas,
320 x 237 cm (126 x 93⅜ in.)
Stockholm, Hilma af Klint Foundation, HaK 111

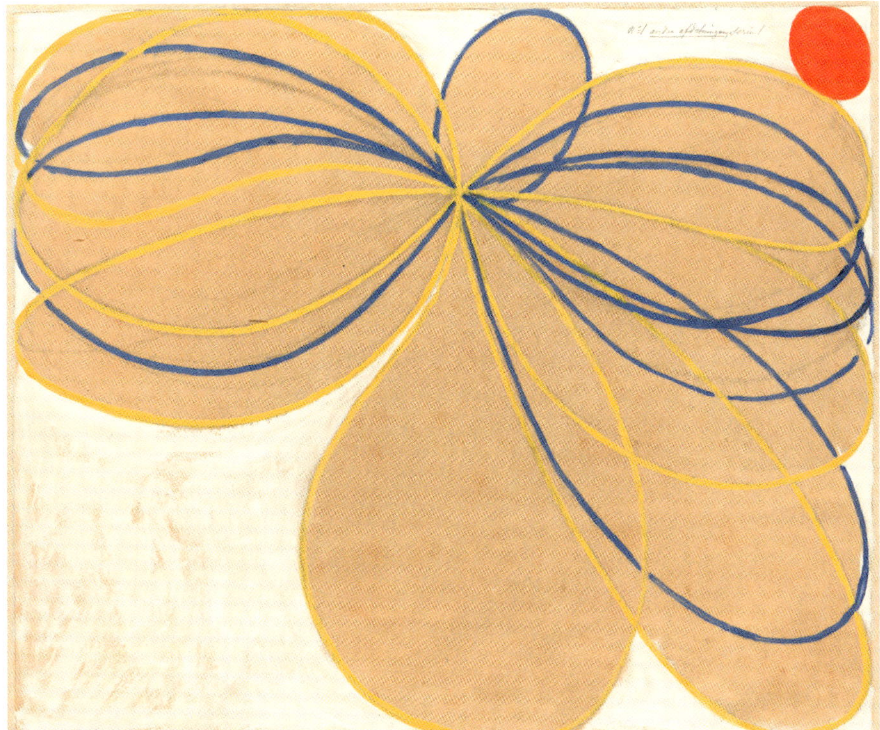

The Seven-Pointed Star, The WUS/ Seven-Pointed Star Series, Group V: No. 1, 1908
Tempera, gouache, and graphite on paper mounted on canvas, 62.5 x 76 cm (24⅝ x 30 in.)
Stockholm, Hilma af Klint Foundation, HaK 48

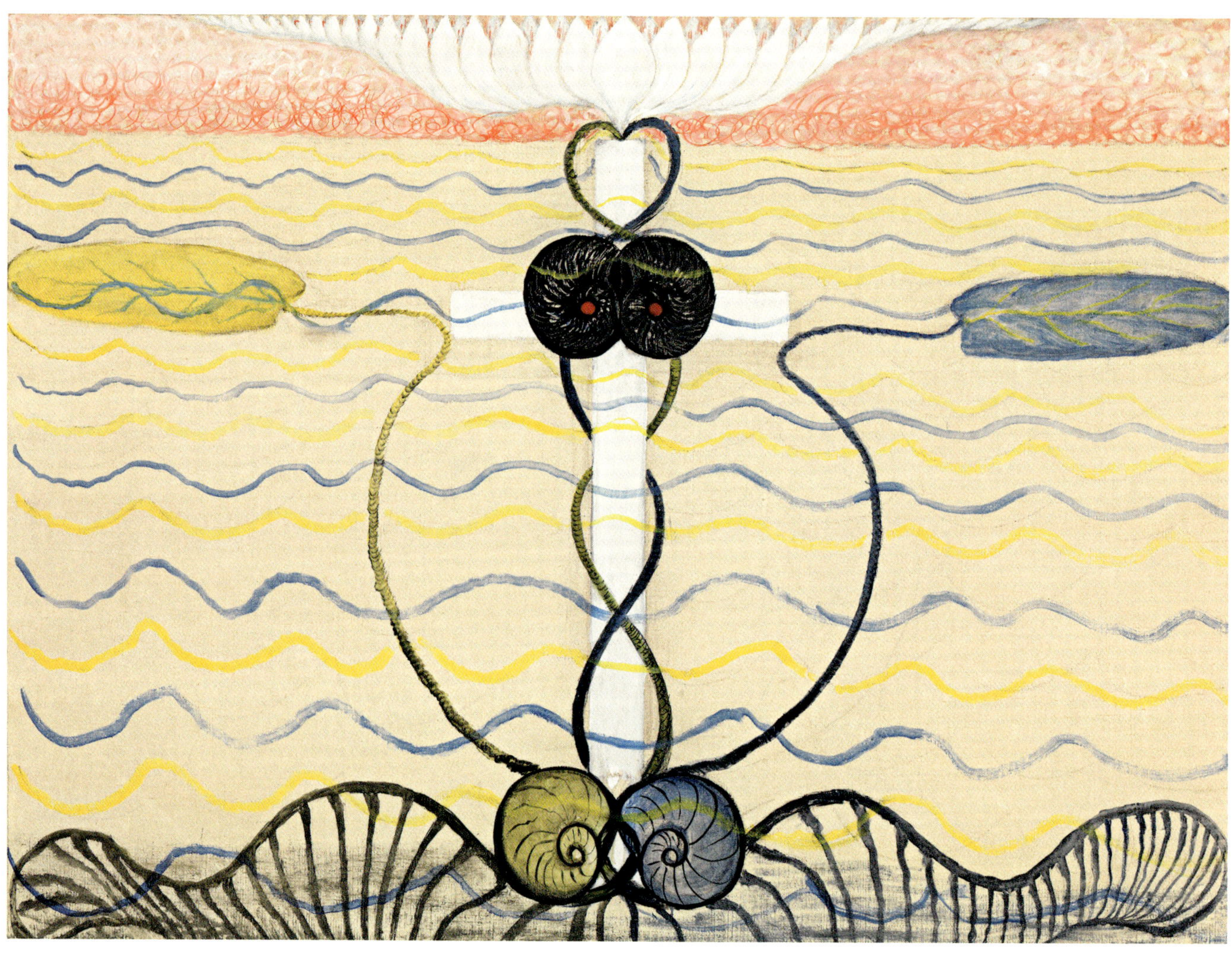

The Evolution, The WUS/Seven-Pointed Star Series, Group VI: No. 6, 1908
Oil on canvas, 100.5 x 132.5 cm (39⅝ x 52¼ in.)
Stockholm, Hilma af Klint Foundation, HaK 74

The Evolution, The WUS/Seven-Pointed Star Series, Group VI: No. 7, 1908
Oil on canvas, 101.5 x 132.5 cm (40 x 52¼ in.)
Stockholm, Hilma af Klint Foundation, HaK 75

spiritual awakening and his union with the divine. In *The Large Figure Paintings, No. 6*, af Klint fastened onto this metaphor of male-female union in her pursuit of self-actualization as a nonbinary person and her own spiritual awakening and transformation.

In *The Large Figure Paintings, No. 7a* (p. 34) af Klint advanced the scene to a more sexualized, frontal union. She superimposed the couple on a softened blue "W"[28] or "omega," the last letter of the Greek alphabet (ω), denoting the end of something. The blue shapes open at the top as a crucible and the couple's lower bodies dissolve into its heat. The pairing of white circles from the previous painting unites into one large circle. Little Venn diagrams speak to the right and left of intersection and combination. An "X" shape of crossing diagonals—one yellow bridegroom line, one blue bride line—reaches from corner to corner in the darkness, reiterating the coupling genitals as geometry. Is the blue crucible simultaneously a woman's truncated upper torso? Do the small white circles between the two drooping "breast" forms depict chakras,[29] or something as banal as blouse buttons? Are there equal parts of touch, spiritual longing, and pain layered here, a forcing together of the everyday with the symbolic? Nothing seems definable.

The next work, *The Large Figure Paintings, No. 7b* (1907), repeats the crucible and background, but now newly formed organs float where humans melted, and a lion's head is suspended emblematically from a winged or feathered heart.

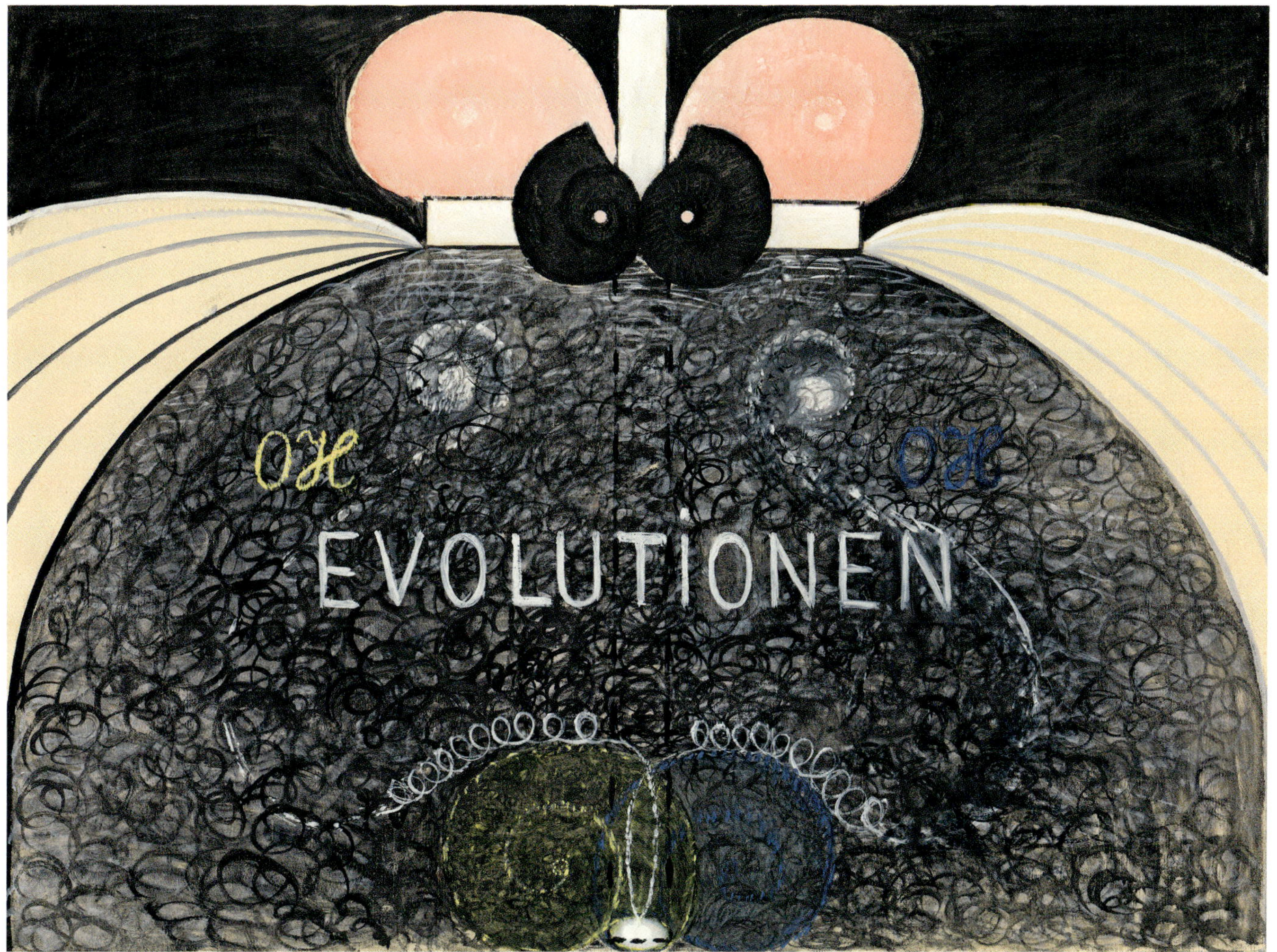

Af Klint's superimposition of an "X" over a circle recalls Leonardo da Vinci's *Vitruvian Man* (*c.* 1490), a drawing of a man standing with arms outstretched and feet spread within a circle that is itself based on the ideal human proportions posited by the Roman engineer and architect Vitruvius. Robert Fludd, one of Rosicrucianism's chief exponents, used a similar image on the title page of his *History of Two Worlds* (1617–21), which addresses the creation of the universe. Af Klint reinterpreted such established uses of geometry to refer to the micro- and macrocosm, showing the human body as a complete world unto itself that mirrors the functioning of the larger divine cosmos around it.

Eerily serene, the last painting of the series pictures a white Rosicrucian altar (cross with central rose), like the altar used by The Five, within a lavender-suffused room. Leadbeater, using his aura color chart, might have read the room as expressive of a love for humanity. Two erect, tiny sentinels flank the altar on each side, one designated yellow, one blue. In their uprightness do they each become a cursive "H," making this Hilma's altar?

When "The Large Figure Paintings" were finished, af Klint had a vision, and she proposed that The Five perform an allegorical marriage-type ceremony based on it. According to Voss, af Klint saw herself and Gusten on two chaises, one blue, one yellow, like the female and male principles. They were holding hands, and according to the spirits, Sigrid Hedman was to lead them to the altar.[30]

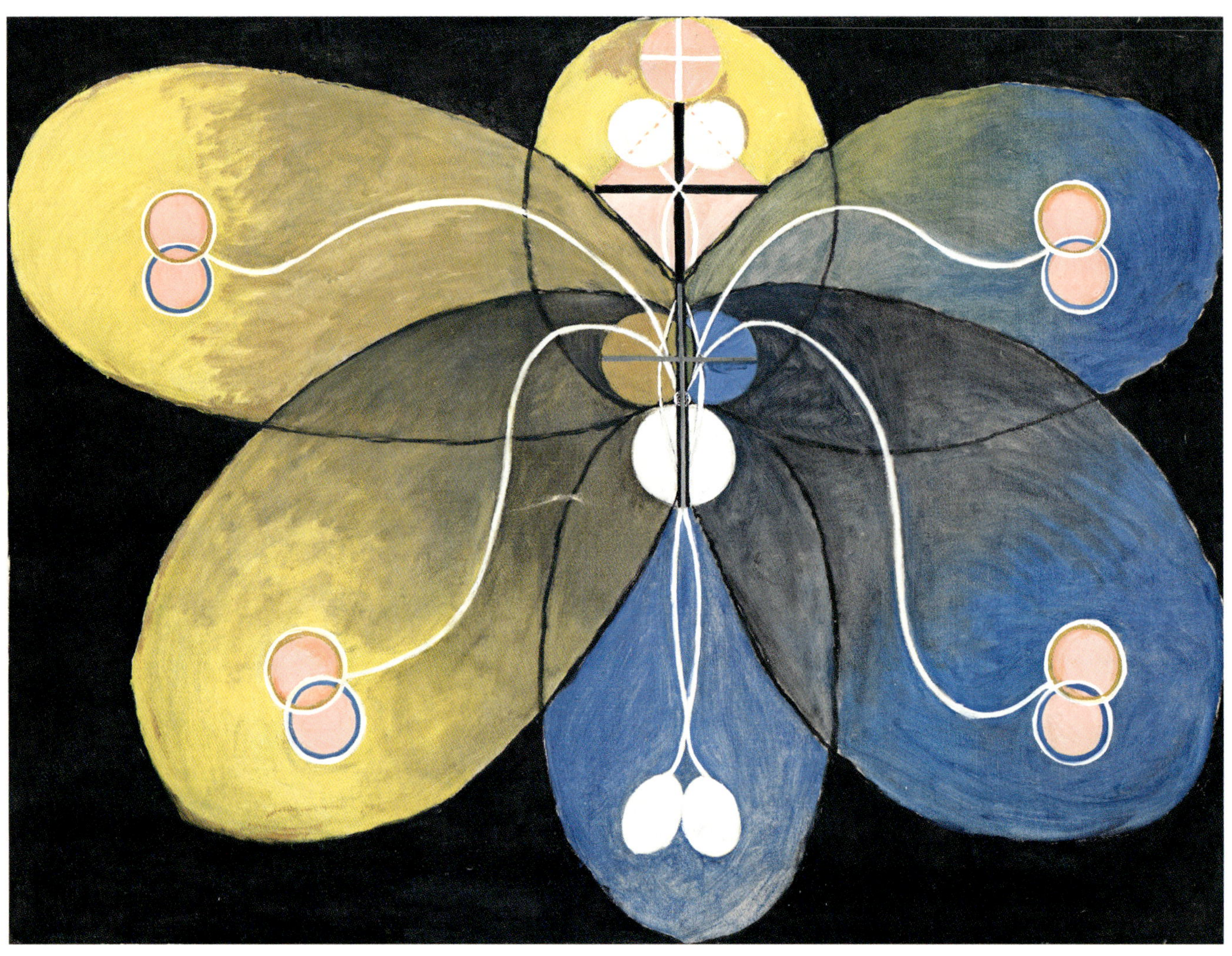

The other women, including Gusten, balked at the nature of the ceremony and refused. Af Klint had gone too far with her suggestion. The artist felt rebuked by the group of women who had sustained and accompanied her up until this point.

"The Evolution—The WUS/Seven-Pointed Star Series, Group VI" (1908)

In all of af Klint's work, the theme of transformative evolution is present. Several of the 16 paintings in her next series, "The Evolution, The WUS/Seven-Pointed Star Series, Group VI," play on cosmic geometry by superimposing a human figure on a circle. The drawings also feature hearts, crucifixes, spirals, bodily organs, pubic hair, androgynous figures, abstracted swan parts, snakes, and a variation on the ouroboros—an ancient symbol of a snake eating its own tail, representing the cycle of destruction and rebirth—that holds eggs in its mouth (pp. 48–49).

Evolution No. 6 and *No. 7* (pp. 46–47) both evoke the female body by assembling it from snail shells, line, and color. In *No. 6* (p. 46), af Klint borrowed the traditional symbol of the caduceus for her subject. As the winged staff carried by the mythical Greek god Hermes, the caduceus also signifies his namesake, Hermes Trismegistos, a legendary ancient writer, teacher, and sage associated with the idea of primeval, divine wisdom. Texts attributed to Hermes Trismegistos went on to influence occult traditions. Af Klint boldly adapts the traditional

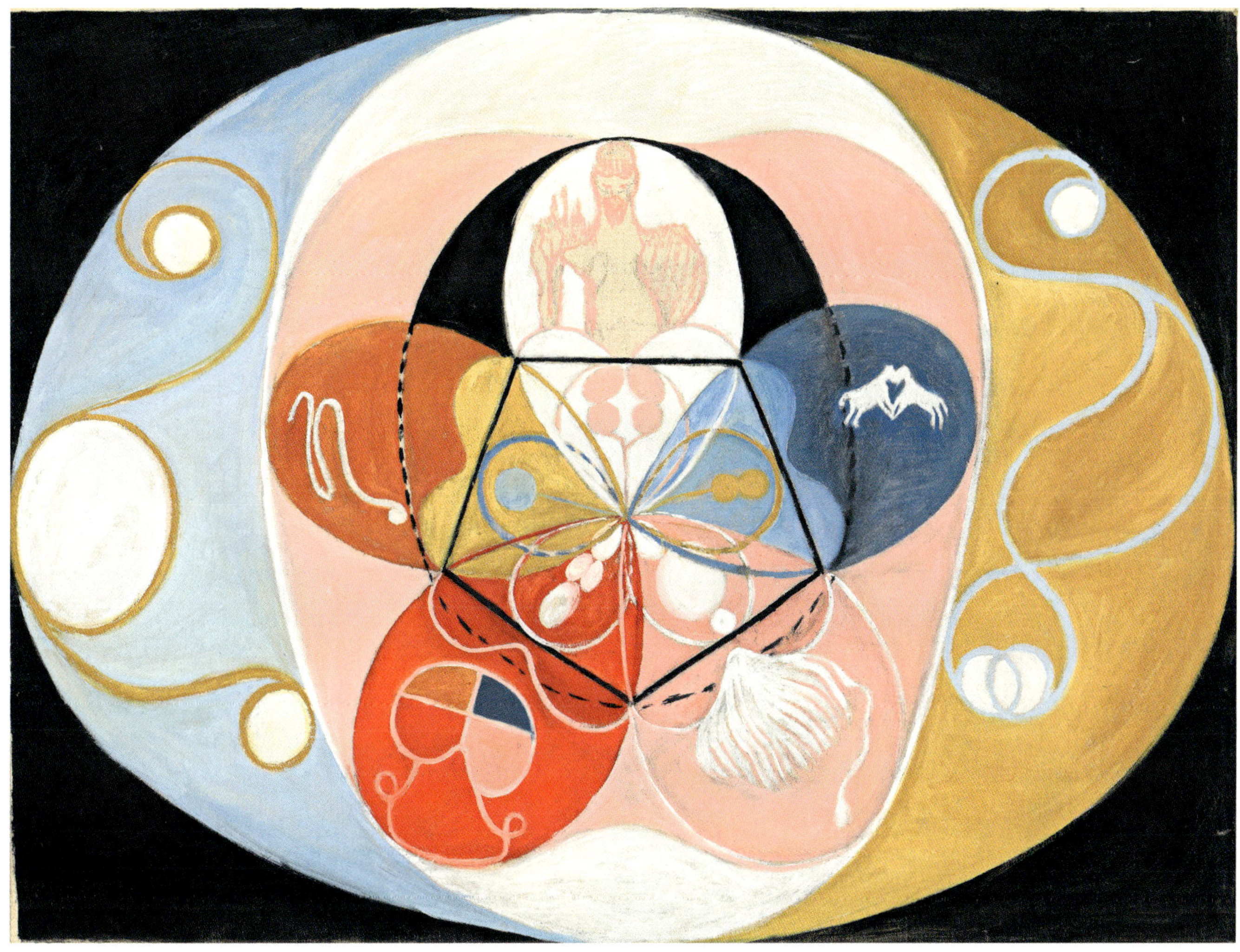

symbol of the caduceus, changing its wings to a combination of swan wing and lotus flower. The staff's winding snakes are reduced to lines that end in a heart. She adds snail shells as breasts with red nipples. Since the caduceus is also associated with alchemy and healing, af Klint is suggesting that spiritual evolution could advance civilization.

"The US Series, Group VII" (1908)

The next series of "Paintings for the Temple" shrank considerably to an easy-to-carry size and used the portable medium of watercolor, as if af Klint felt the need to withdraw and contract. Paintings in "The US Series, Group VII" (1908) include the word "devakan" (Swedish: *devachan*) and "OH" (p. 9), af Klint's letter signification for devachan as noted in her glossary. She was thinking about the place Theosophists believe the advanced initiated soul travels to after death, the blissful intermediate stage between two earth lives or incarnations, just below Nirvana.

Around this time af Klint met Rudolf Steiner in person when he came to Stockholm to lecture. Her notes began to mention him starting in early 1908. Af Klint asked Steiner to put her in touch with the Rosicrucian Brotherhood. She asked if he thought it was possible the Rosicrucians may have already influenced her work.[31] She must have known that they had.

The Evolution, The WUS/Seven-Pointed Star Series, Group VI: No. 9, 1908
Oil on canvas, 101 x 131.5 cm (39⅞ x 51⅞ in.)
Stockholm, Hilma af Klint Foundation, HaK 77

The Evolution, The WUS/Seven-Pointed Star Series, Group VI: No. 14, 1908
Oil on canvas, 99.5 x 129.5 cm (39¼ x 51 in.)
Stockholm, Hilma af Klint Foundation, HaK 82

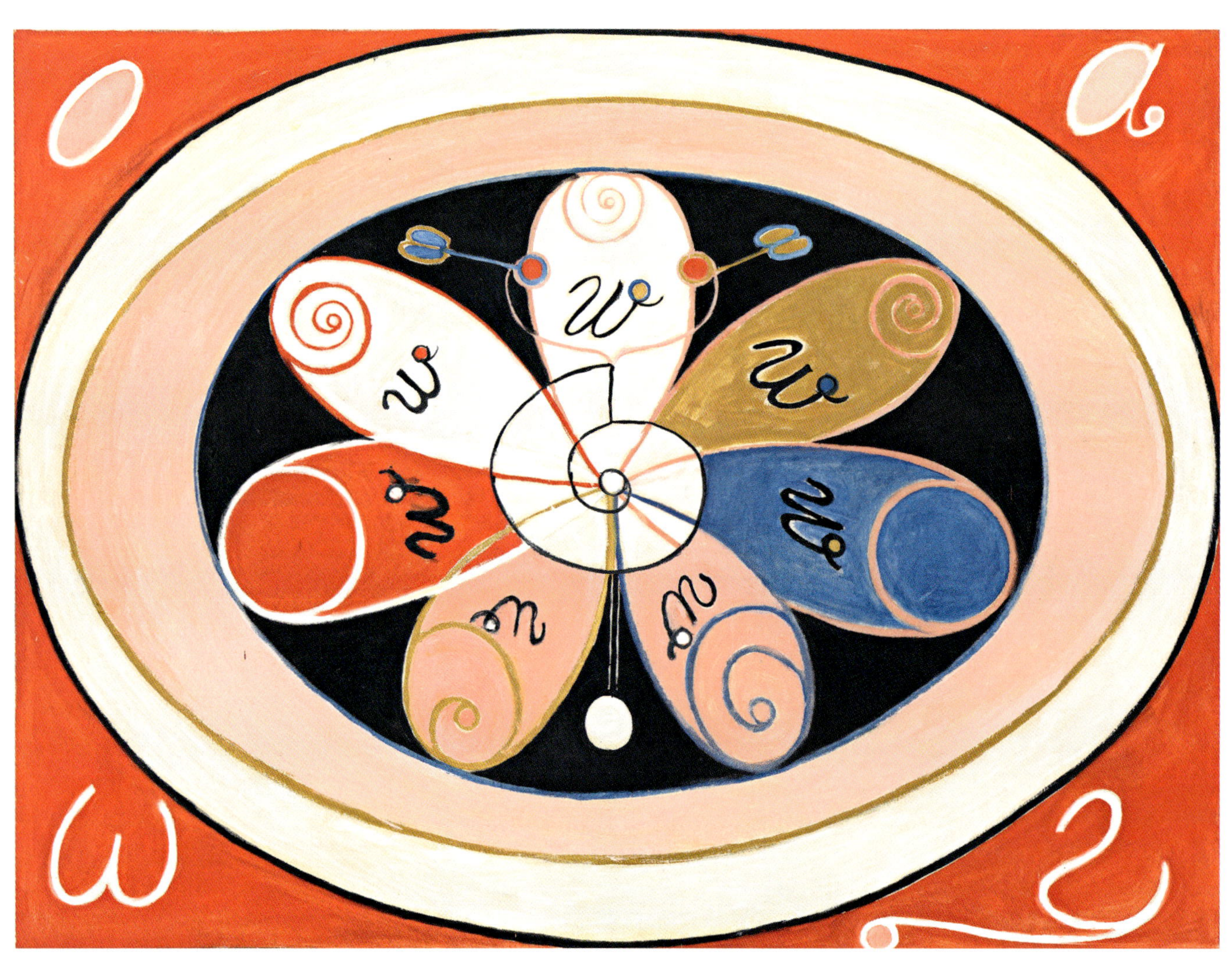

The Evolution, The WUS/Seven-Pointed Star Series, Group VI: No. 15, 1908
Oil on canvas, 99 x 130 cm (39 x 51¼ in.)
Stockholm, Hilma af Klint Foundation, HaK 83

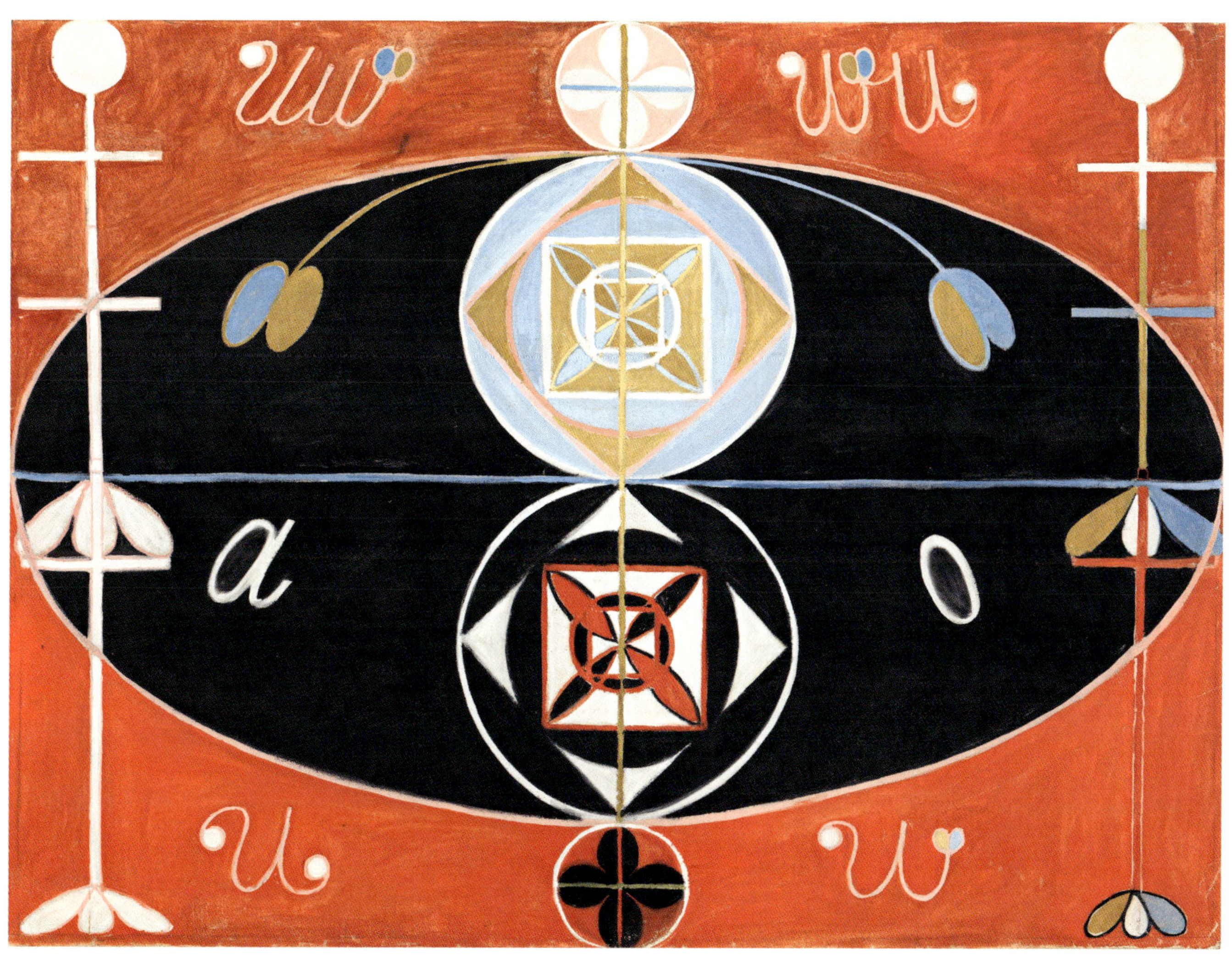

The Evolution, The WUS/Seven-Pointed Star Series, Group VI: No. 16, 1908
Oil on canvas, 104 x 134 cm (41 x 52⅞ in.)
Stockholm, Hilma af Klint Foundation, HaK 84

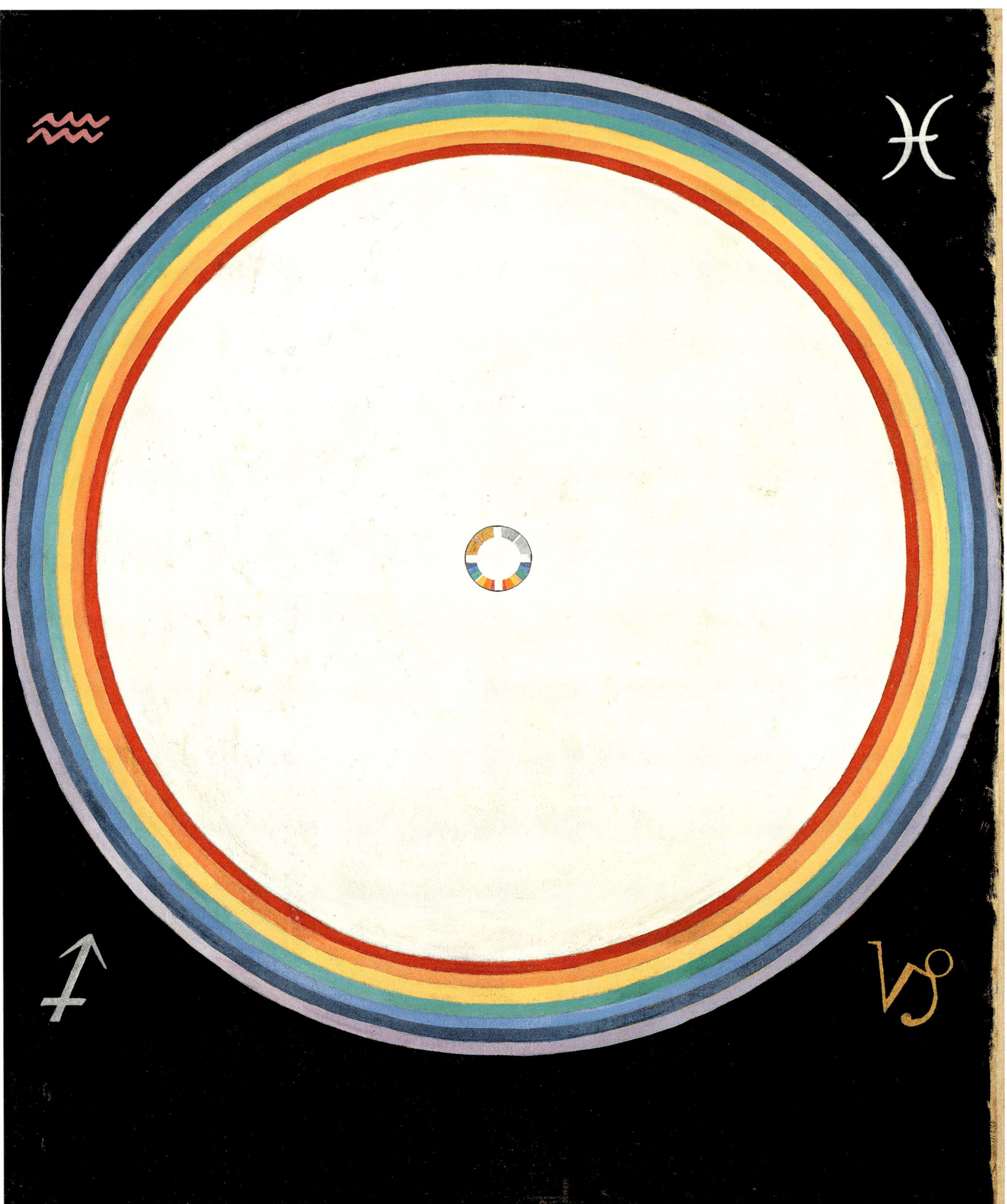

Doubling Down: "The Paintings for the Temple," 1912–15

From 1908 to 1912, af Klint had to pause her "astral" painting for the temple. Her mother had lost her sight in 1908, requiring the artist to change her own life. In an effort to economize, af Klint gave up her separate studio space. She took on paid portrait commissions (p. 53), such as the 1910 posthumous portrait of the Swedish physicist Knut Johan Ångström, designer of scientific instruments, whom af Klint painted from a photograph. To network she joined a women's arts organization, the Association of Swedish Women Artists, and became their secretary for a little over a year, from 1910 to 1911.

In 1909 or 1910 Rudolf Steiner had stopped in Stockholm and responded to the artist's request to look at "The Paintings for the Temple." During his visit to what was probably a provisional workspace, he did not respond effusively, bu made polite comments about a few individual paintings, and grasped the main themes of what she showed. It was a nonspectacular but not totally disheartening encounter. Steiner returned to Stockholm again in April 1912 to deliver a lecture series about "The Three Paths of the Soul to Christ" that af Klint likely attended.[32]

It dealt with the soul's path to the divine through the Gospels, inner experience, and what Steiner termed "initiation." He used the phrase "anthroposophical knowledge" and referenced Rosicrucianism. In December 1912 Steiner broke with the Theosophical Society as it moved in an Eastern-oriented direction under Annie Besant, who had taken over after Helena Blavatsky. He founded the Anthroposophical Society in December 1912, which af Klint herself would later join in 1920. Af Klint probably felt more drawn to anthroposophy than Theosophy because of its esoteric Christian emphasis.

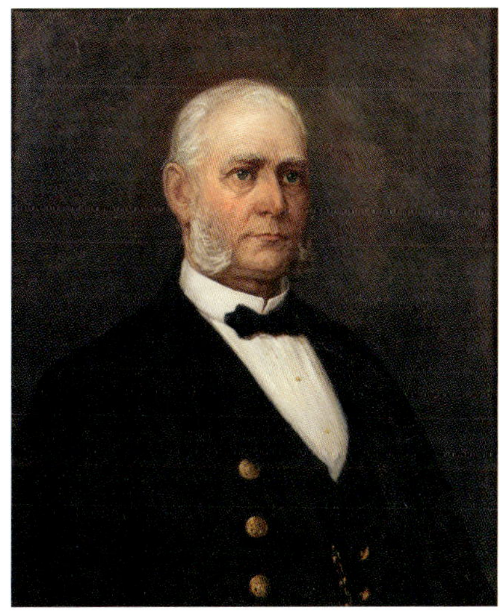

***Portrait, Fredrik Victor af Klint*, n/d**
Oil on canvas, 72 x 51 cm (28⅜ x 20 in.)
Stockholm, Hilma af Klint Foundation, HaK 1781

"The Tree of Knowledge, The W Series" (1913–15)

The pause in "The Paintings for the Temple" between 1908 and 1912 had brought about a shift, a new emphasis on geometry for af Klint. She depended less on spirit guidance and more on meditative and listening skills she had developed within herself. Automatic drawing stopped, and with it the flowing ornamental line reminiscent of cursive handwriting and Art Nouveau. A more rigid, symmetric style emerged, in which fundamental geometric forms replaced or interacted with figures, so that the paintings became an unusual synthesis of diagram and representational scene.

***The Dove, The UW Series, Group IX, Part II: No. 14*, 1915**
Oil on canvas, 154 x 128.5 cm (60¾ x 50⅝ in.)
Stockholm, Hilma af Klint Foundation, HaK 186

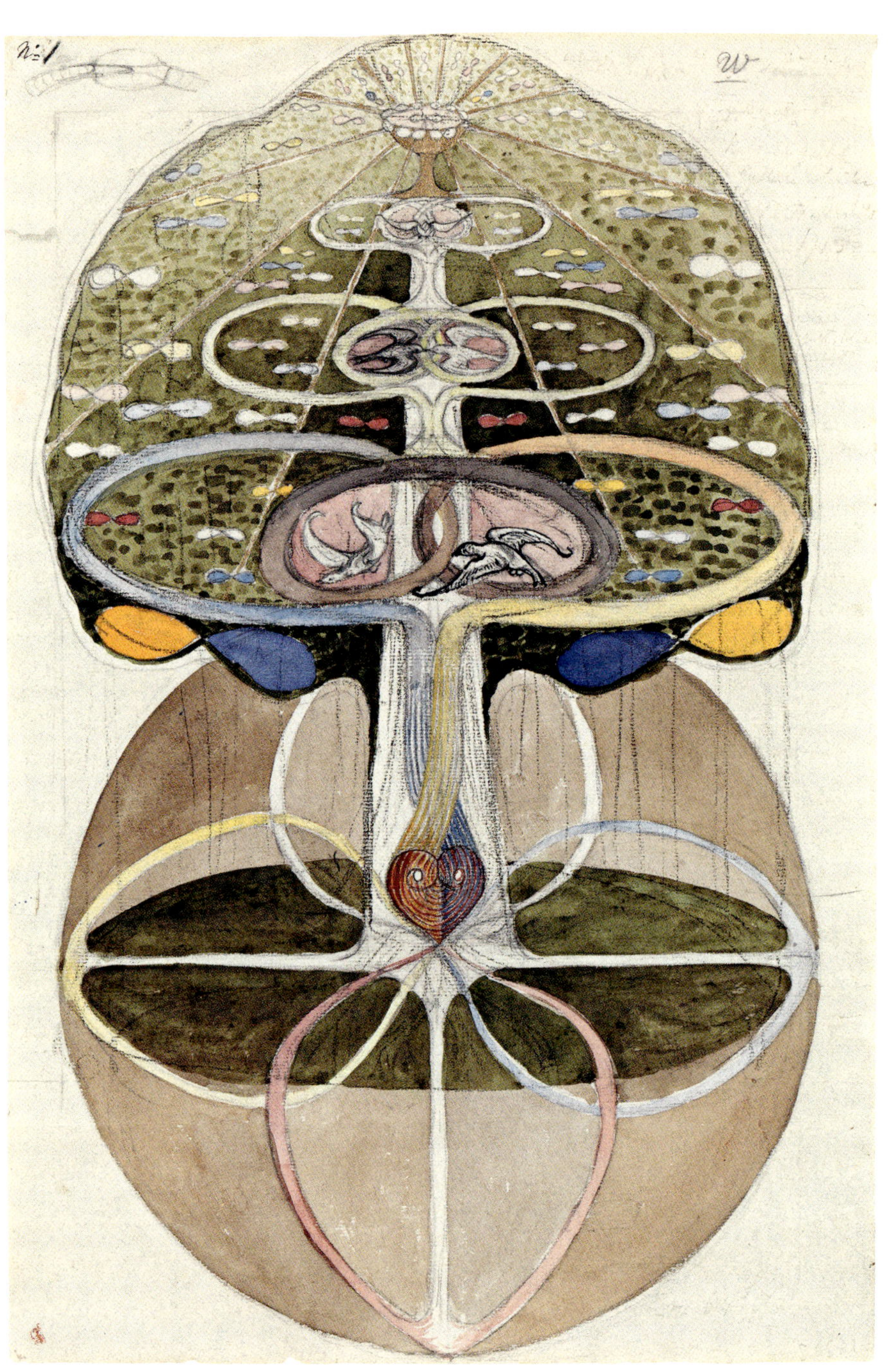

Tree of Knowledge, The W Series: No. 1, 1913–15
Watercolor, gouache, graphite, and ink on paper, 45.7 x 29.5 cm (18 x 11⅝ in.)
Stockholm, Hilma af Klint Foundation, HaK 133

Tree of Knowledge, The W Series: No. 3, 1913–15
Watercolor, gouache, graphite, and ink on paper, 45.8 x 29.5 cm (18 x 11⅝ in.)
Stockholm, Hilma af Klint Foundation, HaK 135

The Greek word *gnosis* means knowledge, but it is used particularly to refer to the knowledge gained through esoteric practices like meditation, repetitive activities, prayer, or dreams. Gnostic Christians favored personally won spiritual insight over orthodox doctrine. The development of such spiritual insight lies at the root of a series of eight drawings af Klint started in June 1913, "Tree of Knowledge" (1913–15). They refer to the tree from which Adam and Eve ate the forbidden fruit, as told in the creation story of the Bible. Buddhism also tells of the Bodhi tree under which Siddhartha Gautama achieved enlightenment. In af Klint's glossary "Letters and Words Pertaining to Works by Hilma af Klint," she wrote "Yggdrasil = the tree of knowledge = the soul." In Norse mythology,

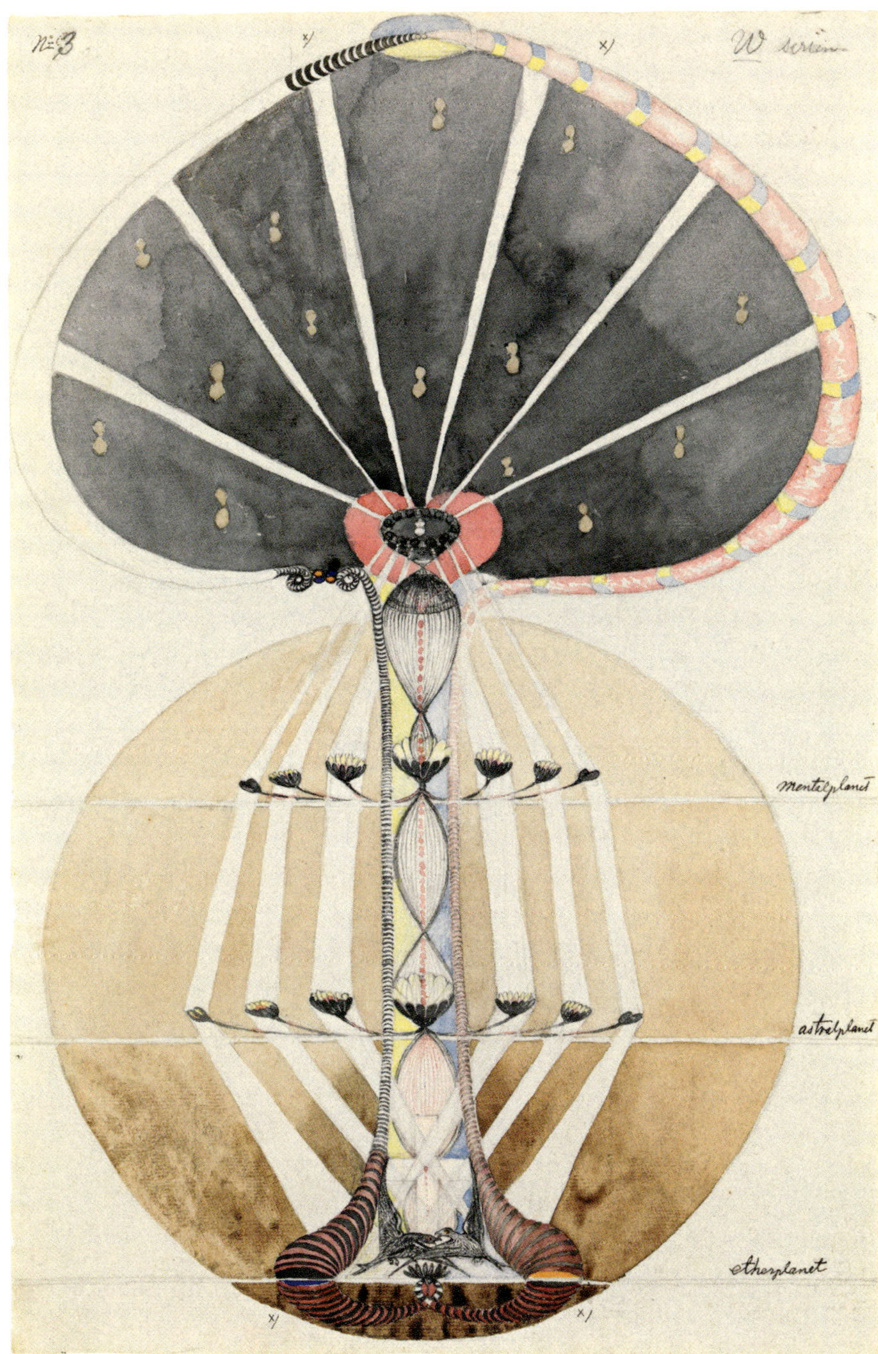

Yggdrasil is an immense and sacred tree, around which the rest of the Norse cosmology forms. As a Theosophist looking for the fundamental truth that resides in all religions, af Klint understood the cultural reach of the tree symbol.

The series begins with a single standing tree, rooted in the center of a green-gray planet. Af Klint centers the trunk of her tree in a heart with two arterial strands. The color-coded female (blue) and male (yellow) circulatory streams rise from an eddying, tidal heart. The heart contains facing spirals, each holding a tiny oval. As Besant explained in her book *Occult Chemistry: A Series of Clairvoyant Observations on the Chemical Elements* (1908),[33] written with Charles W. Leadbeater, she clairvoyantly perceived an atom as a heart-shaped vortex, made

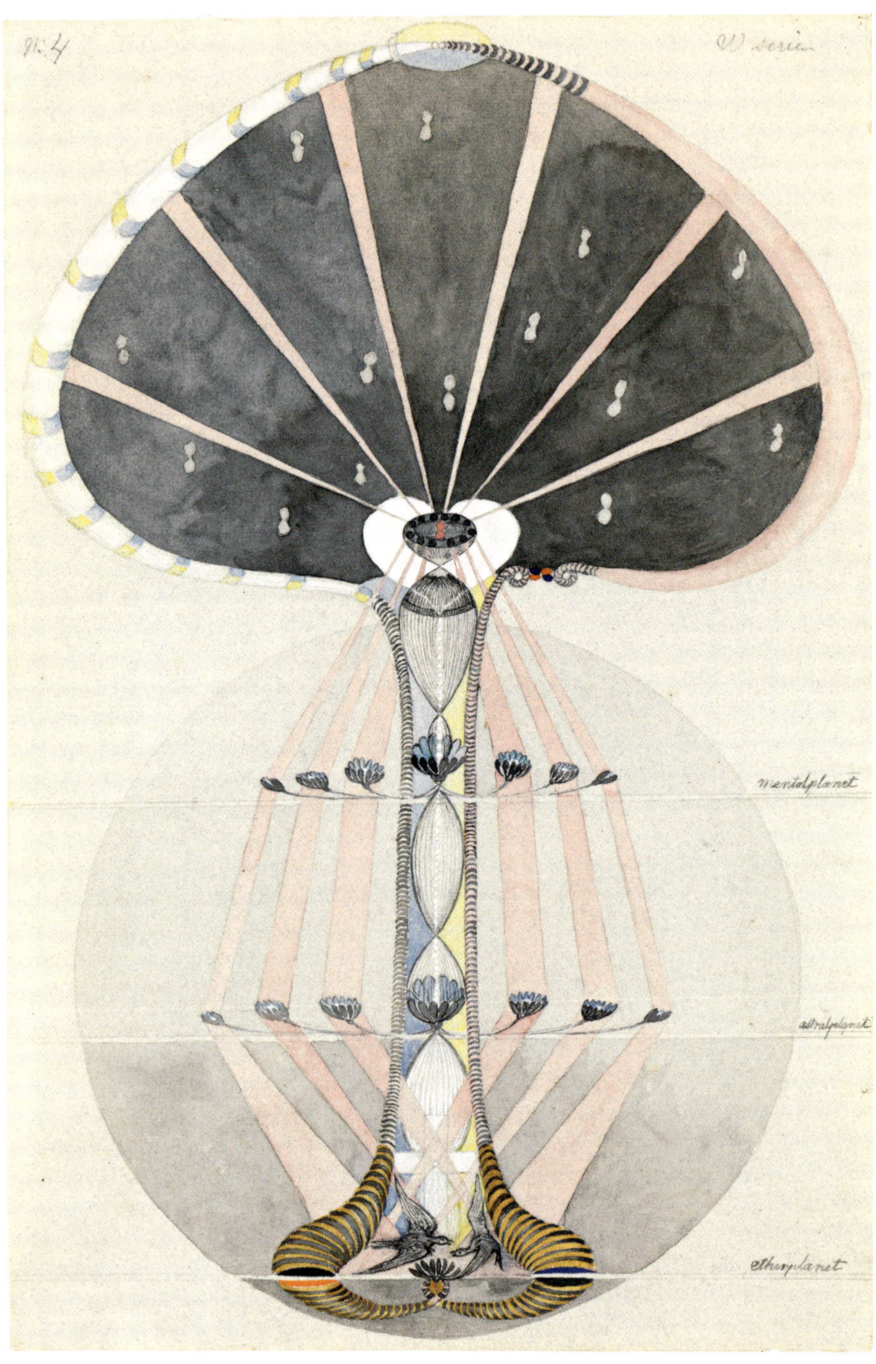

up of spirals containing spirals that contained spirals. Besant illustrated this atom as Plate II in the book. Besant's "ultimate physical atom" occupied the zone between the astral and the material planes, and its heart shape came in male and female versions that spiraled in opposite directions.[34]

In *Tree of Knowledge, No. 1* (p. 54), fluid courses through the tree in tiers of symmetrically pretzeling arteries, decreasing in size as they become more intricate. At the top is a chalice or grail. Twelve rayonnant veins support the membrane of the giant lampshade or umbrella that is the tree's crown. Colored horizontal bulbs couple up, their tips touching, populating the crown as an array of tiny, kissing infinity symbols. The outlines of four simple leaf shapes overlap

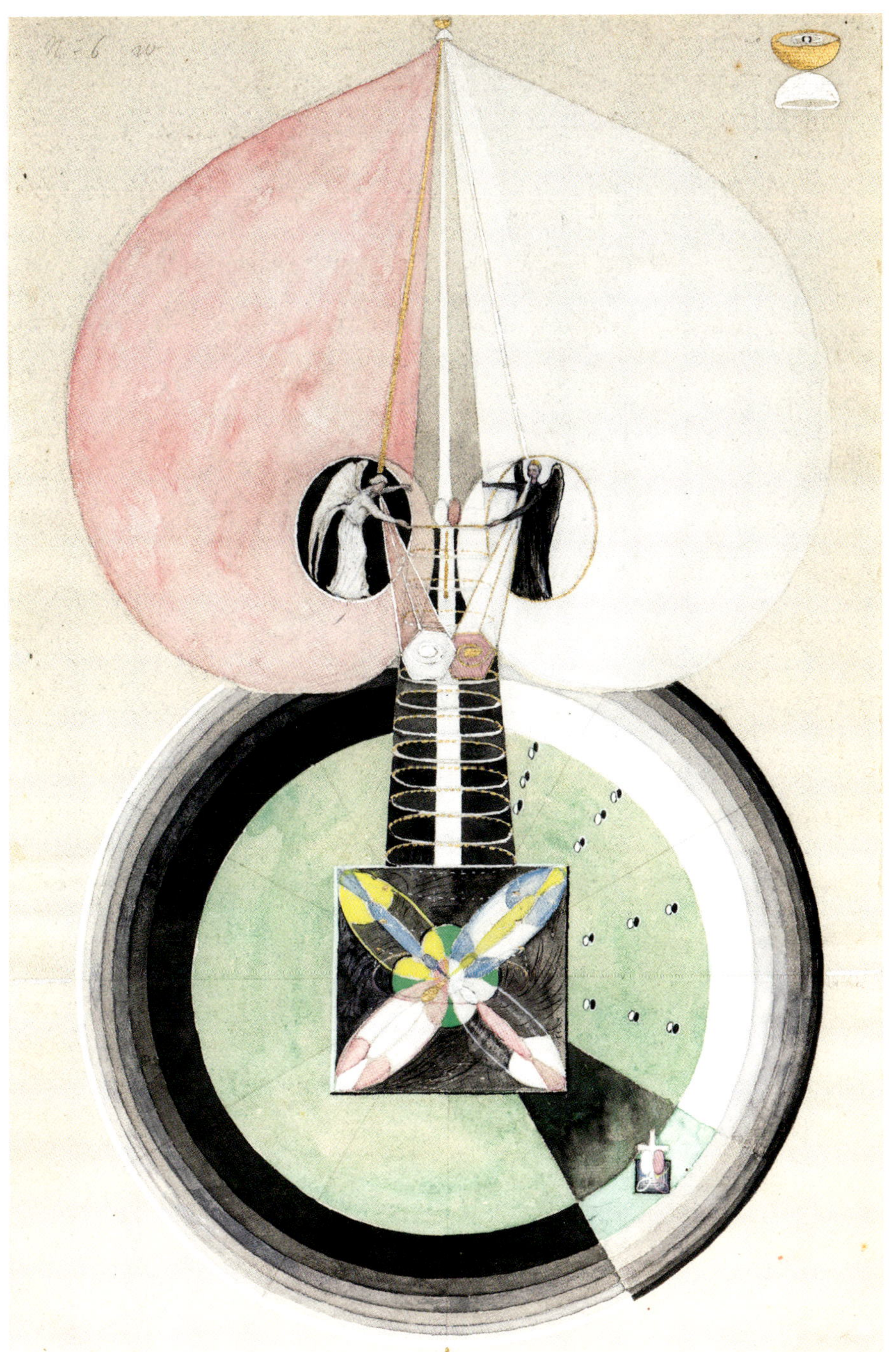

at the base to make up the tree's root system, rising, extending, and descending like the four directions of a compass, contradicting the depth of the planetary orb they cover. The tree's heart throbs at the center of the world. Two pairs of doves hover in the looped openings of each of the sequential tiers, and a single dove floats beneath the chalice in the middle of the top tier.

In the upper left-hand corner of the next drawing, *Tree of Knowledge, No. 2* (first series, 1913), handwriting explains that two arteries labeled "x" and "xx" are "the line of truth" and "the man's line," and also mentions a snake. Also, in the third and fourth drawings (pp. 55–56), the tree has been sectioned into rising layers labeled as "etherplanet," "astralplanet," and "mentalplanet." In his 1902

Tree of Knowledge, The W Series: No. 4, 1913–15
Watercolor, gouache, graphite, and ink on paper, 45.8 x 29.5 cm (18 x 11⅝ in.)
Stockholm, Hilma af Klint Foundation, HaK 136

Tree of Knowledge, The W Series: No. 6, 1913–15
Watercolor, gouache, graphite, and ink on paper, 46 x 30 cm (18⅛ x 11⅞ in.)
Stockholm, Hilma af Klint Foundation, HaK 138

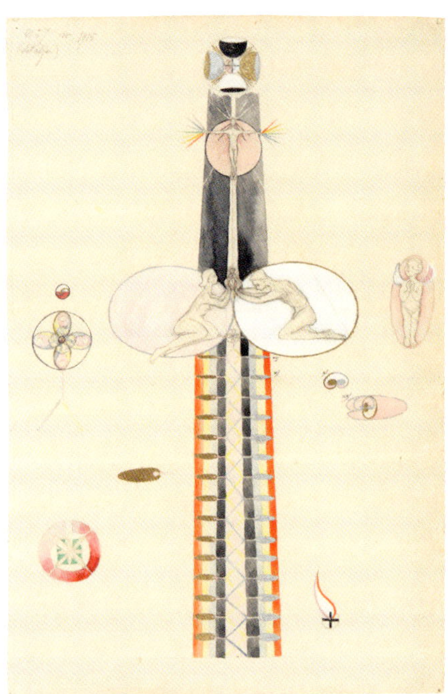

Tree of Knowledge, The W Series: No. 7b, 1915
Watercolor, gouache, and ink on paper,
46 x 30 cm (18⅛ x 11⅞ in.)
Stockholm, Hilma af Klint Foundation, HaK 139b

The Swan, The SUW Series, Group IX, Part I: No. 1, 1914–15
Oil on canvas, 150 x 150 cm (59 x 59 in.)
Stockholm, Hilma af Klint Foundation, HaK 149

book *An Outline of Theosophy*, Leadbeater described the structure of ether, astral, and mental planes not as distinctly separate, but as a layered, interpenetrating interconnectedness.[35] The ether as an all-permeating, invisible medium connected the physical plane of existence with both the astral and the mental planes. Af Klint chooses a tree's rising structure to express this organically. On the verso of the *Tree of Knowledge, No. 2* is a handwritten text in which it sounds like af Klint is being coached by the spirits to understand and trust her perception and not be guided by what she logically "knows." Though vague and hard to understand, the text anchors the "Tree of Knowledge" drawings in desire and its effect:

> It is our intention to present an original image each time we give you a drawing, an original image of a new phase. Thus it is of the utmost importance that you should understand the entire plan … The first of two world trees is … to present the moment of desire's awakening. The second is intended to present the moment when desire has managed to enter that part of the human soul which is not yet liberated from material ties but is still subject to mental meaning.[36]

As the "Tree of Knowledge" progresses to *No. 3* (p. 55), the trunk surrounds itself with powerful beams of light that shine forth from a candelabrum of lotuses. Af Klint summons a radiant, seated Buddha through tubular, striped forms that thicken and thin like folded legs. They rise from the ground, reach from both sides over the tree's crown, and enclose it. As the series continues to *No. 5*, the chalice repositions itself Forms simplify. In *No. 6* (p. 57) standing angels appear along the abstracted trunk, now an axis. One is garbed in white, one in black, and they balance either side as they hang from the chalice at the apex of the composition, whose appearance af Klint clarifies with a detail drawing. The intimation of facing snail shells appears in the two halves (pink and white) of the tree's crown. The final drawing, *Tree of Knowledge, No. 7b* (p. 58), introduces a nude seated woman and kneeling man who hold a winged baby up in their fingertips like a jewel in a pronged setting. The couple place their weight (seated, kneeling) on the base of an equilateral triangle, whose pinnacle marks the heart region of a radiant, slender nude, posed as if crucified and seemingly a realm away in scale. Rays stream from her hands and head. Could the crucified figure stand for the artist?

Af Klint populated her mind with esoteric and scientific readings and lectures. More than any other series in "The Paintings for the Temple," "Tree of Knowledge" shows that af Klint sought images that would communicate spiritual transformation. Art historian Susan Aberth described "Tree of Knowledge" as a "spiritual treatise" that is "symbolically dense, difficult to decipher, and visually alluring as the famed alchemical *Splendor Solis* manuscript (1582) or any seventeenth-century Jakob Boehme mystical illustration."[37] Jakob Boehme, the German philosophical mystic who had begun life as a cobbler, is known to have said, "I compare the whole Philosophy, Astrology, and Theology, together with their mother, to a goodly tree which grows in a fair garden of pleasure."[38] Af Klint's compositions relate to spiritual works of art that she absorbed and distilled, as if they too were "voices" that spoke to her. These influences may be as diverse as Hieronymus Bosch's *The Garden of Earthly Delights* (1490–1500), sculptures of the Buddha on a lotus throne, or illustrations for yoga poses.

"Many who fight in this drama are dressed in the wrong clothing. Many female costumes conceal a man. Many male costumes conceal a woman."
HILMA AF KLINT

Af Klint had lived with her mother since 1899 at Brahegatan 52 in Stockholm, and a few years after consolidating their living arrangements, beginning in 1904,

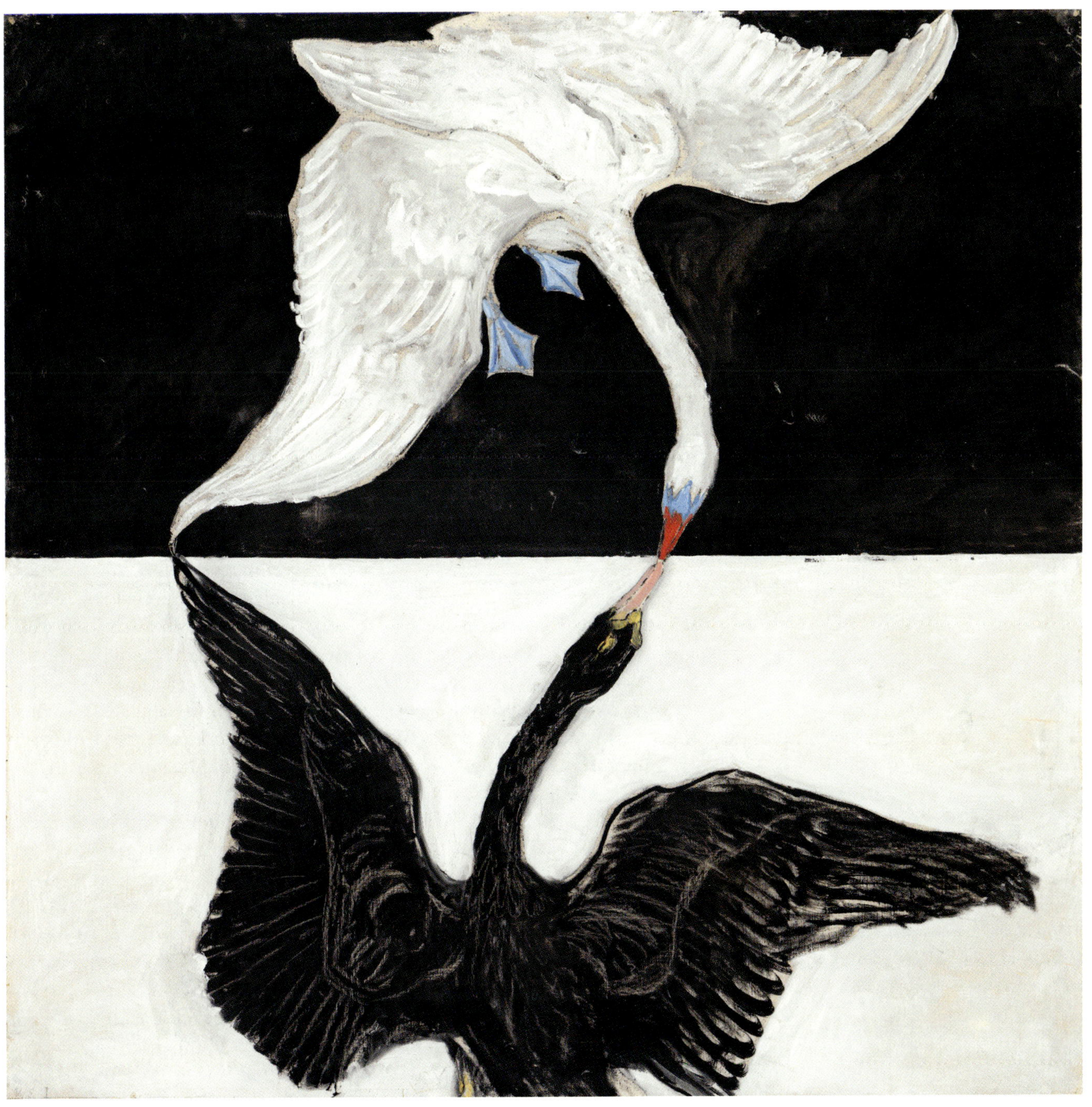

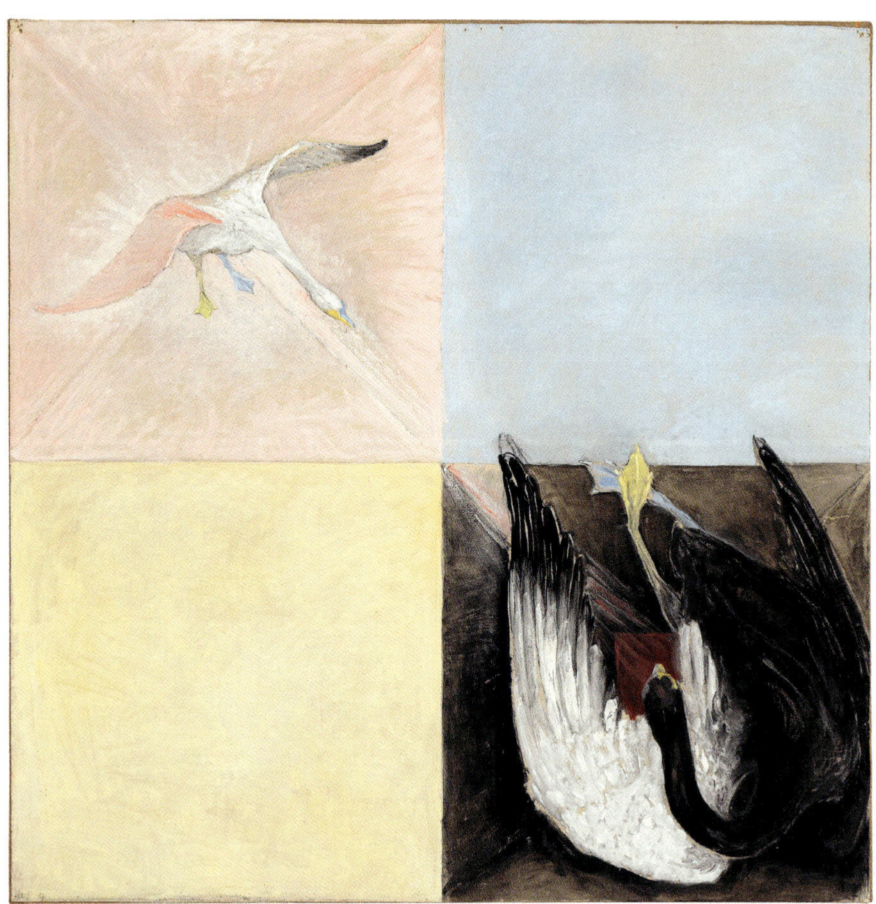

The Swan, The SUW Series, Group IX, Part I: No. 4, 1914
Oil on canvas, 152 x 149 cm (59⅞ x 58¾ in.)
Stockholm, Hilma af Klint Foundation, HaK 152

they took in a female housemate, Sigrid Lancén. Lancén was a gay woman and a friend to af Klint. She felt romantically attracted to af Klint, and the two had exchanged "careless touches" in the past, about which the spirits had warned the artist.[39] Af Klint's notebook records a message from April 21, 1909, which shows the spirits now approved a relationship with Lancén.[40] By 1913 at the latest, the year af Klint turned 51, she and Lancén entered into a physical relationship which may have lasted until 1915. Lancén compared af Klint to Saint George, her hero, a spiritual knight.[41] Lancén was also known as Nr. 8 in the group of The Thirteen—women who, after the disintegration of the original group The Five, had collaborated with af Klint in her art. In a notebook entry from July 1913, Lancén reveals the passion of their relationship as an epiphany: "Half of me felt the flash of joy in my heart when the other half met her dual soul. I felt a connection in those moments between my beloved H. and me that is the answer to the enigma of my life!"[42]

Af Klint recorded in her own notebook the spirit voices she and Lancén heard while clasping hands. They paraphrased the words that Adam said to Eve after she was created: "Believe me, you are part of my being. You are flesh of my flesh, blood of my blood, soul of my soul."[43]

"The US Series, Group VIII" (1913)

In September of 1913, af Klint and Lancén had a cinema date and saw the movie *Quo Vadis*, a love story set during the persecution of Christians under Roman reign. In the course of the film, one era ends and another begins:

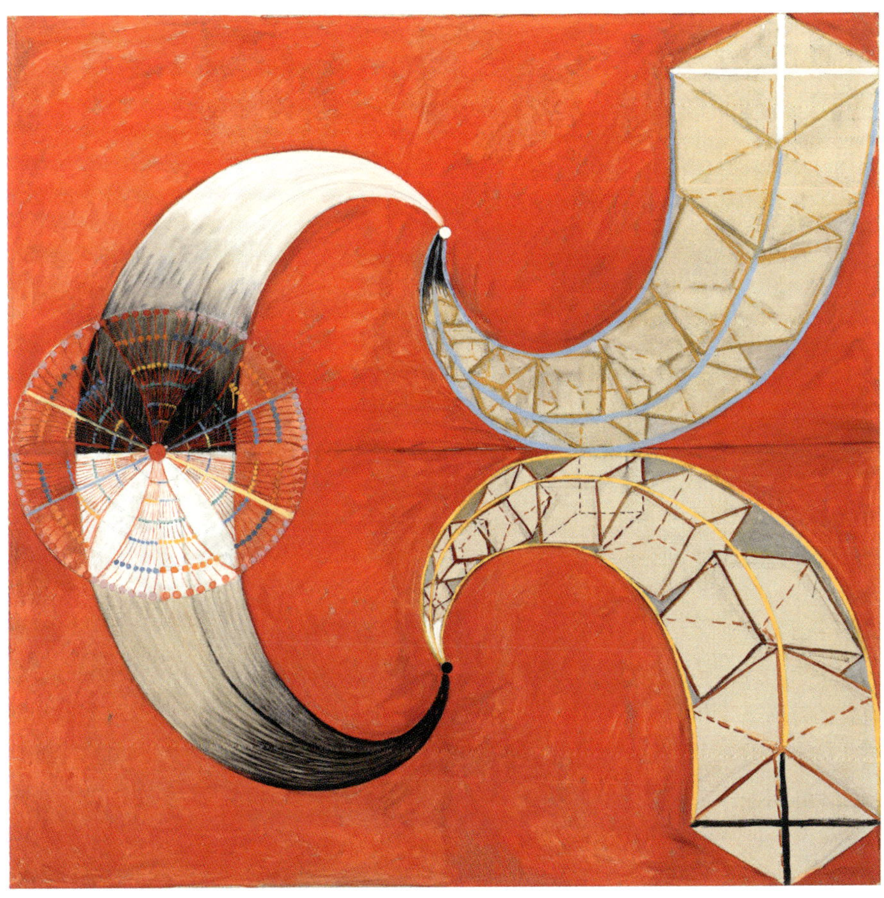

The Swan, The SUW Series, Group IX, Part I: No. 9, 1915
Oil on canvas, 149.5 x 149 cm (58⅞ x 58¾ in.)
Stockholm, Hilma af Klint Foundation, HaK 157

corrupt, decadent Rome gives way to Christianity. The main couple in the movie eventually gain freedom and can live and love as Christians. The last scene shows Christ centered on high, standing in front of a glowing crucifix.

Af Klint created her next series for "The Paintings for the Temple"—titled "The US Series, Group VIII"—days after seeing the movie, and she acknowledged that Lancén inspired it. It is significant that she may have channeled feelings about a modern, popular medium like film and her relationship to a lover into her work. This makes the work more hers, not only a product of guiding spirits. "The US Series, Group VIII" comprises seven vertical paintings—three medium-sized (about 73 x 53 centimeters, or 29 x 21 inches) and four large (about 152 x 111 centimeters, or 60 x 44 inches). Af Klint placed one or more crucifixes at the center of every composition. The most startling painting is *No. 5* (p. 61), which depicts five crucified individuals on three crosses, the central of which is a hypercubic cross. The hanging bodies are seen as if by x-ray, with bones visible. Af Klint also shows colored organs, like each martyr's one blue and one yellow lung, along with their exterior facial features and hair color. She used the hypercubic cross to extend into a fourth dimension and referenced x-rays' ability to pass through material to radically "dematerialize" the body and see it as a system of organs.

The crucified, rather modern-looking individuals of *Group VIII: No. 5*—androgynous males and females—do not suffer unduly, especially those in the center, who hang back-to-back on the thick, hypercubic cross. In an inward-directed, manneristic fashion, they meditate and levitate and wear a kind of

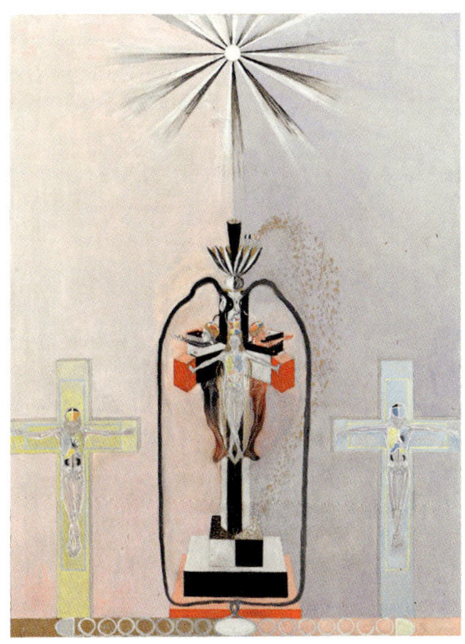

The US Series, Group VIII: No. 5, 1913
Oil on canvas, 156.5 x 114.5 cm (61⅝ x 45 in.)
Stockholm, Hilma af Klint Foundation, HaK 130

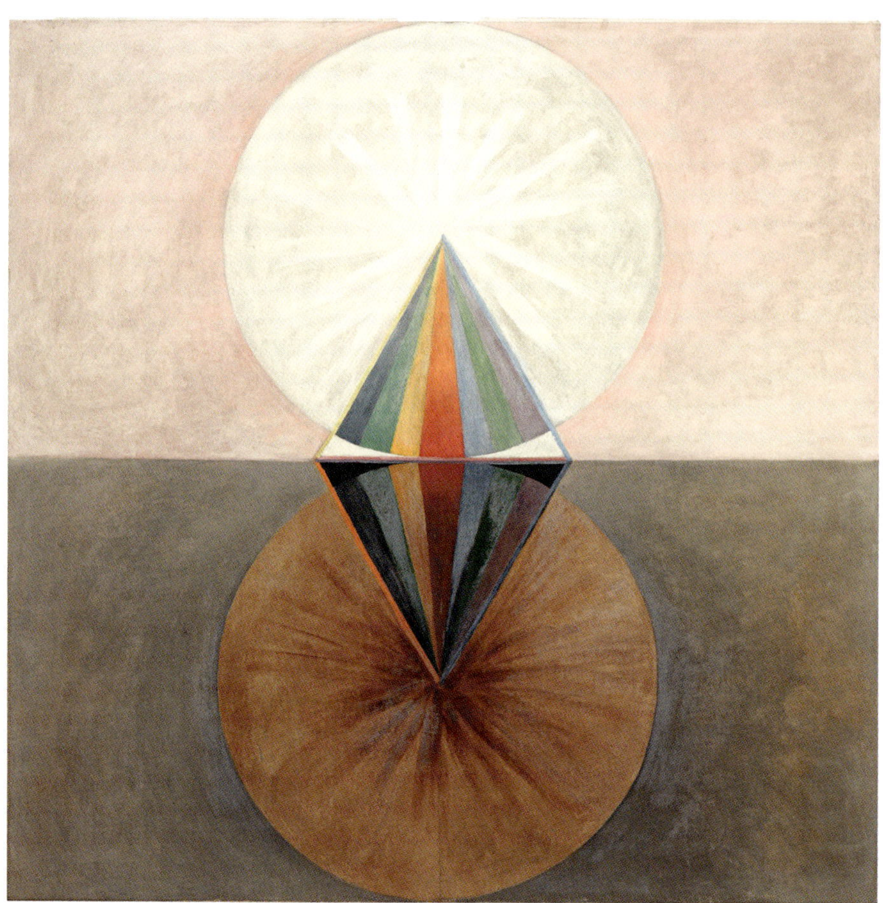

The Swan, The SUW Series, Group IX, Part I: No. 12, 1915
Oil on canvas, 151.5 x 151 cm (59¾ x 59½ in.)
Stockholm, Hilma af Klint Foundation, HaK 160

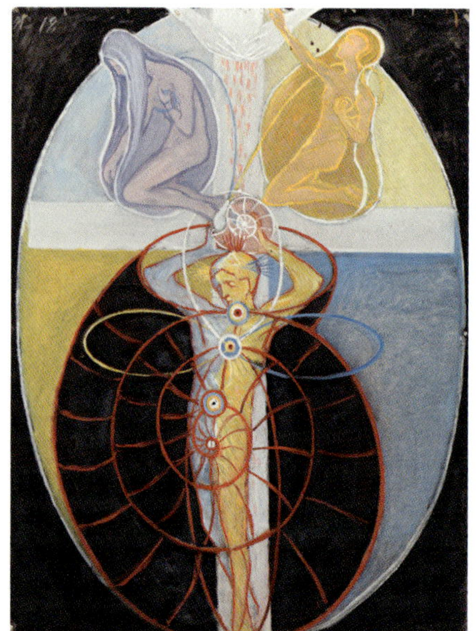

The US Series, Group VIII: No. 1, 1913
Oil on canvas, 74 x 53 cm (29¼ x 20⅞ in.)
Stockholm, Hilma af Klint Foundation, HaK 126

skullcap that marks them as people of the cross. The background bisects into a bluish-purple half with a blue cross, and a bluish-pink half with a yellow cross. In the center, the tall hypercubic cross carries three visible bodies. The artist emphasizes right angles and the black and white geometry of squares at the base of the cross and in its crossbar. Bright red paint accents the bottom staging of the central cross, and the central crucified figure, a female, pushes red boxes away with her hands, a liberating gesture that may refer to an unfolding of the hypercubic crucifix into a fourth dimension. Dark snakes form a containing outline around the center cross, ending in two yin-yang heads whose tongues connect to the heads of the crucified. A diagram of *The Three Outpourings*, Plate III in Leadbeater's *Man Visible and Invisible* (1903), probably inspired this outline. That diagram shows curving lines that descend and ascend through lines designating the planes of nature and relates to how Jesus became human through his mother while embodying God because of his father. At the top of the cross in Klint's painting, the stamens of a 12-petaled lotus, the Buddhist and Hindu symbol for the heart chakra, scatter golden pollen to the wind, but it blows back, and the pollen fertilizes the base of the cross.

Another complex composition, the first painting in *The US Series, Group VIII: No. 1* (p. 62) introduces the theme of youthful male and female bodies and the cross. Contained by their auras, a blue female and a yellow male rest on the cross bars between dripping, ghostly hands. A half-blue, half-yellow figure stands below them in front of the cross, arms raised, holding a snail or nautilus shell on their head. This main figure's body is marked by four chakras. These

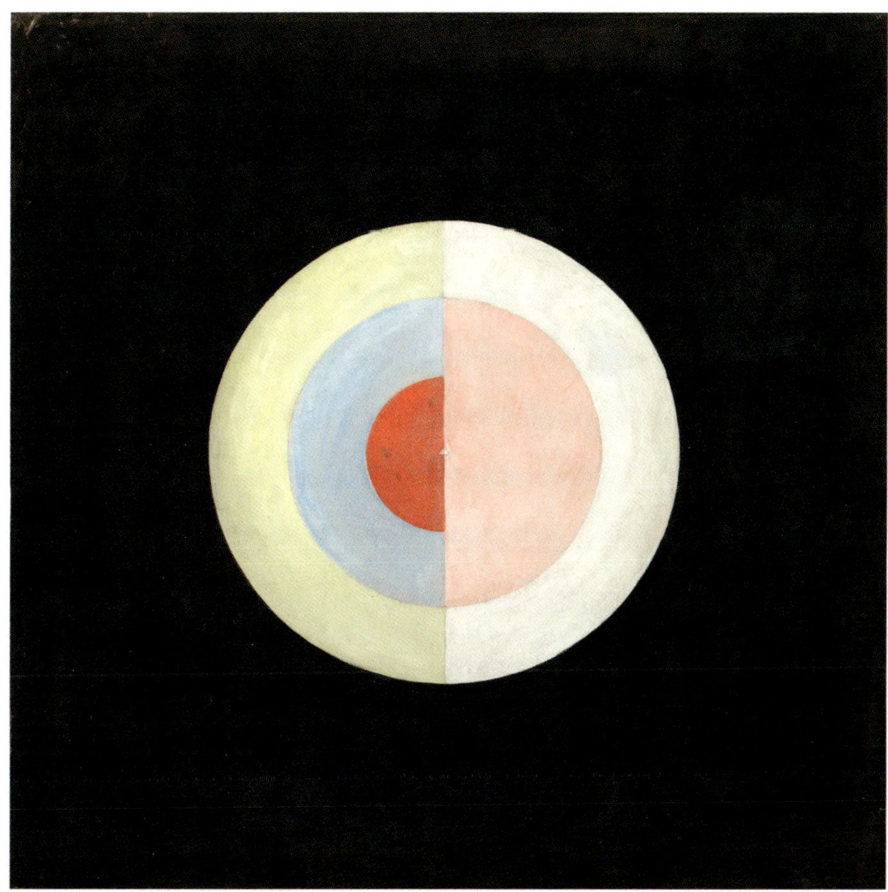

The Swan, The SUW Series, Group IX, Part I: No. 16, 1915
Oil on canvas, 154.5 x 151 cm (60⅞ x 59½ in.)
Stockholm, Hilma af Klint Foundation, HaK 164

force centers or wheels of energy appear at the genitals, navel, heart, and throat. Simultaneously, the chakras sit one above the other along the curves of a spiraling shell superimposed as a red line drawing on the figure. The black shell should hide the figure, but af Klint enabled the viewer to see through the spiraling shell and perceive the figure about to emerge from it with a new shell.

As in so many af Klint compositions, here complexities of colored line complicate and structure the painting—line may be rayant, spiraling, roping, never-ending, segmenting, connecting, or containing. Lines can recall a chart or a lined notebook page. The artist draws her figures expressively and uses color symbolically. As the background for all the figures, a brightly colored egg shape stands out against darkness. Af Klint liked to isolate and highlight figures and scenes within her rectangular canvases with rounded medallion shapes. The artist's biographer Julia Voss understood this round form as a reference to petri dishes, those flat, round vessels designed to hold samples for a microscope. The form also echoes the ovoid auras of *Man Visible and Invisible* (p. 33). The last two works in this series inspired by the movie date with Lancén may suggest the projected cone of light in a cinema and the abstracted spatial separation of audience and elevated curtained stage and screen (*The US Series, Group VIII*: *No. 7*, p. 65). Af Klint arrives at a high level of geometric abstraction here as she orders and repeats symbols and considers light scientifically, culturally, and spiritually.

Lutheranism was the foundation of af Klint's cultural background, yet her widened spiritual and emotional perspectives made her paintings heretical to that

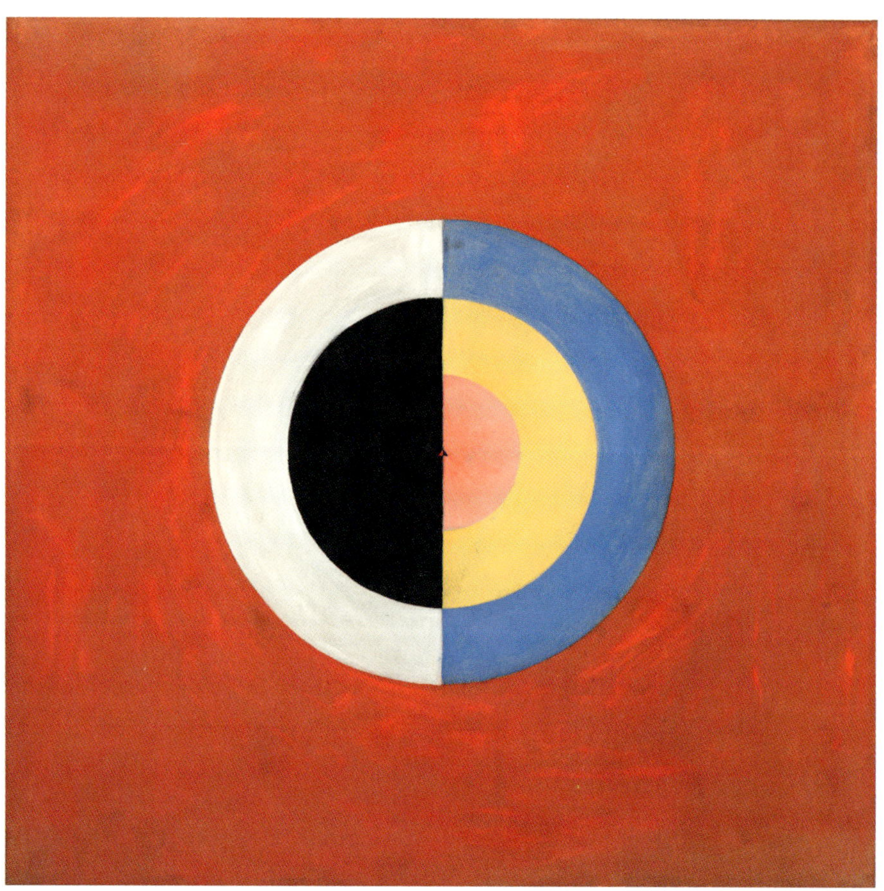

The Swan, The SUW Series, Group IX, Part I: No. 17, 1915
Oil on canvas, 150.5 x 151 cm (59⅜ x 59½ in.)
Stockholm, Hilma af Klint Foundation, HaK 165

religion. Between 1917 and 1918, af Klint produced a more than 2,000-page handwritten book entitled *Studies of the Life of the Soul*, in which she posited that humanity would evolve to a higher spiritual plane where rigid gender divisions would be overcome. Society would need to acknowledge the "manwoman" and the "womanman." She knew that such people already existed—she herself was one. Voss quotes a passage where af Klint refers to people mistakenly clothed as the opposite gender: "Many who fight in this drama are dressed in the wrong clothing. Many female costumes conceal a man. Many male costumes conceal the woman."[44] In her era, when many women, including her own sister, fought for equal rights and the right to vote, af Klint perceived the acceptance of gender fluidity as part of human evolution. The resolution of oppositions would lead to peace and a new spirituality. She considered *Studies of the Life of the Soul* a fifth Gospel, thus comparing it in its importance to the first four books of the New Testament.

The overcoming of divisions is central in anthroposophical writing. One of Steiner's 1912 Stockholm lectures dealt with "The Path of Initiation." Essentially, the "initiate" was any person who had approached the divine, whether it be through Christianity, Buddhism, Judaism, or any world religion. Steiner says that spiritual science is the point of departure for understanding the way to initiation and real insight into the secrets of the spiritual world. Mystery and the secret nature of this knowledge is inherent to Steiner's concept.

When at the end of the same lecture he speaks about Rosicrucianism, he seems to be explaining a recommended policy about the secrets of spiritual growth,

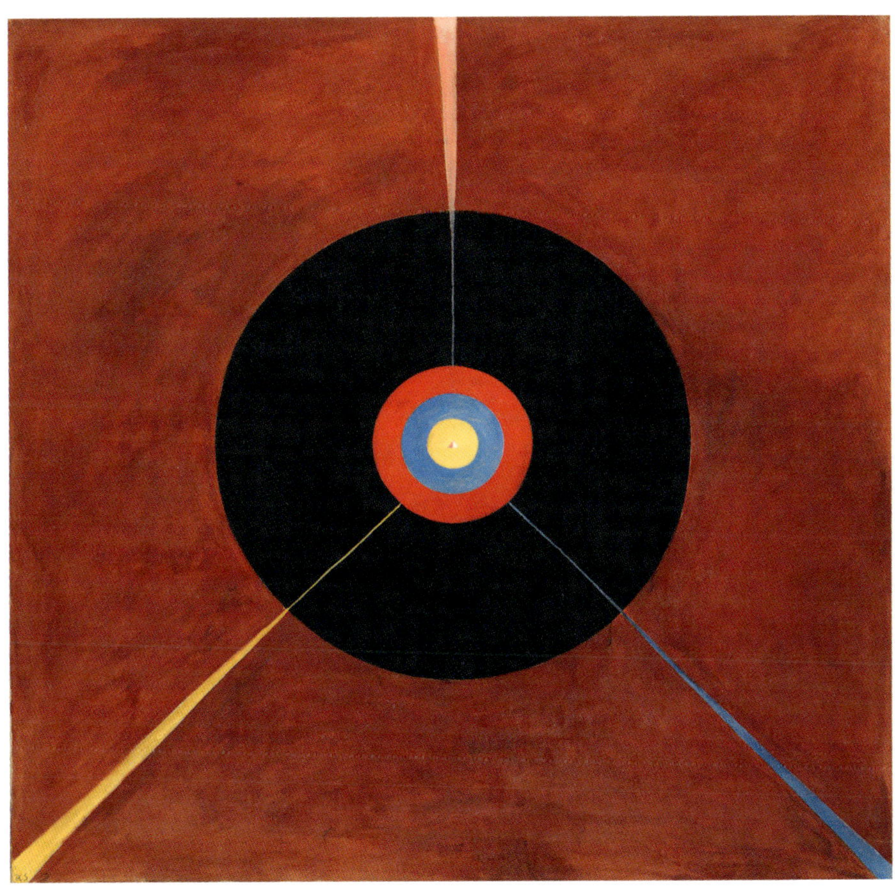

The Swan, The SUW Series, Group IX, Part I: No. 18, 1914
Oil on canvas, 149 x 152 cm (58¾ x 59⅞ in.)
Stockholm, Hilma af Klint Foundation, HaK 166

which should be a path each individual finds for themselves. He says that the leaders of those entrusted with attending to spiritual growth are not identifiable, that they keep their identity secret, and only a century after their death are their names known. Like Steiner's Rosicrucians, af Klint entrusted her work and fame to a future generation and kept information about her personal life to a minimum.

"The Swan, The SUW Series, Group IX: Part I" (1914–15) and "The Dove, The UW Series, Group IX: Part II" (1915)

The two penultimate series in "The Paintings for the Temple" are both named after birds that have recurred in af Klint's work: the swan and the dove. There are 24 oil paintings in the group "The Swan," all of them square and roughly the same size at about 150 x 150 centimeters (just under 5 x 5 feet). The artist began painting them in October 1914, only a few months after the beginning of the First World War. Discord, aerial battle, sex, and suffering play out in the first five paintings of the series, where the swans exist as large organic forms against a flat, minimalistic background that is divided into halves or quarters (pp. 59–60). Af Klint's choice of the swan may have to do with Helena Blavatsky, who rather suddenly introduces a white swan's egg into her discussion of human evolution in part two of her book *The Secret Doctrine* (1888), in the chapter "The Evolution of the Sweat-Born." The swan's egg hatches a "man-swan" (part human, part swan). The egg-born human is first a hermaphrodite, before evolving into distinctly gendered men and women. While it is not possible to follow her story

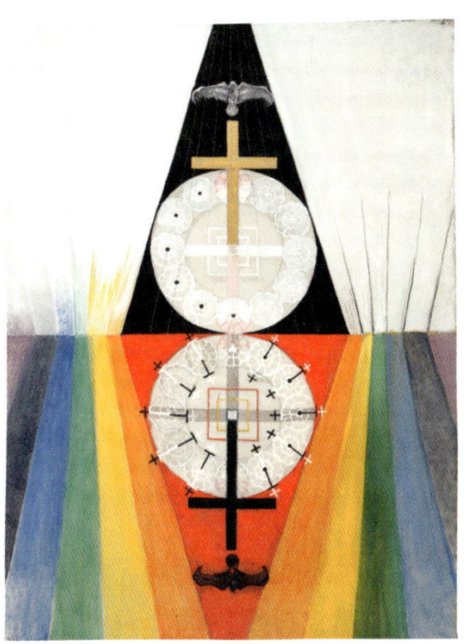

The US Series, Group VIII: No. 7, 1913
Oil on canvas, 156 x 116 cm (61½ x 45¾ in.)
Stockholm, Hilma af Klint Foundation, HaK 132

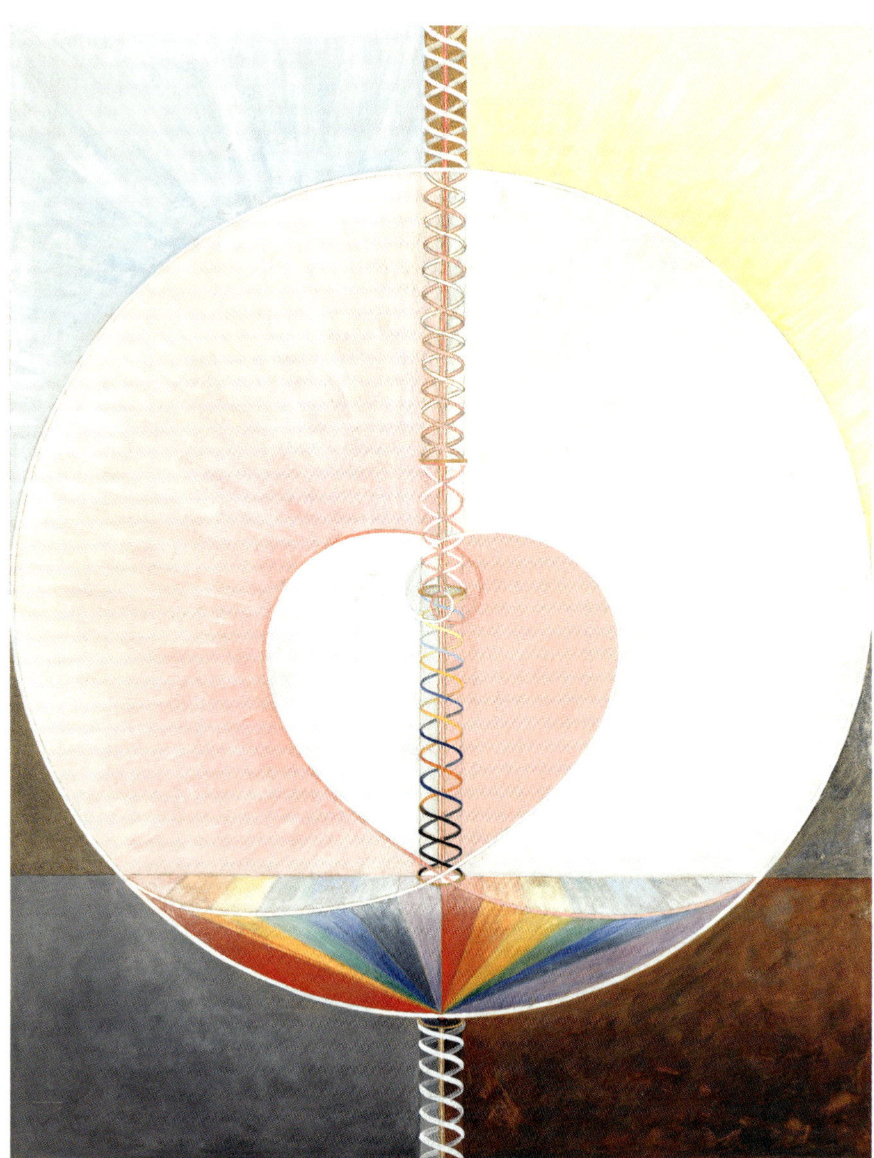

The Dove, The UW Series, Group IX, Part II: No. 1, 1915
Oil on canvas, 151 x 114.5 cm (59½ x 45 in.)
Stockholm, Hilma af Klint Foundation, HaK 173

logically, the swan as a progenitor embodies both hermaphroditism and its resolution.

The Swan, No. 1 (p. 59) introduces the series in one of the most beautifully lyrical works af Klint created. As if recalling Pyotr Ilyich Tchaikovsky's 1877 ballet *Swan Lake*, the swans begin a pas de deux with graceful contact at wingtip and beak, positioned above and below in a mirrored pose. Black and white create stark contrasts. The female white swan has blue feet, with some blue around her red beak; the male black swan's beak and barely visible feet are yellow. Af Klint is not overly fine in her brushwork—she is also drawing with paint, pulling the paint into the outline of feathers and around the muscles of the birds' bodies. In *The Swan, No. 2*, the partnering action continues with a wounding, and the birds bleed into each other's realms, with the white swan lifted above the black swan. Af Klint shows tangled bodies, impact, pain, dual explosive hits. The vulnerable necks of the swans arc and touch. The black swan's beak is bloodied. In the next canvas, *The Swan, No. 3*, the birds mate. Their beaks have changed color—his is now white, and hers is black. They may

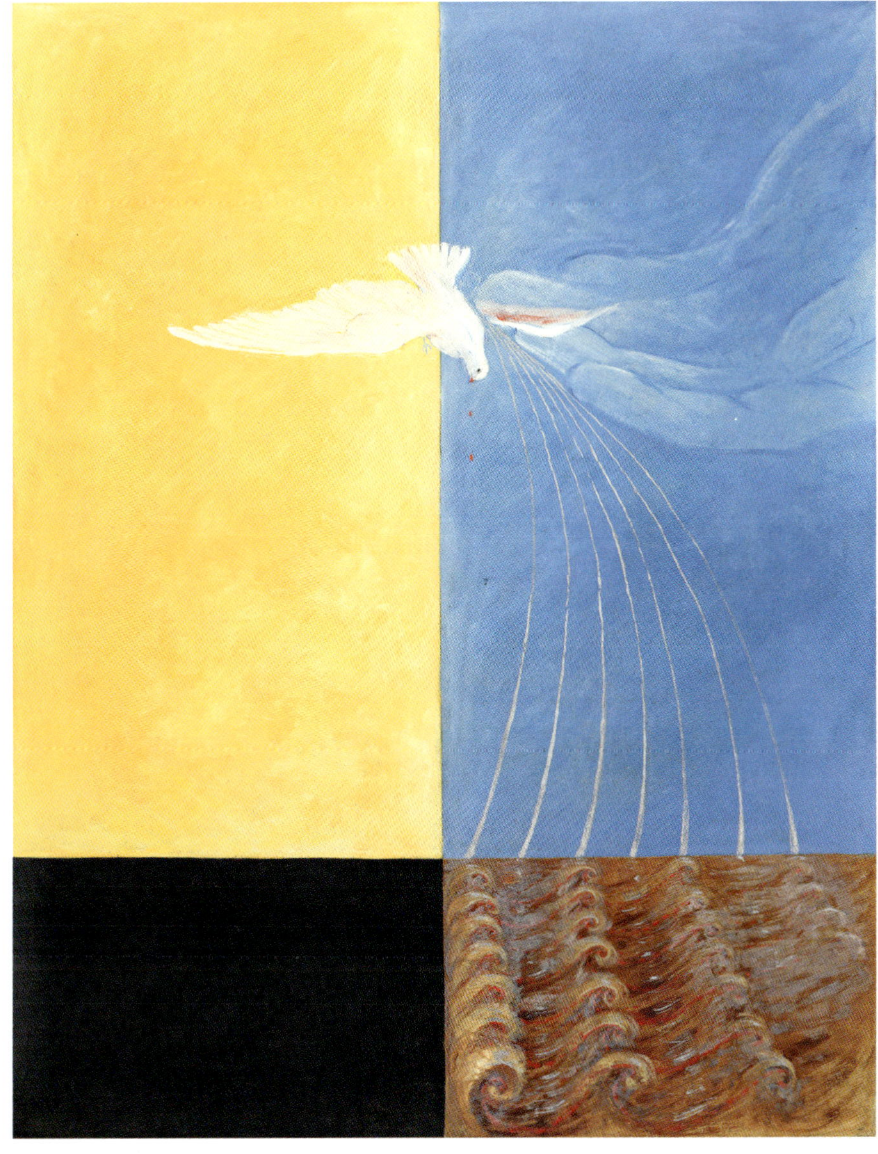

The Dove, The UW Series, Group IX, Part II: No. 4, 1915
Oil on canvas, 152.5 x 115.5 cm (60 x 45½ in.)
Stockholm, Hilma af Klint Foundation, HaK 176

be dying, or have died or climaxed, and transformed into a male-female that escapes to a higher plane as a single organism.

With *The Swan, No. 6* and *The Swan, No. 7* the series shifts into partial abstraction and its swans become a propeller or a wheel, attached by their beaks to the central heart. Rough brushstrokes further dematerialize their bodies, which begin to rotate, even spiral. Starting with *The Swan, No. 8*, af Klint fully abstracts her swans, representing them as concentric circles of cubes held together by ray-like forces. This sudden visual leap surprises. The artist referenced crystal systems and tools used for passing light through them. The cube is one of seven different motifs according to which the atoms of a mineral can crystalize, forming a crystal system. From where did this idea arrive?

When geologist and writer William Glassley (1947–2023) attended the Hilma af Klint exhibition at the Solomon R. Guggenheim Museum in New York in 2018, he noted the scientific references in the artist's work.[45] For Glassley, af Klint's representation of light that resembled the way it was used in polarizing microscopes. We have already suggested that af Klint knew, through Steiner, of

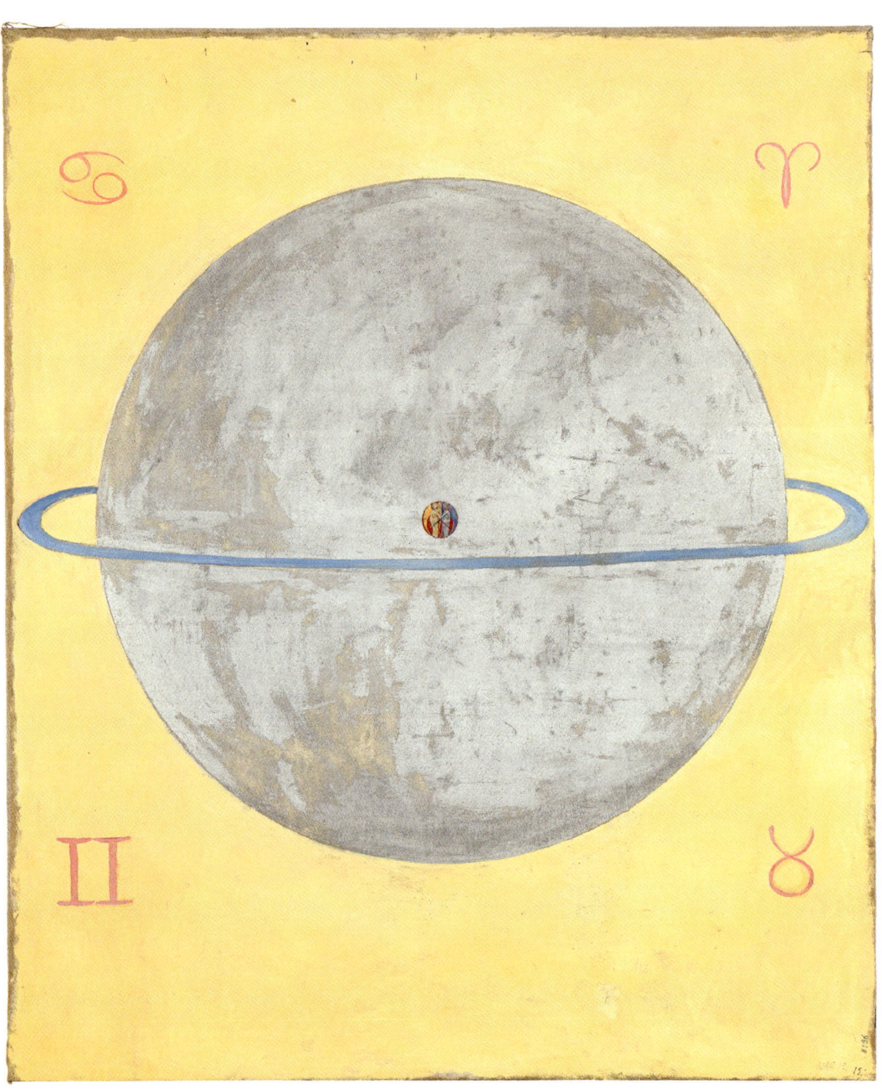

The Dove, The UW Series, Group IX, Part II: No. 12, 1915
Oil on canvas, 157 x 129 cm (61⅞ x 50⅞ in.)
Stockholm, Hilma af Klint Foundation, HaK 184

Goethe's experiments with light and color. A modern instrument would interest her even more, according to Glassley, and research into polarizing microscopes was being published across Europe in the early 20th century.[46]

Glassley's observations revealed that af Klint used illustrations of scientific research techniques and diagrams of scientific instruments to inform her spiritual paintings. *The Swan, No. 9* (p. 61), for instance, has a distinctly diagram-like composition. The two "swans" become funnels of cubes that rotate and decrease in size. They touch wing tips with another pair of funnels which meet in a straight edge anchored by a spinning, colorful propeller shape. Glassley compares this painting to an 1879 diagram representing experiments with feldspar crystals, the most common mineral of the earth's crust. When researchers rotated the feldspars under a microscope, the crystals revealed their structure by the way they refracted light, alternately showing bright colors and then going dark. Feldspars have "twins," which are mirror images of each other. Glassley maintains that *The Swan, No. 9* "essentially depicts this same diagram":

> There is a line dividing the twins, represented by the blue and yellow curving lines, and the cubes within those lines represent crystal structures. The

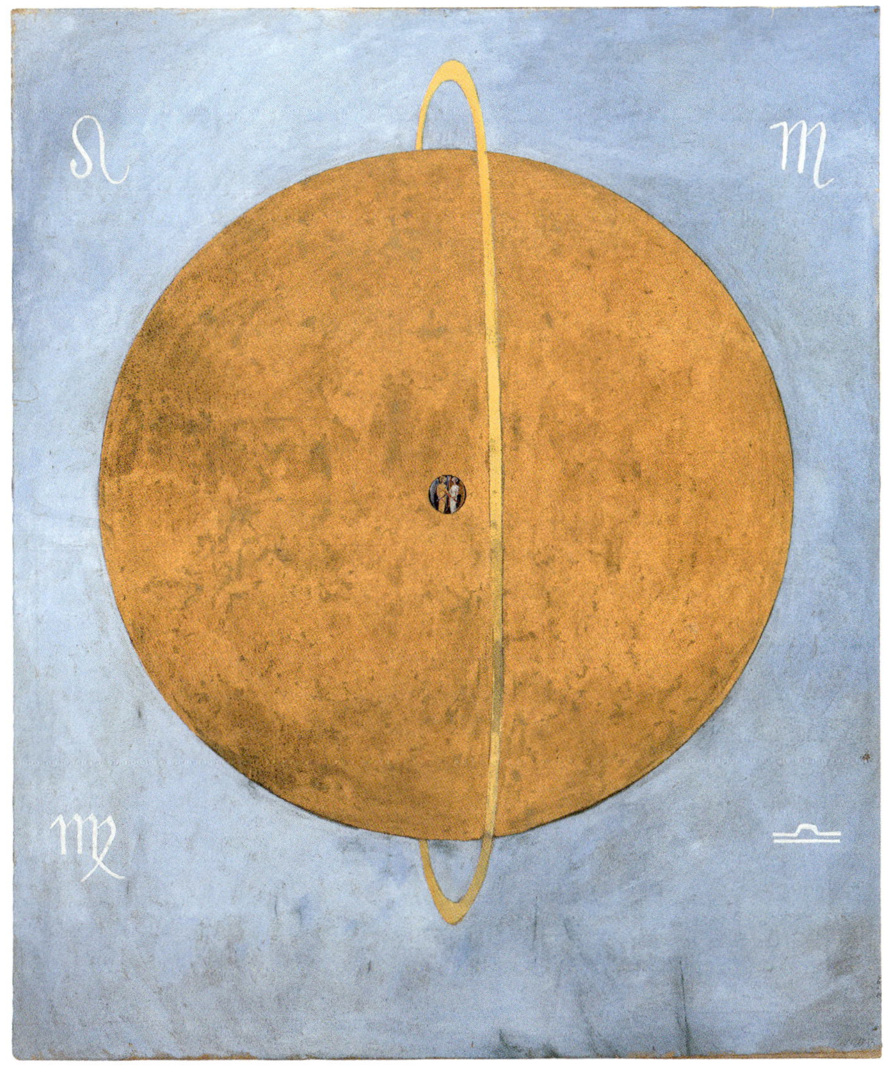

The Dove, The UW Series, Group IX, Part II: No. 13, 1915
Oil on canvas, 155 x 130 cm (61 x 51¼ in.)
Stockholm, Hilma af Klint Foundation, HaK 185

> variation in the orientation of the cubes results from rotating the crystals. The winglike forms connected to the cubes that progress from black to white, but in opposite directions, precisely depict how the colors seen in the microscope would change for each twin as the sample is rotated.[47]

Another scholar, the astronomer Britt Lundgren, suggests that the physicist Thomas Young (1773–1829) may have inspired af Klint with the plates in his published lectures (1807).[48] Young helped establish the wave theory of light through experiments on refraction and diffraction. He and Goethe were aware of each other's work, which overlapped. As "abstract" as af Klint's work may appear, especially after 1912 it has concrete reference points in science without being rigorously scientific.

In a painting like *The Dove, No. 5* (1915), af Klint returns to symbolic organic forms. Huge, ghostly hands hold aloft an upended dove with bloodied, plucked wings, whose tail fans out over the tiny, pastel holy family sheltering almost unseen in a temple of the night. Af Klint employs scale and grisaille painting to suggest immanence or invisible presences. Here she floats the vision of the biblical holy family in the darkest of modern times: 1915 was a bloody year in Europe.

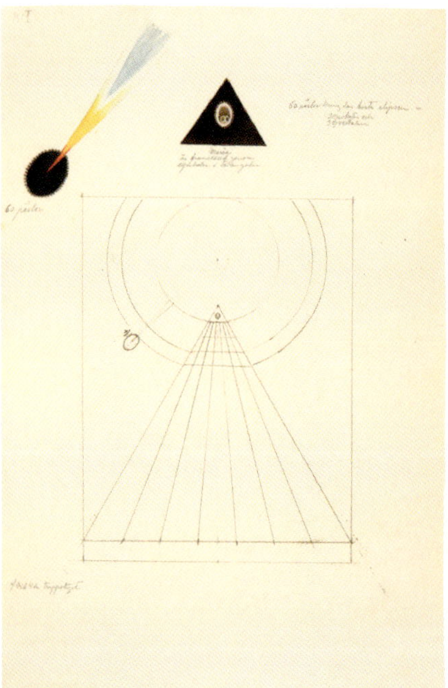

Sketch for Altarpiece No. 1
(Skiss till Altarbild Nr. 1), 1915
Graphite and watercolor on paper, 46 x 30 cm
(18 x 11¾ in.)
Stockholm, Hilma af Klint Foundation, HaK 190

Altarpieces, Group X: No. 1, 1915
Oil and metal leaf on canvas, 237.5 x 179.5 cm
(93⅝ x 70¾ in.)
Stockholm, Hilma af Klint Foundation, HaK 187

PAGE 72
Altarpieces, Group X: No. 2, 1915
Oil and metal leaf on canvas,
238 x 179 cm (93¾ x 70½ in.)
Stockholm, Hilma af Klint Foundation, HaK 188

PAGE 73
Altarpieces, Group X: No. 3, 1915
Oil and metal leaf on canvas,
237.5 x 178.5 cm (93⅝ x 70⅜ in.)
Stockholm, Hilma af Klint Foundation, HaK 189

The dove is a Christian symbol of Mary and is the creature that returned to Noah after the Flood carrying an olive branch, signifying a new beginning as the First World War raged on.

Another recurrent subject in *The Dove* series (pp. 4, 52, 66–69), which features 14 painting, comes unexpectedly: Saint George, who appears with his dragon on five canvases. The monochrome backgrounds of the first four alternate between angry, negative black and red (pp. 66, 4). On each canvas, two ghostly, hairless heads are sketched into the lower corners of the undefined background. They scream, glare, pray, howl, or sigh, and their energy connects them to the dragon that Saint George must vanquish. The saint is surrounded by his aura, and stands with his sword raised, appealing for divine wisdom and strength. On the final white canvas, peace has come.

"Altarpieces, Group X" (1915)

Three large canvases make up the final group of "The Paintings for the Temple" (pp. 71, 72–73).They are all about the same size (238 x 179 centimeters or 94 x 70 inches), painted in oil and metal leaf on canvas, and are meant to be shown next to each other in a dynamic grouping. Each painting features a gold circle, interpreted sometimes as a version of the Buddhist Wheel of Dharma, or as a planet. In the painting that is usually shown at the center of the three (*Altarpieces, Group X: No. 3*, p. 73), one circle asserts dominance. In the paintings usually shown to the left and right, the gold circles are smaller, and both occupy the top third of their canvases. Beneath them af Klint used equilateral triangles in distinctly different ways. In *Altarpieces, Group X: No. 2* (p. 72), the downward pointing triangle may suggest descent. An orb spins in alternating yellow and blue orbits. Its pendant triangle, *Altarpieces, Group X: No. 1* (p. 71), points upward, recalling a pyramid clad in colorful steps. These colors rise to the golden orb, a chain of chakra wheels separating permutations of blues from yellows.

Preliminary sketches hone in on small, almost hidden details within the altarpiece paintings, contained like the relics that invest a pilgrimage site with meaning. In *Sketch for Altarpiece No. 1* (p. 70), the sketch detail identifies the symbol in the black triangle pointing into the sun as standing for Maria. In *Altarpieces, Group X: No. 2*, the detail shows a yellow, blue, and pink prism embedded at the base, the meeting point of two small, curling yin yang waves. In *Altarpieces, Group X: No. 3*, the theosophical symbol of the six-pointed star comprising superimposed upward- and downward-pointing equilateral triangles rests at the midpoint of the gold circle.

Seen together, the altarpiece paintings speak of cosmic integration and spiritual evolution, communication between the physical world and the most elevated plane. The viewer, acutely aware of being incarnated on earth and not fully able to decipher these mysterious forms, faces off with af Klint's invitation to embark on a journey: The final goal is the resolution of opposites and a resulting unity with the cosmos.

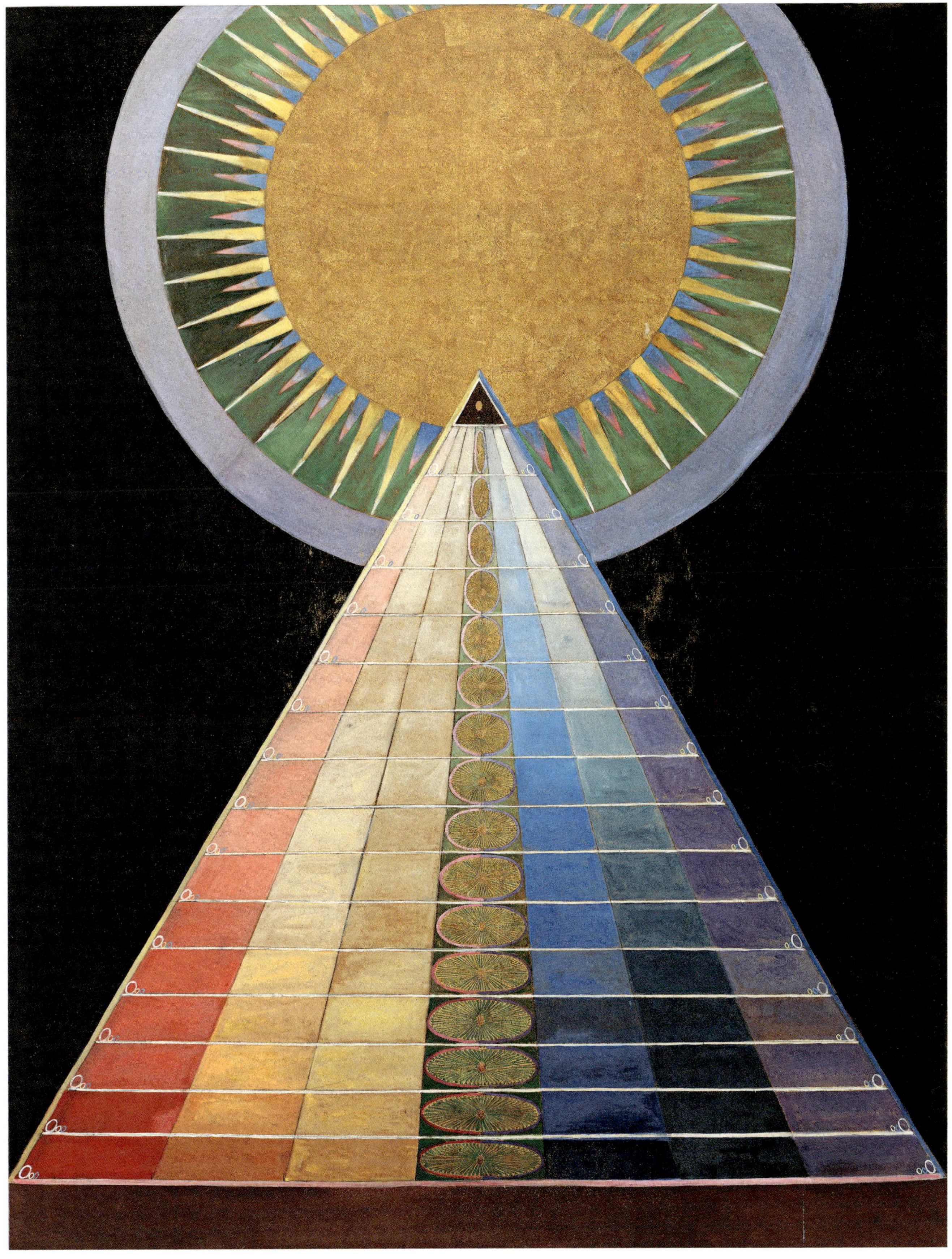

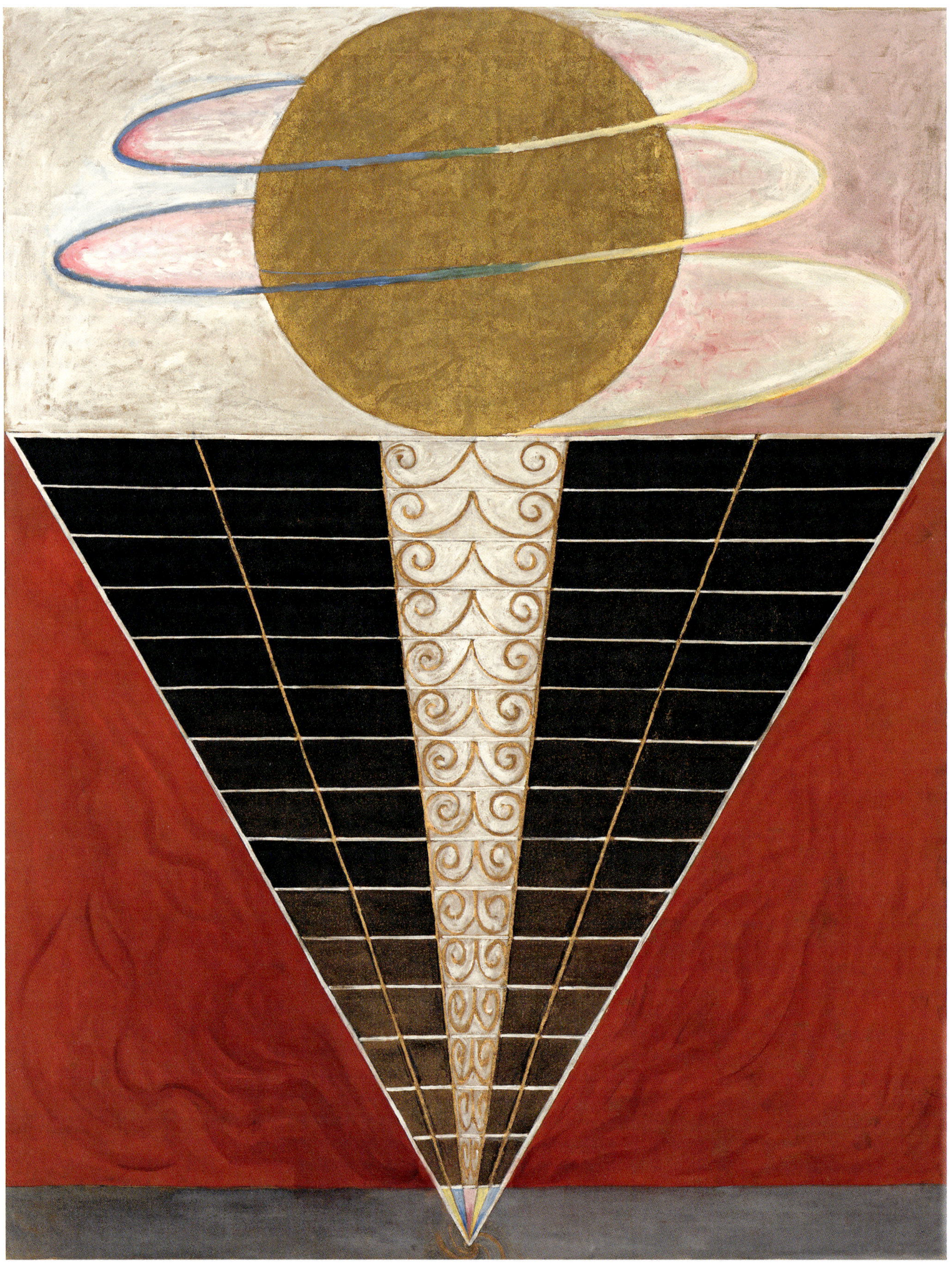

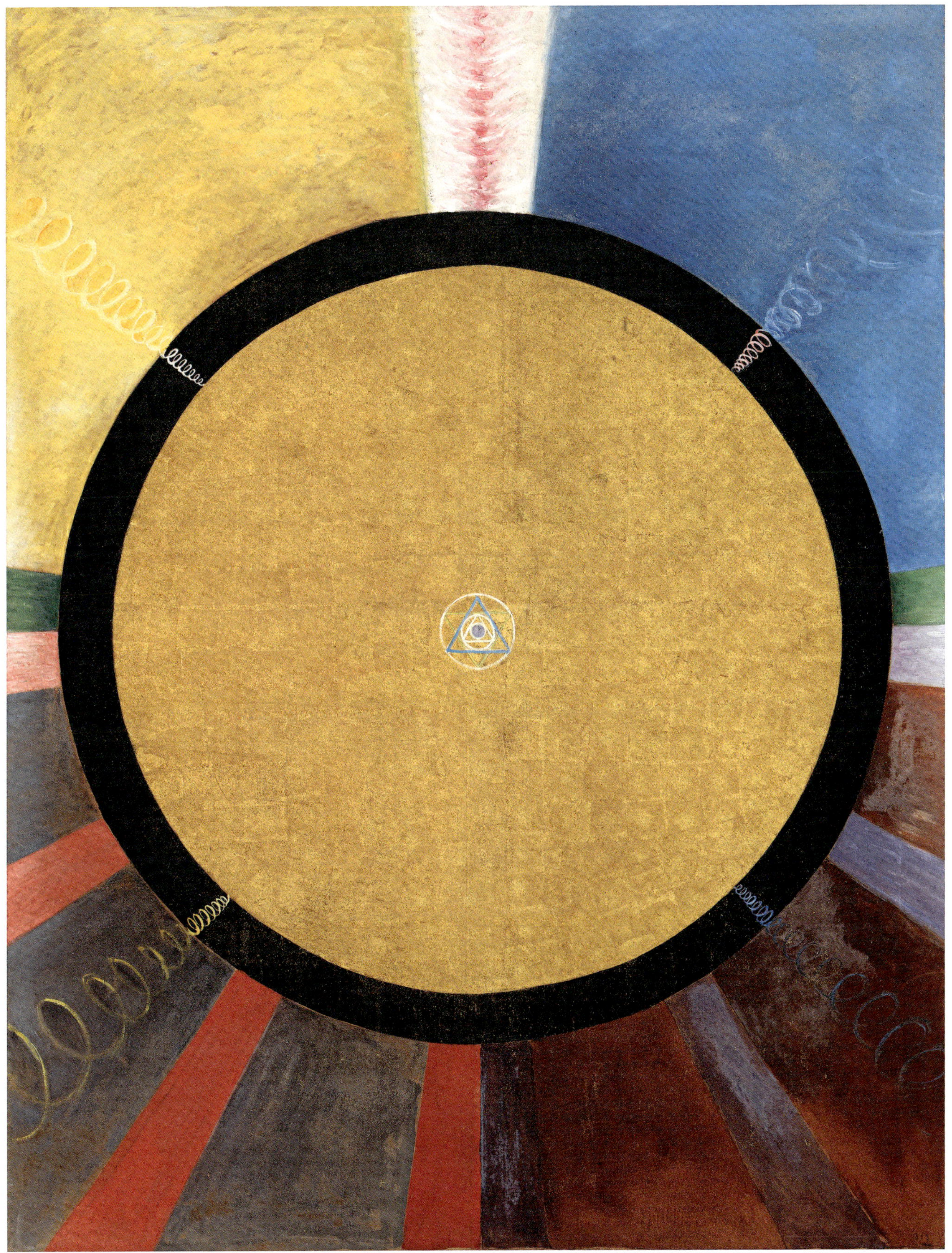

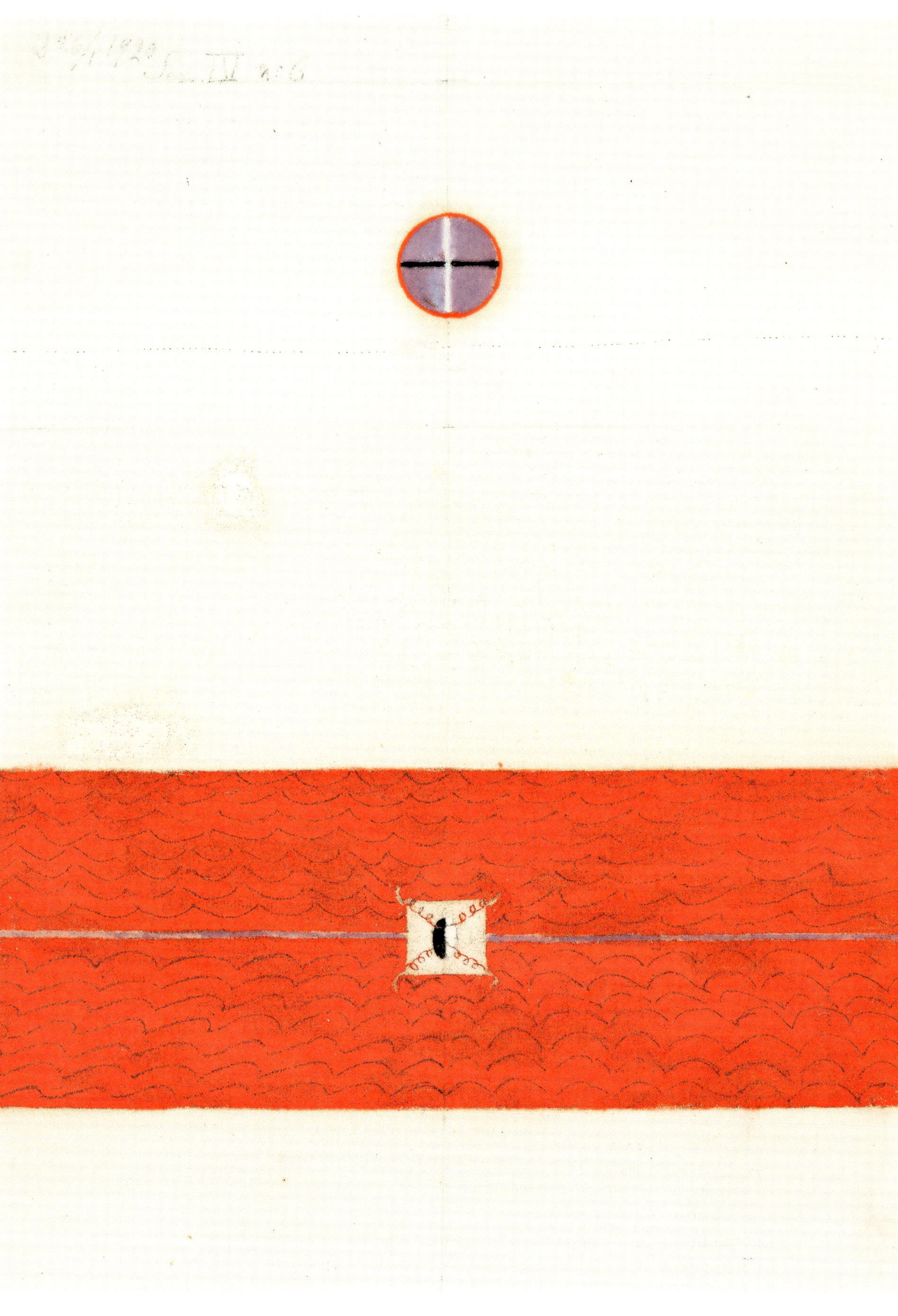

Preparing for Posterity

Abstraction and Legacy

The First World War had caused several artists to move through Stockholm, the capital of a neutral nation. Two artists welcomed by the cosmopolitan art scene there were the German Gabriele Münter (1877–1962) and the Russian Wassily Kandinsky (1866–1944). Münter showed paintings in a private gallery in Stockholm in spring 1916 as well as at a show that had been organized by the Association of Swedish Women Artists, the same group af Klint had joined and for which she had worked as secretary for a year. Kandinsky was also invited to exhibit in Stockholm. His nonrepresentational works did not sell but were nonetheless discussed in the press.[49] Kandinsky, just four years younger than af Klint, had in common with her the fact that he had joined the Theosophists in 1909, much enthused by Annie Besant and Charles W. Leadbeater's book *Thought-Forms: A Record of Clairvoyant Investigation*. Kandinsky's work featured color as an expressive agent, and he leaned away from representational art towards suggestive abstract forms. His treatise *Concerning the Spiritual in Art* from 1912 (p. 75) was widely read.

By the end of March 1916 Kandinsky had already left Stockholm. However, it is hard to imagine af Klint not following the reception of Münter's and Kandinsky's work. She must also have known about Sonia Delaunay-Terk's (1885–1979) first major exhibition outside of France that same year, held at Stockholm's Nya Konstgalleriet. Delaunay-Terk showed paintings that blended figuration and abstraction using concentric arcs and rings of color. Her color contrasts created a sense of motion, a push and pull, using the color theory of Michel Eugène Chevreul. These were dynamic works intended to energize the world, not depict it. Delaunay-Terk collaborated with the poet Blaise Cendrars by offering up geometric color experiences parallel to his poems, such as *La Prose du Transsibérien et de la Petite Jehanne de France* (*The Prose of the Trans-Siberian and of Little Joan of France)* (1913) with its "big red Christ of the Russian Revolution."[50] This poem spoke of imaginary travel in a collision of places and times, published as an accordion-folded sheet of paper nearly seven feet long. It would not have been impossible for af Klint to have seen such artist books.

While af Klint was not uninformed about goings on in European avant-garde art, she felt herself part of a spiritual vanguard—her art leaned toward the future and the divine. She reached though time to the cosmic pulse behind all religions,

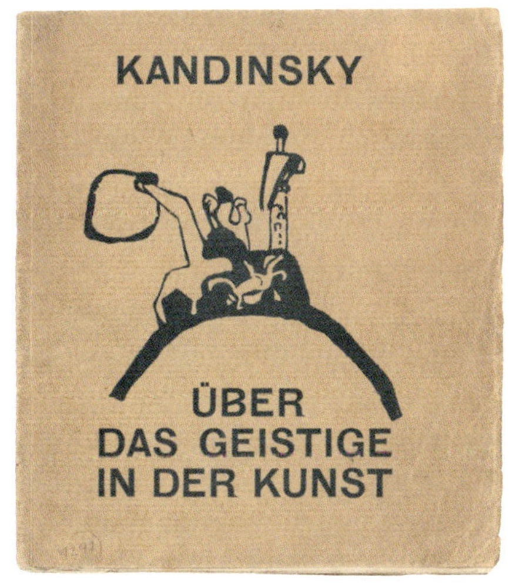

Wassily Kandinsky
Concerning the Spiritual in Art
(Über das Geistige in der Kunst), 1912
Bound volume with text, woodcuts, and photomechanical illustrations on laid paper, plus woodcut illustrations on upper and lower covers, 21 x 18.3 x 1 cm (8 1/4 x 7 3/16 x 3/8 in.)
Washington, D.C., The National Gallery of Art

Geometric Series IV: No. 6, January 26, 1920
Oil and graphite on canvas,
38.5 x 28 cm (15¼ x 11 in.)
Stockholm, Hilma af Klint Foundation,
HaK494

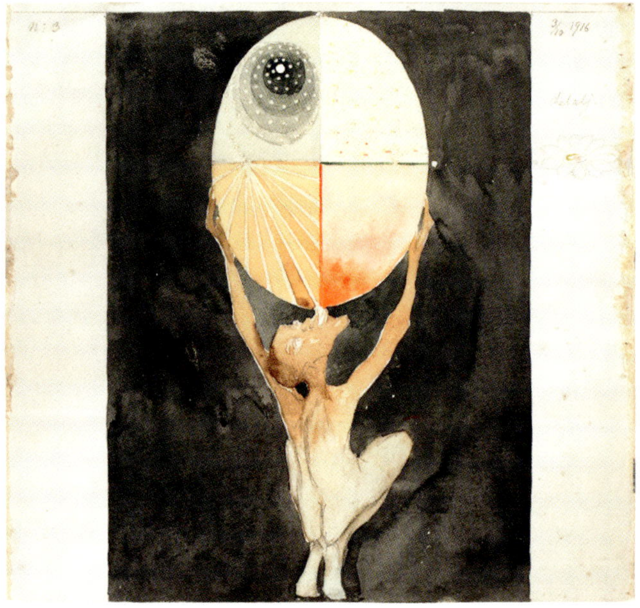

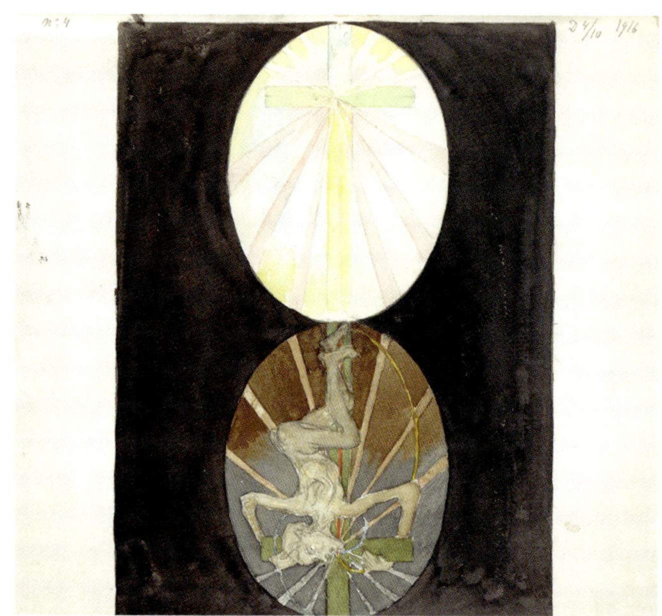

The Parsifal Series, Group I: No. 3, Detail,
October 3, 1916
Watercolor and graphite on paper,
28 x 26 cm (11 x 10¼ in.)
Stockholm, Hilma af Klint Foundation, HaK204

The Parsifal Series, Group I: No. 4,
October 4, 1916
Watercolor and graphite on paper,
25 x 26 cm (9⅞ x 10¼ in.)
Stockholm, Hilma af Klint Foundation, HaK205

a life force she saw corroborated by the scientific inquiry of her time. Her spiritual evolution and search for ancient, eternal truths ran parallel to her attending public lectures, listening to radio, seeing moving pictures, and taking trains and streetcars. While she did not network with international artists through magazine or manifesto publication, she owned a telephone book filled with the numbers of friends and contacts. She wrote private notebooks and sought the input of like-minded anthroposophical associates. In 1916 af Klint's work saw a shift that showed she "read" her own time intuitively and accurately. She began to move radically towards minimal content and abstraction, beginning with "The Parsifal Series."

"The Parsifal Series" (1916)

This series comprises 144 highly structured small watercolor and graphite sketches divided into four groups, including "Group II: The Ether Convolute," "The Convolute of Astral Forces," "The Convolute of the Mental Plane," and "The Convolute of the Physical Plane." The series takes af Klint's established themes and presents them delicately in an approximately 25 x 25 centimeter (10 x 10 inch) format. The title was borrowed from *Parsifal* (1882), Richard Wagner's (1813–1883) opera about Christianity, conceived by the composer on Good Friday, thus linking it to the Easter story and to resurrection/reincarnation. The opera is based on a 13th-century epic poem about a knight's quest for the Holy Grail. Steiner lectured about Wagner in 1906, observing that "there is in Wagner and in his works a very large measure of occult power."[51] Through sound, his music introduced leitmotifs and evoked imagery such as the shimmering of light.

Af Klint's first "Parsifal" sketch invites the viewer on a journey through the dark and on into the light in a tight spiral. Interestingly, almost all the first group's 57 drawings picture an upright rectangle divided by graphite lines into vertically climbing planes. Sometimes one or more of the subdivided planes carry a pale color wash. Art historian Briony Fer suggests that af Klint's occult belief system gave her permission to work completely outside the conventional framework of her training. She was able to look to diagrams in printed books

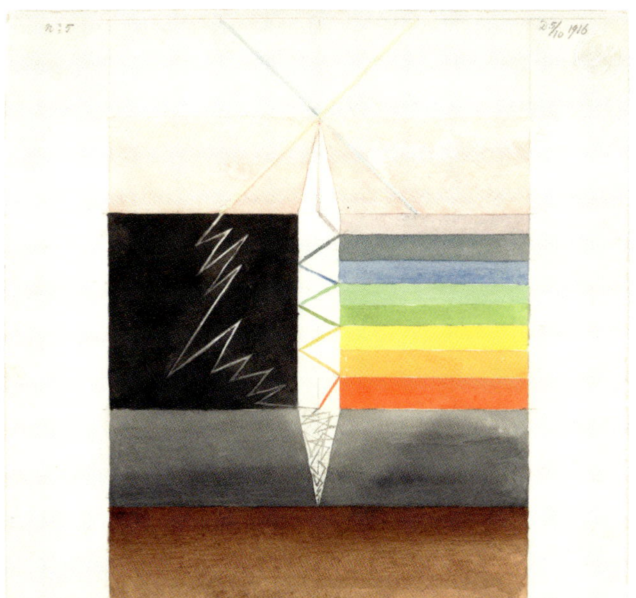

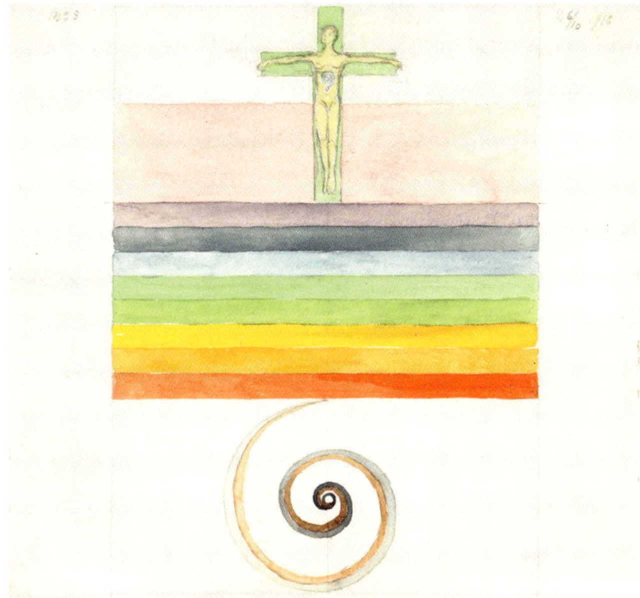

The Parsifal Series, Group I: No. 5,
October 5, 1916
Watercolor and graphite on paper,
28 x 26 cm (11 x 10¼ in.)
Stockholm, Hilma af Klint Foundation, HaK206

The Parsifal Series, Group I: No. 8,
October 6, 1916
Watercolor and graphite on paper,
25 x 26 cm (9⅞ x 10¼ in.)
Stockholm, Hilma af Klint Foundation, HaK209

like Charles W. Leadbeater and Annie Besant's *Thought-Forms: A Record of Clairvoyant Investigation*, as well as in Johann Wolfgang von Goethe's published color theory of 1810, which dealt with the color of light, not the color of pigments.[52]

In *No. 3* and *No. 4* of "The Parsifal Series" (p. 76), "Group I," af Klint introduces what may be an alter ego, a thin, androgynous, rather desperate-looking character seemingly about to tumble into a spiritual journey to a higher plane. In *No. 5* (p. 77), a triangular prism hangs like an energized dagger and splits light into colors. Above the prism two beams of light cross, one yellow and one blue. The prism touches five separate planes distinguished by their colors, including the top plane, which uses the color of the paper as implied immateriality. The planar separation bears comparison to Leadbeater's Plate IV in *Man Visible and Invisible* (1903), listing the physical, astral, mental, buddhic, nirvanic, paranirvanic, and Mahaparanirvanic planes for minerals, vegetables, animals, humans, and the spiritual. In that chart, a similarly shaped form spans the physical to the nirvanic plane.

The series then begins an operatic story, without explanatory text, open to conjecture. Seen through the prism, a crucified female reincarnates as a boy child (*Parsifal, Nos. 8* and *9*, pp. 77–78). It takes several drawings for the boy to mature. In *Parsifal, Nos. 14* (p. 78), *15*, *16*, and *17*, a rose and a lily form a pair within a green plane. A girl child then generates and matures in subsequent drawings. These two humans eventually form a pair, with the male holding a grail in *No. 28*. The watercolor drawings are all concentric, layered in planes, with varying symbolic figuration in the plane centers. In *Parsifal, No. 31*, a pink circle and a first tiny apex triangle—af Klint's shorthand for a prism—appear. The small triangle has yellow, blue, and red sides, and stands for the kind of triangular prism that Goethe used in his experiments.[53] Under the pink circle stands Parsifal in the physical plane, surrounded by Wagner's Flower Maidens, out to seduce him and derail his spiritual quest, to no avail. Later, in *No. 41*, the circle has grown to a frame-bursting, breast-like, lavender-pink wholeness punctuated by a tender aureole pooling at its center. A narrow band of green light is visible along its

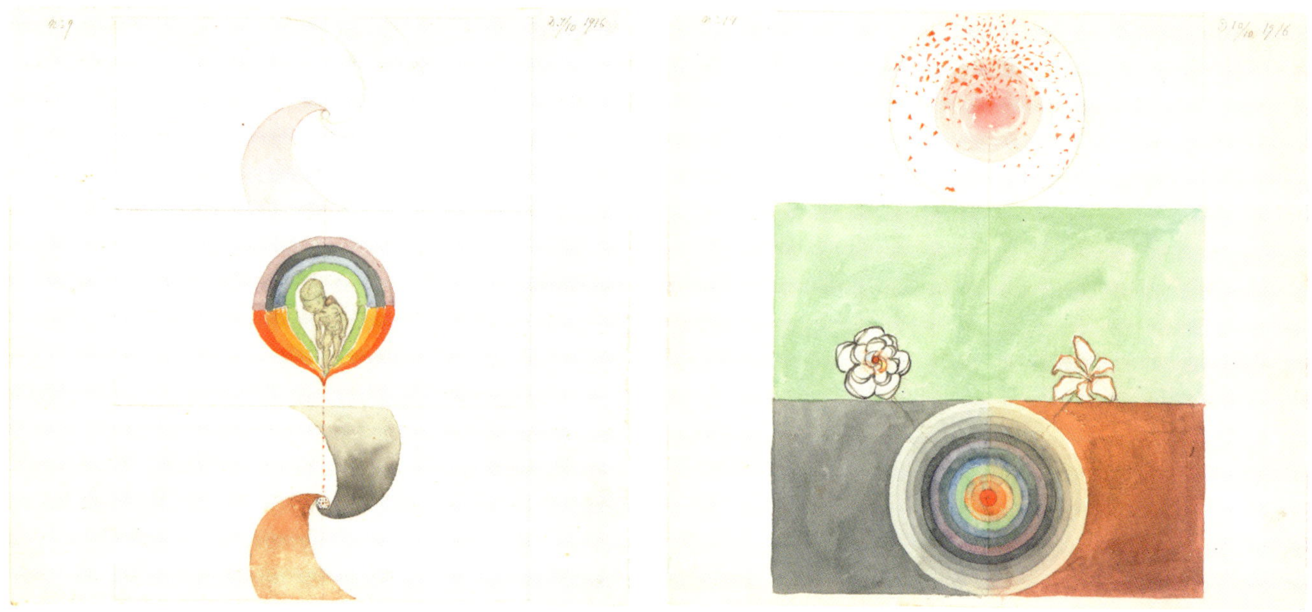

The Parsifal Series, Group I: No. 9,
October 7, 1916
Watercolor and graphite on paper,
25 x 26 cm (9⅞ x 10¼ in.)
Stockholm, Hilma af Klint Foundation, HaK210

The Parsifal Series, Group I: No. 14,
October 10, 1916
Watercolor and graphite on paper,
25 x 26 cm (9⅞ x 10¼ in.)
Stockholm, Hilma af Klint Foundation, HaK215

perimeter, a phenomenon Goethe noted when he described colors nestling along the edges of objects viewed through a prism. Af Klint innovatively combined the yellow and blue light that Goethe saw, her symbol for the uniting of genders.

Now dwarfed by the enlarged circle of *No. 41* behind it, the triangle prism floats quietly, having fulfilled its mission of effecting a new vision. Af Klint used the tool of the prism as a symbol for transformation that manifests in humanity as spiritual growth. The circle's light lavender-pink color may be intended to align with Leadbeater's color chart (p. 27) from *Man Visible and Invisible*, which in that case would read as "Love for Humanity." A sense of touch and refinement communicates itself in the delicately brushed surface. A dawning green love, resurrection, and the rebirth of nurturing spring all resonate here.

In "Group II" af Klint shifts to working with a square on the roughly square paper. She creates meditative images that show a square of one single color wash—blue, red, yellow, green, and lilac. The squares vary minimally—only in color application, not in size. Goethe's illustrative tables from his *Theory of Colours* showing experiments with candles, reflections, refractions, and prisms offered visual prototypes and a sense of proportion to af Klint as she was considering philosophical and spiritual aspects of light symbolism and the representation of planes. An example of this is the way the yellow square in *The Ether Convolute, No. 62* (p. 79) resembles Goethe's yellow circle, showing the reflection of a burning candle on a white wall, seen on the first plate in *Theory of Colour* (p. 30). In place of Goethe's small, centered candle flame, af Klint places an ambiguous form, either a seed about to open or a bivalve, right in the center of the yellow color field. The proportional vastness of the yellow field compared to the minute form increases its mystery.

Af Klint synthesized Goethe's earnest optical science. She submersed herself in the careful watercolor brushing of each square. In some works, she introduced words lettered gothically as if taken from an old German book, placing them horizontally or vertically within or adjacent to the color fields. The words are sometimes seen in reverse, as if the viewer is looking at writing on a colored

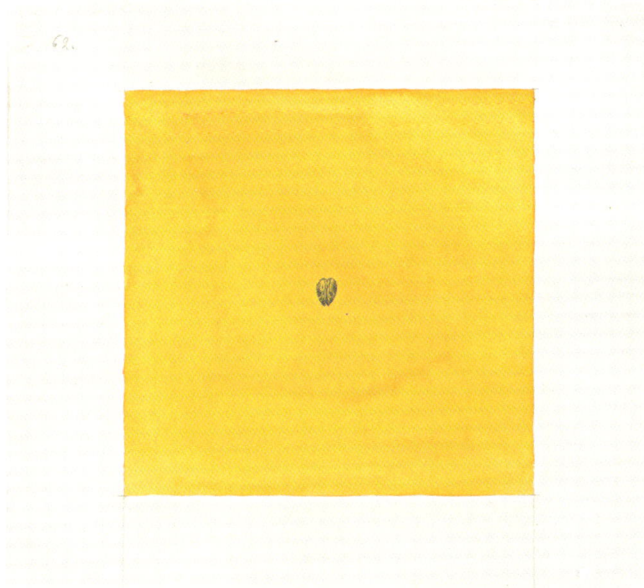

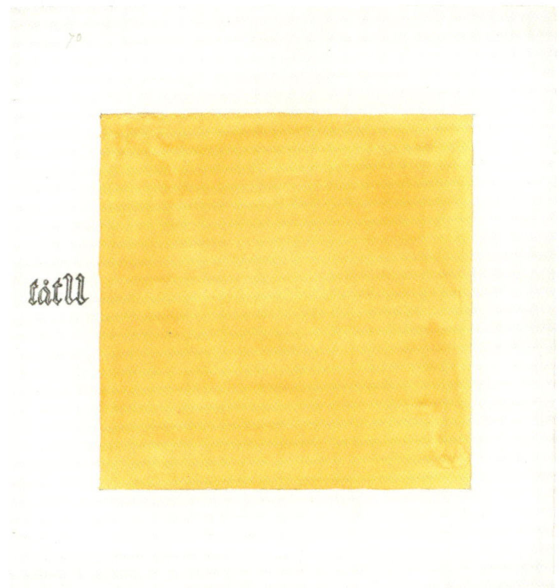

pane of glass, but from the outside, forcing them to consider their position (*The Convolute of Astral Forces, No. 70*, p. 79). Af Klint's filmic ascending rose crosses from "Group III" of the "Parsifal" series astound with their graceful lightness (*The Parsifal Series: Group III, Nos. 94–97*, pp. 80–81). She painted the resurrecting rose crucifix two years before Kazimir Malevich (1879–1935) painted a square with one corner lifting in his *White on White* (1918), an icon of the Russian revolution and a symbol of radical change.

In the final subgroup of the series ("Group IV"), af Klint brushes delicate pastel watercolor onto pencil drawings, conflating the cosmic with the microscopic and suggesting the bombardment of earth with life-bringing astral matter, or the creation of a zygote. Macrocosmos and microcosmos unite in these beautiful, cerebral paintings. Af Klint's interest in science also extended to research on the atom, about which she made an entire series of works in 1917 called "The Atom." Besant and Leadbeater's book *Occult Chemistry: A Series of Clairvoyant Observations on the Chemical Elements* (1908) claimed that a clairvoyant person could see atoms with the third eye, and diagrams accompanied their text. In "The Atom," af Klint used variations of square diagrams in the upper left and lower right corners of her paper and balanced them against text in the upper right corner. These penciled texts make parallel statements, such as, "Every atom has its center, but every center is directly connected to the center of the universe." Another drawing with a sizzling or radiating square reads, "The atom gains strength because it feels and acknowledges its dependence on Divine power; it is inexhaustible and incomprehensible life itself." Color is held to a minimum in this series, and the graphite writing is part of the drawing, not an explanation of it.

"The Blue Books" (1919)

In 1913, shortly before the First World War began, af Klint had been able to take over a lake house on the island of Munsö, off the coast of Stockholm. It was only a short, rowable distance from Adelsö, where she had summered with her family in her youth. In 1916 she decided to design and build a studio near the

The Parsifal Series, Group II, The Ether Convolute: No. 62, 1916
Watercolor and graphite on paper, 27 x 25 cm (10¾ x 9⅞ in.)
Stockholm, Hilma af Klint Foundation, HaK271

The Parsifal Series, Group II, The Convolute of Astral Forces: No. 70, 1916
Watercolor and graphite on paper, 27 x 25 cm (10¾ x 9⅞ in.)
Stockholm, Hilma af Klint Foundation, HaK280

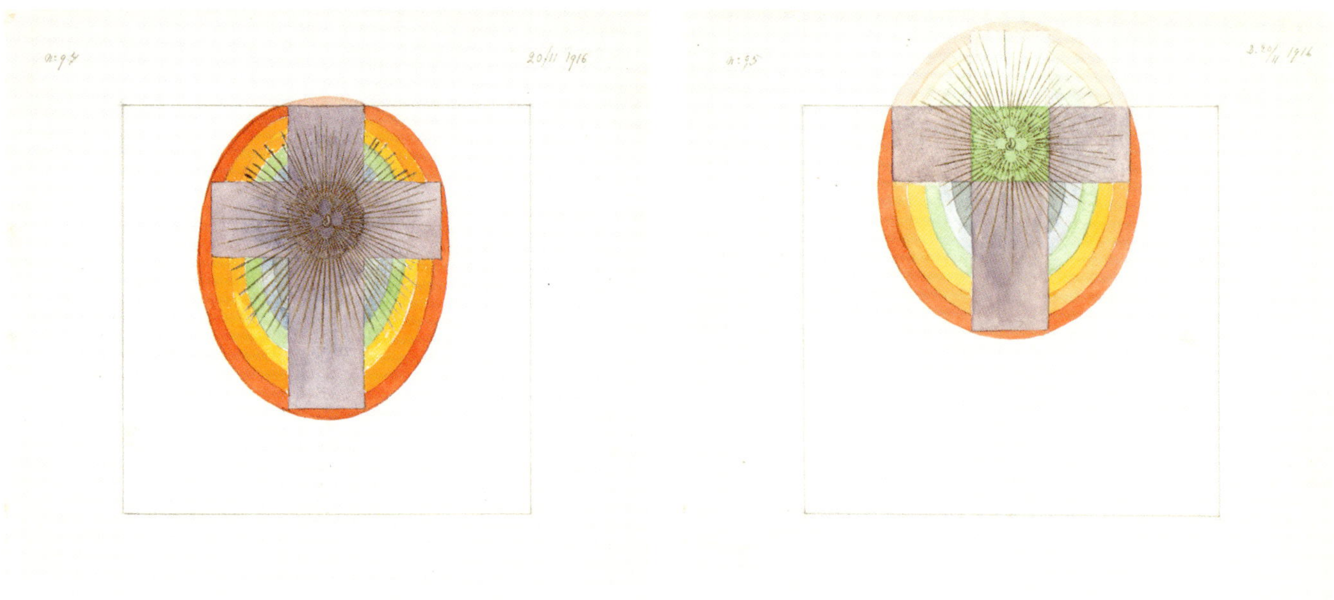

The Parsifal Series, Group III: No. 94, November 20, 1916
Watercolor, graphite, and metallic paint on paper, 25 x 27 cm (9⅞ x 10¾ in.)
Stockholm, Hilma af Klint Foundation, HaK304

The Parsifal Series, Group III: No. 95, November 20, 1916
Watercolor, graphite, and metallic paint on paper, 25 x 27 cm (9⅞ x 10¾ in.)
Stockholm, Hilma af Klint Foundation, HaK305

new lake house. By 1918 she had relocated there more permanently with her mother and the nurse Thomasine Andersson (*c.* 1880–1940). The studio was not a temple, but at least most of the works from "The Paintings for the Temple" could be hung in one church-like building. A high ceiling accommodated "The Ten Largest." A prayer room was the most unusual feature for an artist studio. Upstairs, an apartment could absorb guests. Af Klint's ideal form for the studio had originally been an oval space, although in the end a rectangular building was created, which her school friend and former romantic interest Anna Cassel (1860–1937) and others helped to finance.[54]

During this time, Andersson became af Klint's final life partner as well as her mother's nurse. Because Andersson spoke German, she could help af Klint write in that language, which was also the language of Rudolf Steiner. The move to Munsö, although it had begun with the artist's dream of communal creative effort, resulted in distancing af Klint from The Thirteen. The other women did not see themselves as equals in the arrangement. Andersson became Hilma af Klint's main helpmate and support, and because her studies in medicine had included medicinal botany, af Klint's interest in plants began to grow. Instead of only listening for voices from the spirits, she directed her listening towards nature. She may have considered herself an adept, having advanced to the point where she was able to "read" the spiritual content of her surroundings. It was reported that she could heal by the laying on of hands.

In 1919, after the war had ended, af Klint and Andersson decided to document "The Paintings for the Temple" in an attempt to gain an audience for them and place them in a collection, such as Steiner's Goetheanum in Dornach. They hired a photographer to take pictures of af Klint's paintings outdoors, positioned in bright, even light. Over 200 photographs were taken that rendered almost all the paintings into small, black-and-white images. Af Klint then carefully painted miniature watercolor replicas of the photographed works. She enlarged important details to enhance understanding. After months of work, the color replicas and black and white photographs were mounted in albums on facing pages, color paintings on the left and the photographs on the right. The dimensions,

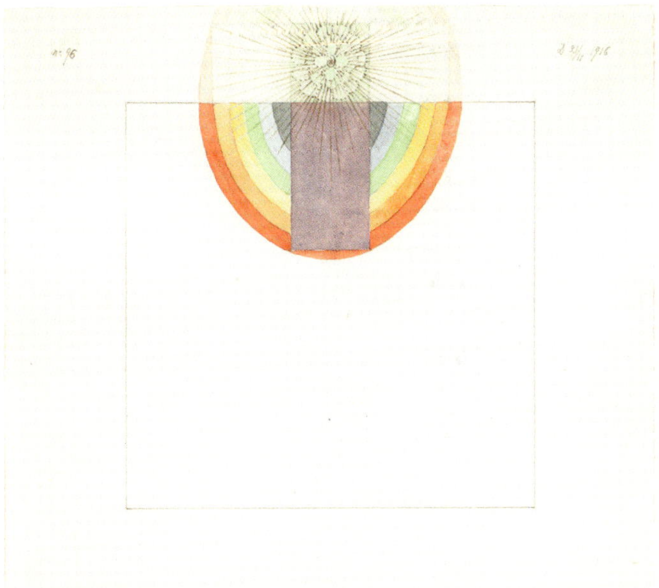

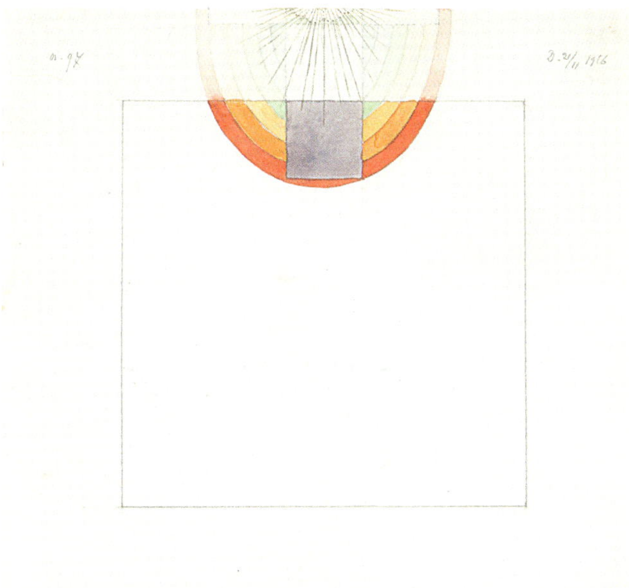

The Parsifal Series, Group III: No. 96,
November 21, 1916
Watercolor, graphite, and metallic paint on paper, 25 x 27 cm (9⅞ x 10¾ in.)
Stockholm, Hilma af Klint Foundation, HaK306

The Parsifal Series, Group III: No. 97,
November 21, 1916
Watercolor, graphite, and metallic paint on paper, 25 x 27 cm (9⅞ x 10¾ in.)
Stockholm, Hilma af Klint Foundation, HaK307

dates, and titles of the originals were included. Ten such custom albums came into existence, all blue, in a horizontal format and of a size and weight easy to hold (17 x 23 centimeters, or about 7 x 9 inches). These came to be known as "The Blue Books" (p. 83).[55]

With Andersson's help, af Klint had gained a tool for presenting the full context, colors, and compositions of her paintings to interested parties. Sometimes called a "suitcase museum," one might also consider "The Blue Books" a first "temple," or even a kind of hymnal. Today, they can be regarded as artist's books and as a conceptual art project in their own right. Their making gave af Klint the chance to reflect on what had begun as Amaliel's commission and brought about her own spiritual coming of age. They embody her desire to show "The Paintings for the Temple" in their entire context in one place.

Restoring Nature

As the industrialized violence and destruction of the First World War negated Western society's faith in itself as a set of civilized countries, af Klint felt the need to restore the landscape. She began working on texts written in German with Andersson's help, complemented by drawings and small watercolor paintings. These works focused on plants. Steiner, whose interest she hoped to gain for her paintings, had written and lectured extensively about the plant, animal, and mineral worlds on their own and in relation to human spirituality. He recommended observation and experience of the natural world, combined with introspection, to develop a clairvoyant consciousness, as opposed to listening for spirit voices, which he feared could veer into the obscure and inauthentic. Steiner lectured, "If someone empathizes with the plant-Soul, then he can share in the knowledge of all nature and feel with it. If we make ourselves confidants of the whole of nature, then our Soul will be tuned to also empathize with the other human beings."[56]

Af Klint wrote on January 7, 1917: "First I will attempt to understand the flowers of the earth… finally I will penetrate the forest exploring the silent mosses, the trees, and the many animals that inhabit the cool, dark undergrowth."[57] A set of exquisite sketches in pencil, ink, and watercolor on paper (50 x 27 centimeters, or about 19 x 10 inches), starting in spring 1919, show af Klint's study of flowers plucked from the awakening landscape around her. She collected entire plants and looked at roots, stems, flowers, and leaves. Grouped today as the "Dornach Nature Studies,"[58] these botanical drawings began with recording two tips of a hazel branch with catkins, and a clump of liverwort, the blue-flowering relative of the buttercup (p. 84). Next to every plant is a geometric diagram that embodies the organism on a higher plane. The drawings go from the physical to the spiritual; they try for a new synthetic science.

The liverwort is represented by a six-pointed star formed from two equilateral triangles with a circle in the middle, while the hazelnut branch corresponds to a square bisected in two directions to form quarter sections, one of which has diagonal lines in it. These small geometric diagrams resemble some of af Klint's larger paintings without figures. Af Klint labelled the diagrams with the word "Riktlinier," meaning "directing lines" or "guidelines." The nature sketches continue on 46 sheets, extraordinarily delicate and keenly observed. There are three sheets that show only diagrams. On one drawing, a bee buzzes across the top. On the bottom of another lies an immobile white wagtail bird. A mosquito and a red ant accompany multiple stalks of sweet vernal grass that grow from one base root.

Af Klint used the botanical drawings to assemble a scientific notebook, *Flowers, Mosses, Lichens* (p. 85). This distilled her new way of looking at plants, as it only contained diagrams, now somewhat enlarged and augmented with more text than had been written on the botanical drawings. Af Klint set herself the goal of divining what defined the plant—its lines of intent, direction, or self-guidance. For her, plants had an emotional signature. She recognized their

BELOW
Temple Design, pp. 50–51, 1930–31
Ink and graphite on paper, spread:
21 x 34 cm (8⅜ x 13½ in.)
Stockholm, Hilma af Klint Foundation,
HaK1047

OPPOSITE
Blue Book 4, The Ten Largest: No. 102—11, 1907
Watercolor and black-and-white photographs
on notebook paper, 23 x 17 cm (9 x 7 in.)
Stockholm, Hilma af Klint Foundation

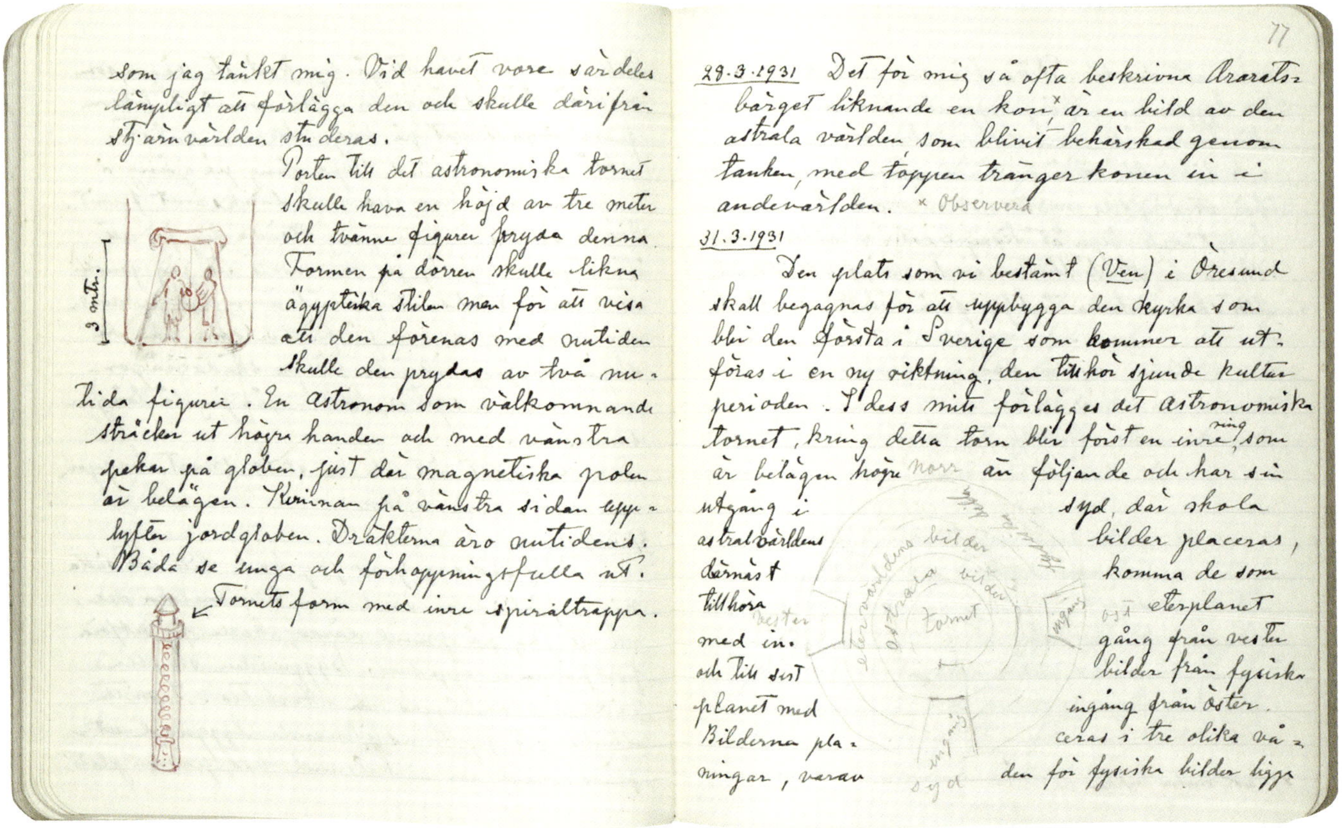

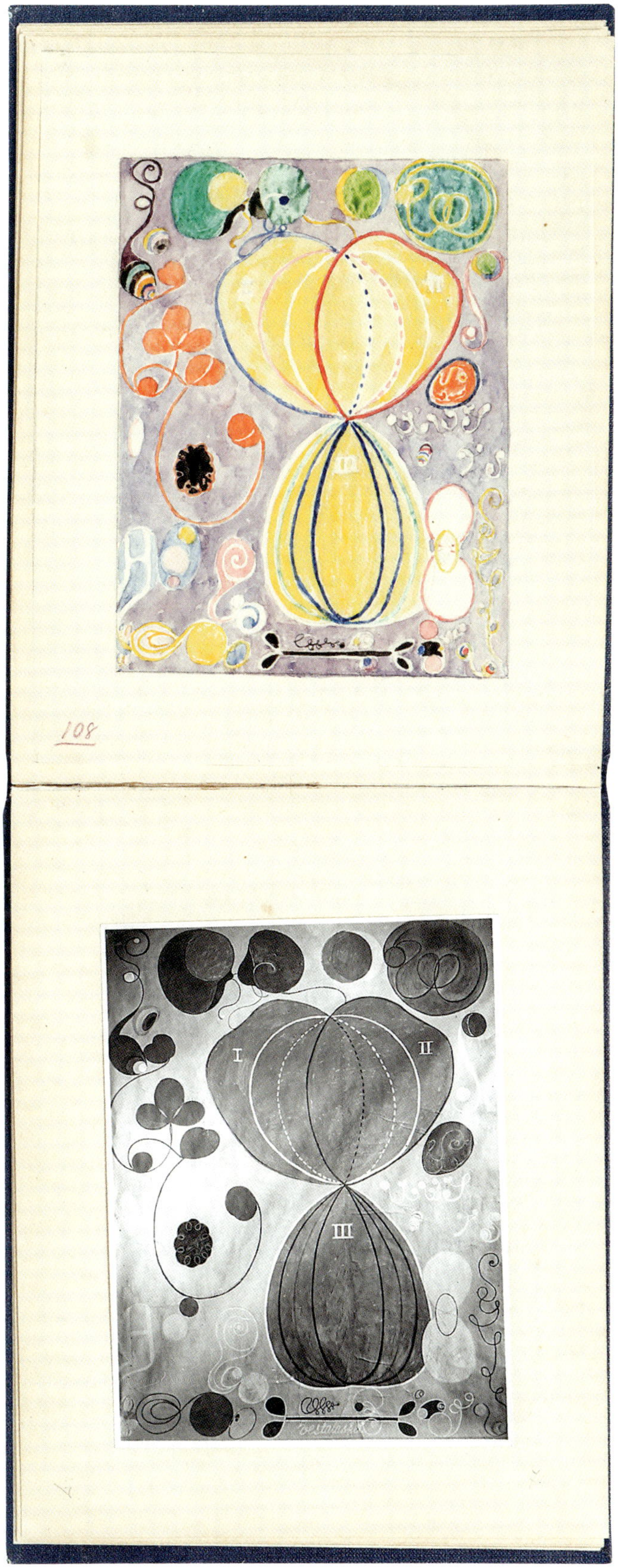

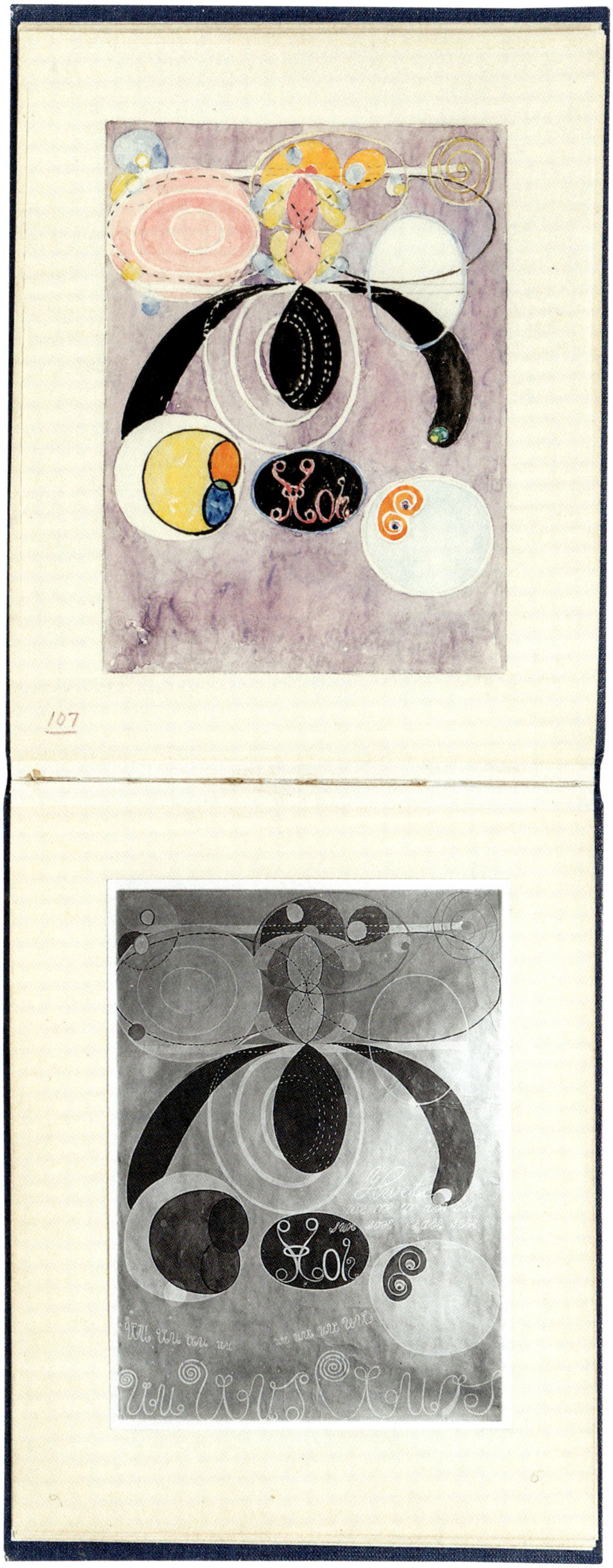

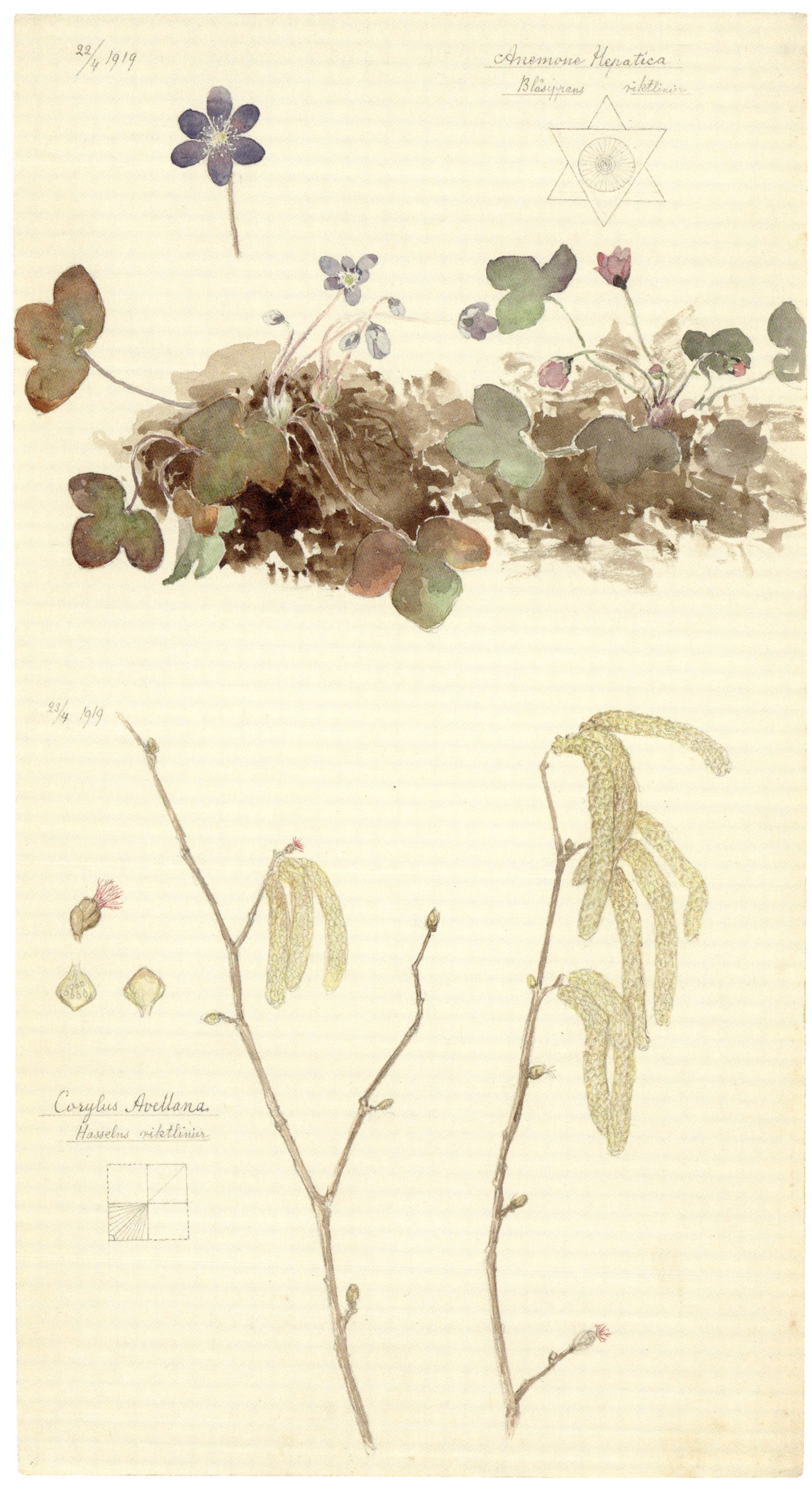
22/4 1919
Anemone Hepatica
Blåsippans riktlinier
23/4 1919
Corylus Avellana.
Hasselns riktlinier

consciousness and their fellow company. At this point in her life, through her work as an artist, spiritual seeker, and theosophist, af Klint had developed a high degree of attunement. She acted as a clairvoyant or clairsentient, feeling herself able to tap into an organism's energy. At the highest level of this capability, she would also feel able to redirect that organism's energy, and affect it, heal it, communicate with it. She pictured herself entering through the etheric plane, which was a bridge between the physical level and the astral plane of the plant.

The artist's mother, Mathilda af Klint, died in 1920, the year af Klint painted a series of eight small works dealing with world religions ("Series II"). Most of the titles include the word "standpoints," and after the first horizontally oriented Starting Picture, each canvas "stood" in a vertical format. To make them, af Klint drew a large circle onto raw canvas. She then painted and accented each circle abstractly. Alternating regions of black and white in *Series II, The Current Standpoint of the Mahatmas* recall successive reincarnations in Hinduism. Buddha's Standpoint in Worldly Life suggests balance and peace. The purely black and white world religion images recall Goethe's experiments with viewing black and white circles: colored crescents appeared on their rim when they were seen through a prism. All religions, when seen through an anthroposophical lens, share the colors of fundamental divine wisdom.

In 1920, af Klint's painting formats decreased in size but gained in focus. She had begun to turn to watercolor and pencil on paper, and the paper's areas of blankness may have prompted her to also allow the texture and color of untreated canvas to enter her work as an aesthetic element, or as a sign of simplicity, release, and honesty in materials. She mixed drawing with graphite and painting with oil on canvas in works like *Series IV, No. 6 (January 1920)*. This

Hepatica nobilis (Hepatica), Corylus avellana (Common Filbert), sheet 1 from ***Nature Studies***, portfolio of 46 drawings, April 22–23, 1919
Watercolor, pencil, and ink on paper, 49.7 x 26.9 cm (19⁹⁄₁₆ x 10⁹⁄₁₆ in.)
New York, The Museum of Modern Art, Committee on Drawings and Prints Fund and gift of Jack Shear

Flowers, Mosses, Lichens, pp. 24–25, 1919–20
Ink, watercolor, and graphite on paper, spread: 21 x 34 cm (8⅜ x 13½ in.)
Stockholm, Hilma af Klint Foundation, HaK 586

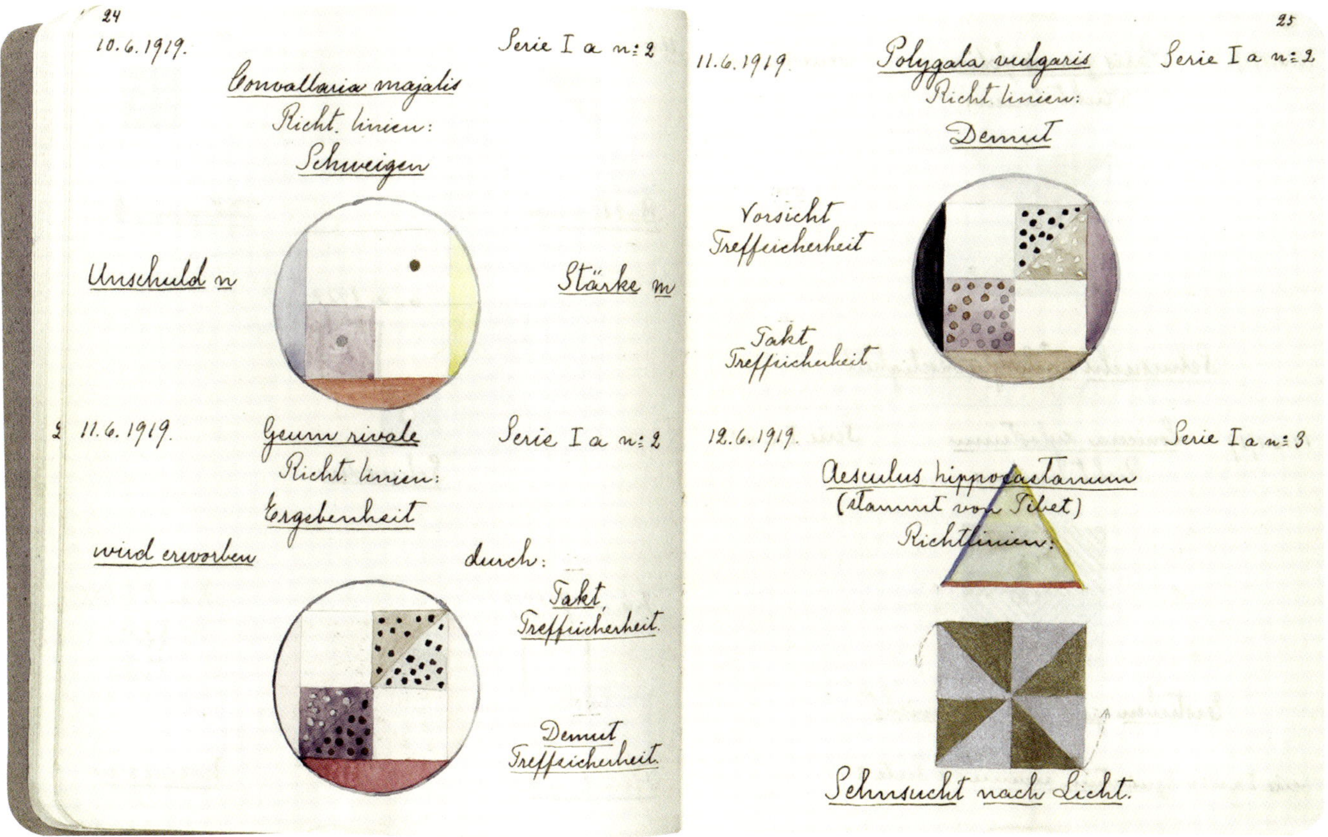

Portrait Study, Woman's Head [Emilia Giertta] (Porträttstudie, kvinnohuvud [Emilia Giertta]), 1918
Charcoal and crayon on paper,
50 x 40 cm (19¾ x 15¾ in.)
Stockholm, Hilma af Klint Foundation, HaK 1247

Portrait Study, Woman [Anna Cassel] (Porträttstudie, kvinna [Anna Cassel]), n/d
Charcoal and crayon on paper,
50 x 40 cm (19¾ x 15¾ in.)
Stockholm, Hilma af Klint Foundation, HaK 1417

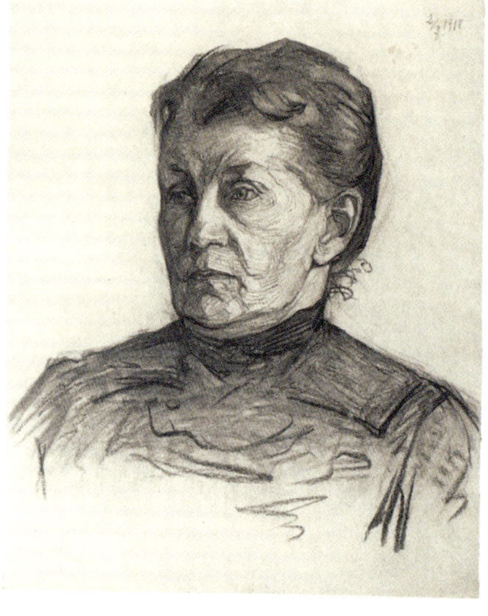

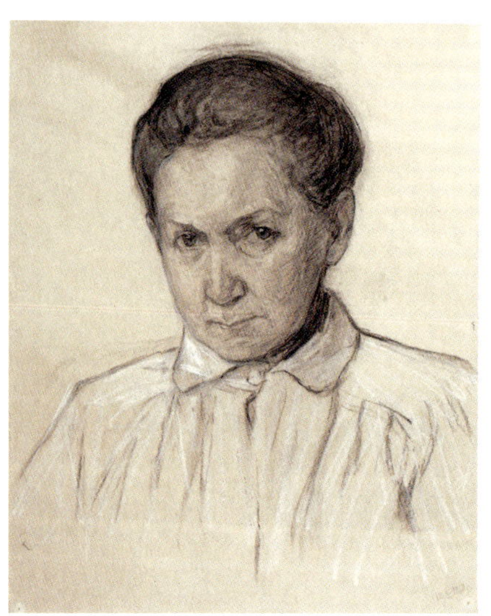

highly structured, delicate image is both energetic and meditative. The artist had arrived at minimal means, formats, and materials, and acquired lightness of touch; she welcomed space, and the natural ground of her pictures. At this point, she was happy to show relationships, life's movement—upward or downward—and connection to the spiritual, sometimes even in the conceptual company of the highest-ranking angels.

After 1922 af Klint, who had rheumatism in her hands, painted almost exclusively in watercolor on paper, using a wet-on-wet technique propagated by Steiner. Her themes also recurred in this technique, and she created many jewel-like abstractions, but also figurative works and portraits.

Building a Legacy

In 1925 Steiner died, and with him af Klint's last hope of getting "The Paintings for the Temple" a home at his Goetheanum in Dornach. Steiner had never accepted her suggested donation of the paintings, nor did he even consider exhibiting them for a short time. Nonetheless, af Klint and Andersson traveled to Dornach nine times between 1920 and 1932. They felt themselves among the like-minded there, and enjoyed the cultural life of the Goetheanum, which fostered artistic expression, spiritual exploration, and the development of new social and educational initiatives. Af Klint probably felt that the spirits were also disappointed that "The Paintings for the Temple" would not hang there.

The idea of building a permanent home for her paintings became more acute as af Klint aged. In 1931 she conceived of a spiral-shaped temple and sketched it in a notebook. No sponsor stood ready to build it, but it existed as an idea, that necessary first step towards anything utopian. The temple she sketched had three floors that climbed to an apex around a central spiral staircase. The staircase was a kind of tower in the middle of the building with an observatory on top. It looked like a lighthouse surrounded by a snail shell. The paintings and a library would find space there (*Temple Design*, p. 82).

Af Klint deemed Ven, an island between Sweden and Denmark, the perfect location for the temple. The 16th-century Danish astronomer Tycho Brahe had once constructed an observatory for Frederick II on Ven, where Brahe had made important observations and developed new astronomical instruments. The location suited af Klint's ambition of bringing humanity onto a higher plane. Yet her spiral temple was not built in her lifetime, or since.

Nor was her work picked up by existing spiritually oriented venues, despite the artist's and her friends' efforts. Noteworthy was an invitation to exhibit in an anthroposophical context at the World Conference on Spiritual Science in London in 1928. A selection of her large format works from "The Paintings for the Temple" traveled to London, but they did not garner much attention. Af Klint gave an introductory talk in Swedish. A neutral comment by the British magazine *Anthroposophy* summed up the paintings as "Rosicrucian symbolism." The mainstream British newspaper *The Times* ignored her in its arts coverage of the multifaceted conference.

By 1928 af Klint was actively preparing for posterity, as well as painting new work. She and Cassel looked through and edited the early notebooks of The Five, a process that continued into the 1930s. The two artists recopied notebooks, omitting parts, exercising control over how they would be seen and understood. On the first page of a 1932 notebook, af Klint drew a symbol or formula: a "+ x" housed in a little box. It looks like the plus sign keeps company with another self, tipped to the side. As she explained in the notebook, she would mark some of her

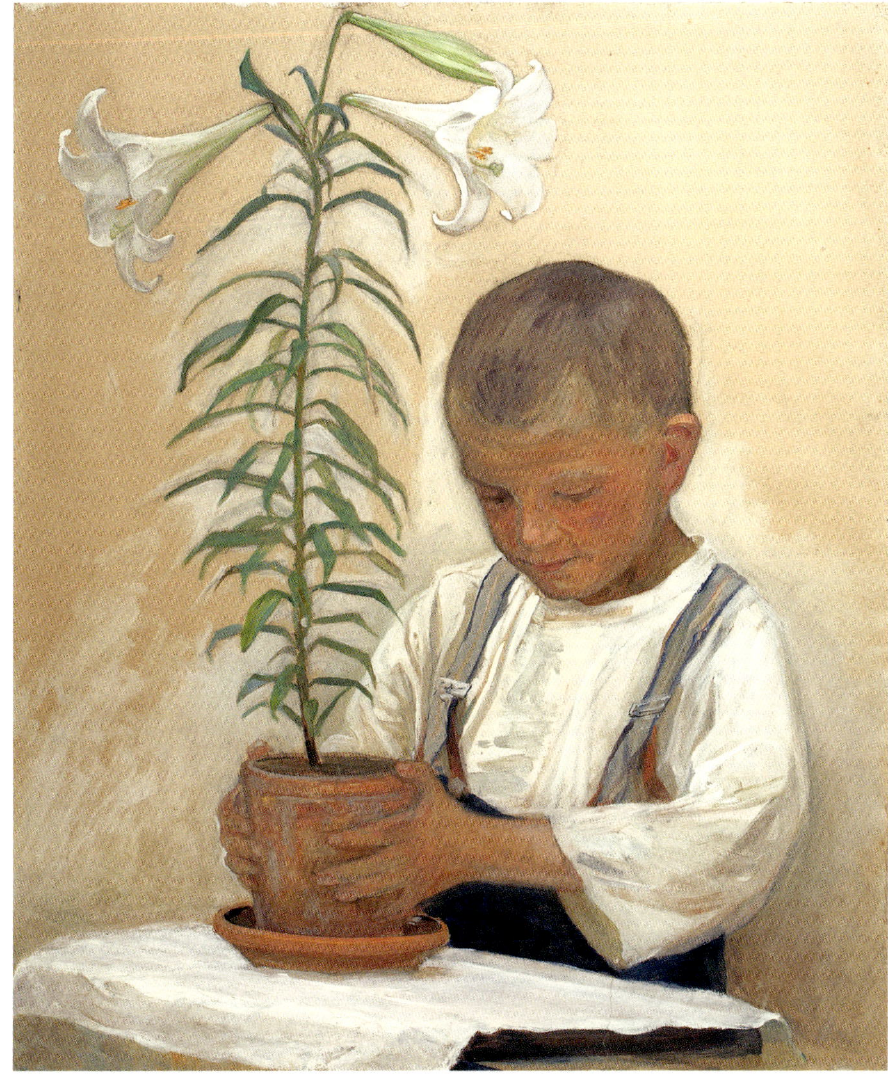

Figure Study: Boy with Flower (Figurstudie, pojke med blomma), n/d
Charcoal and oil on paper,
77 x 63.5 cm (30⅜ x 25 in.)
Stockholm, Hilma af Klint Foundation,
HaK 1429

works with this sign, and those things should not be viewed until 20 years after her death. There is a lack of certainty in the art historical literature about which things could not be viewed. Perhaps af Klint meant only her notebooks were not to be viewed, since "+ x" was written on them, including "The Blue Books." Because "The Blue Books" documented "The Paintings for the Temple," one might conceivably interpret the ban extending to those works, too. It seems she did not mark any paintings directly with the sign.

Anna Cassel died in 1937, followed by af Klint's beloved "force" Thomasine Andersson in 1940. At the end of her life af Klint moved in with her cousin Hedvig in a suburb of Stockholm. In 1943 she rejected a well-meant offer to have her paintings absorbed into the collection of the Protestant Sigtuna Foundation because it was not anthroposophically inclined. Her own death in 1944 following a streetcar accident came just days before her 82nd birthday. In her will, af Klint passed her paintings to the only family member she trusted to be an excellent steward: her nephew Erik af Klint (1901–1981), a naval officer who was initially none too eager to accept the job.

Af Klint's family disregarded her request to be buried with Andersson. To place two unmarried and unrelated females, Hilma and Thomasine, not sisters

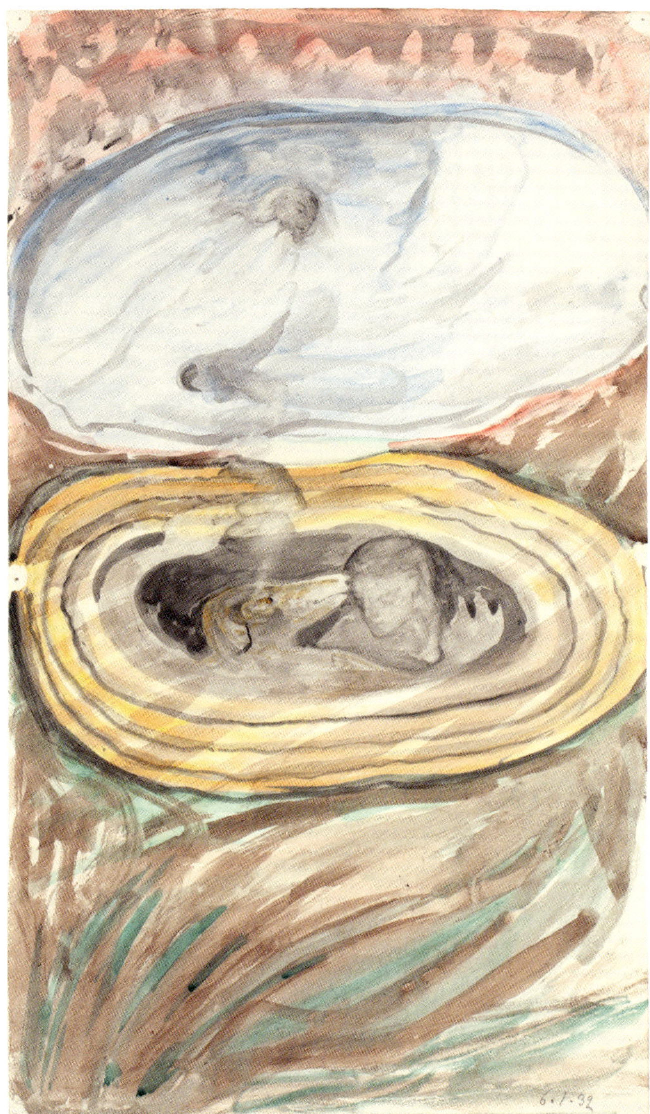

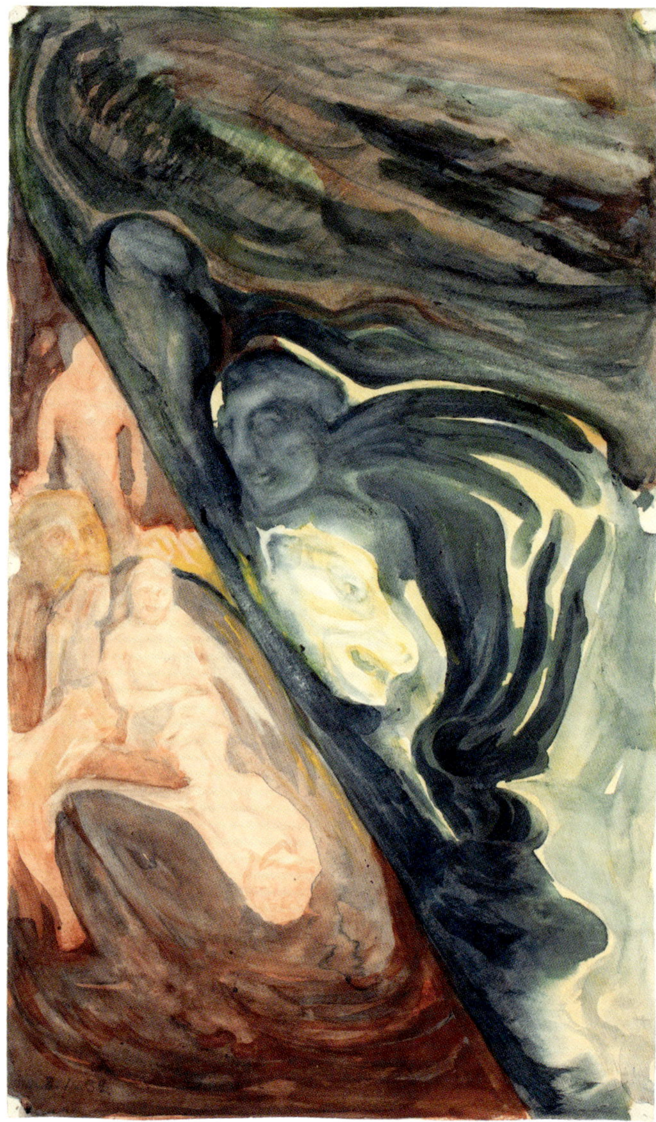

January 6, 1932
Watercolor on paper, 46.5 x 27 cm (18⅜ x 10¾ in.)
Stockholm, Hilma af Klint Foundation, HaK846

January 8, 1932
Watercolor on paper, 46.5 x 27 cm (18⅜ x 10¾ in.)
Stockholm, Hilma af Klint Foundation, HaK847

but partners, in the same grave would have been an acknowledgment of their emotional allegiance to each other and of their gay relationship. Af Klint's cremated remains were laid to rest in the family gravesite, with no individual name marker, like those of her sister Hermina.

Along with af Klint's unexpected death came the surprise that her Munsö house and studio, still full of her paintings, belonged to the Giertta family, whose matriarch, Emilia Giertta, had been the longtime soulmate of Cassel (p. 86). With all the women now dead, the buildings were no longer wanted. The teardown ordered by Giertta's son purged the land of what had been a female creative center. It would take place within three months, and the buildings needed to be cleared. Erik af Klint was in the navy and it was the height of the Second World War, so he was not able to pack up af Klint's paintings. He turned to an artist and fellow anthroposophist, Olof Sandström, who, together with his wife, had recently gotten to know af Klint and experienced her art as a significant spiritual statement. Sandström moved to Munsö and took Hilma af Klint's work down from the studio walls. He created an index of the notebooks, drawings, and works on paper that is still used today. The works were appropriately rolled, protected, crated, and taken to Erik af Klint's house, where they were stored in an attic without climate control until after Erik retired in 1966. He formed a foundation in 1972. The Anthroposophical Society in Stockholm agreed to store the art. Slowly, little by little, curators and art historians were able to see and appreciate af Klint's work.[59]

It took longer than 20 years for her art to be shown to the public: The unknown in the formula of "+ x" turned out to be 42 years. In 1986 an exhibition titled "The Spiritual in Art: Abstract Painting, 1890–1985" opened at the Los Angeles County Museum of Art. In it, af Klint's work was hung next to that of male artists thought to have established abstraction in art, such as Kandinsky, Malevich, and Piet Mondrian. Her unknown work woke people up. Art historian Sixten Ringbom, writing in the exhibition catalogue, thought af Klint was a kind of test case for his findings that Theosophy and esoteric literature had pushed imaginative, inventive artists into using abstract forms, because af Klint had done this on her own, without contact with the mainstream art world.[60]

In *Devachan*, the heaven that Theosophists pictured on the mental plane, a person connects with their invisible inner life as real and perceives the things seen in the outer world as illusory. Hilma af Klint accepted her inner life—that which could not and should not be seen—as the most real part of herself. *Devachan* modeled an unseen world where she could love and survive.

"Where war has torn up plants and killed animals there are empty spaces which could be filled with new figures, if there were sufficient faith in human imagination and the human capacity to develop higher forms."

HILMA AF KLINT, FIRST PAGE, HAK 431

PAGE 90
A Map: Great Britain (En karta: Storbritannien), June 11, 1932
Watercolor and graphite on paper,
70 x 48.5 cm (27⅝ x 19 in.)
Stockholm, Hilma af Klint Foundation, HaK883

PAGE 91
A Map: The Iberian Peninsula (En karta: Iberiska halvön), June 12, 1932
Watercolor and graphite on paper,
70 x 48.5 cm (27⅝ x 19 in.)
Stockholm, Hilma af Klint Foundation, HaK884

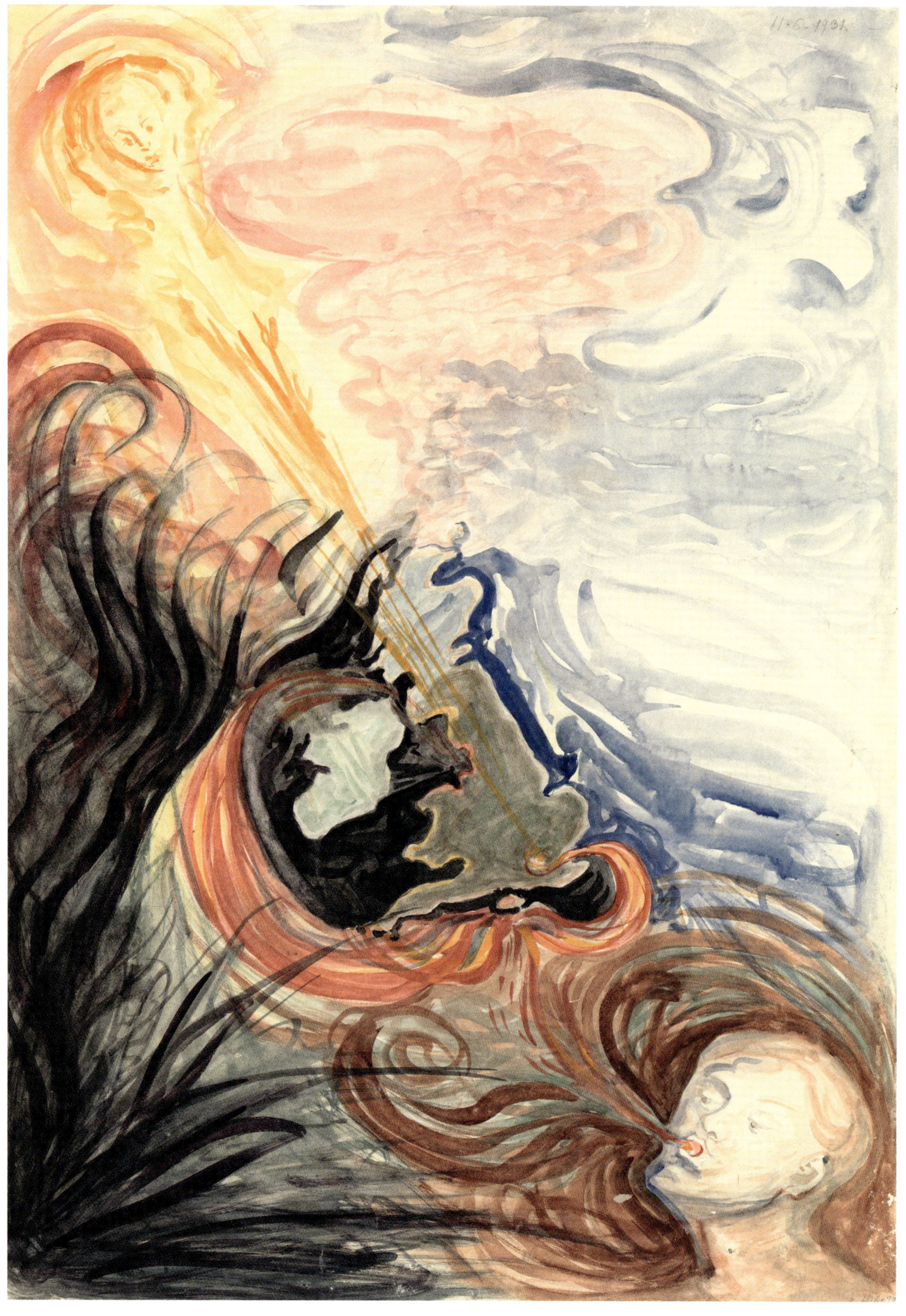

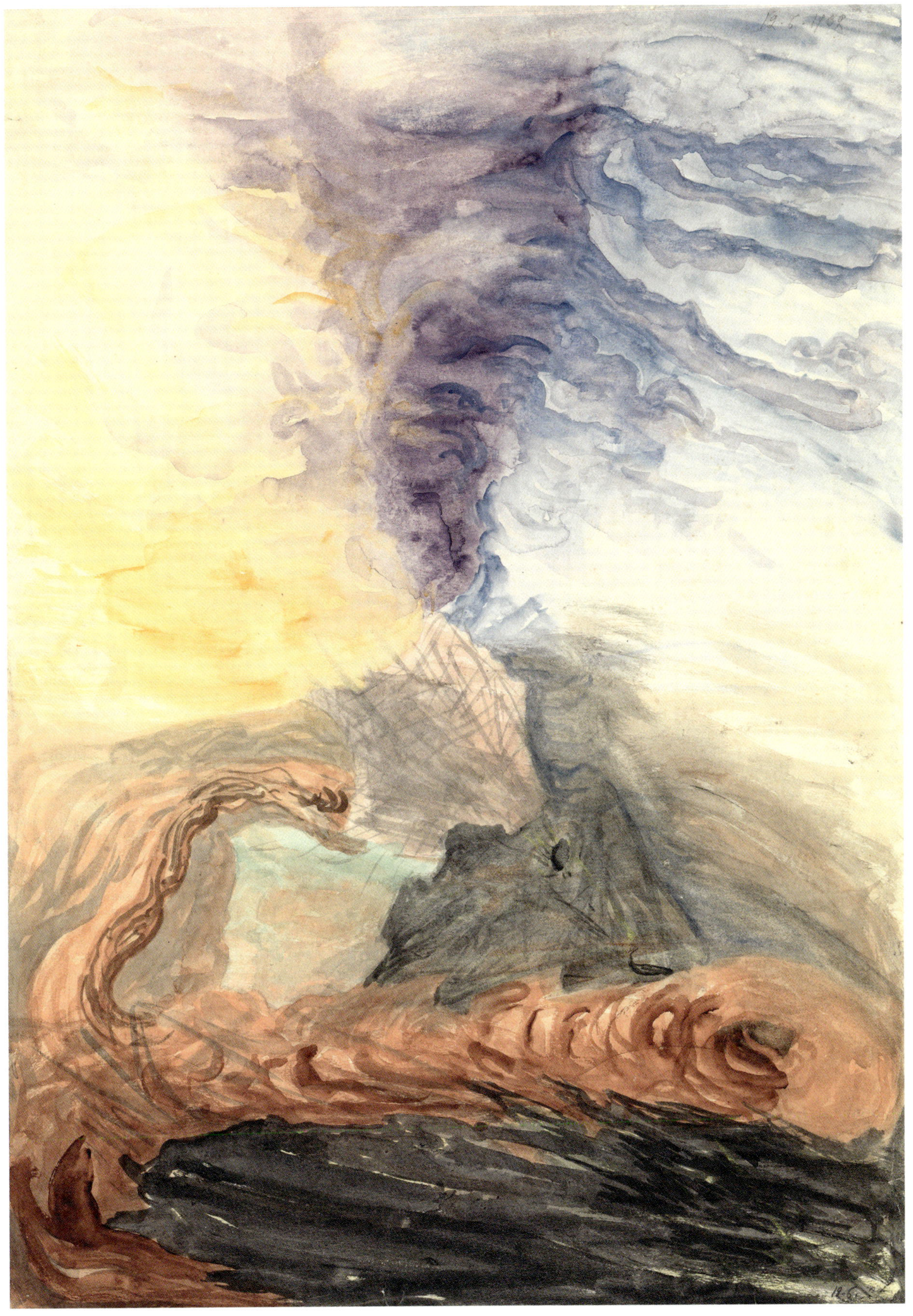

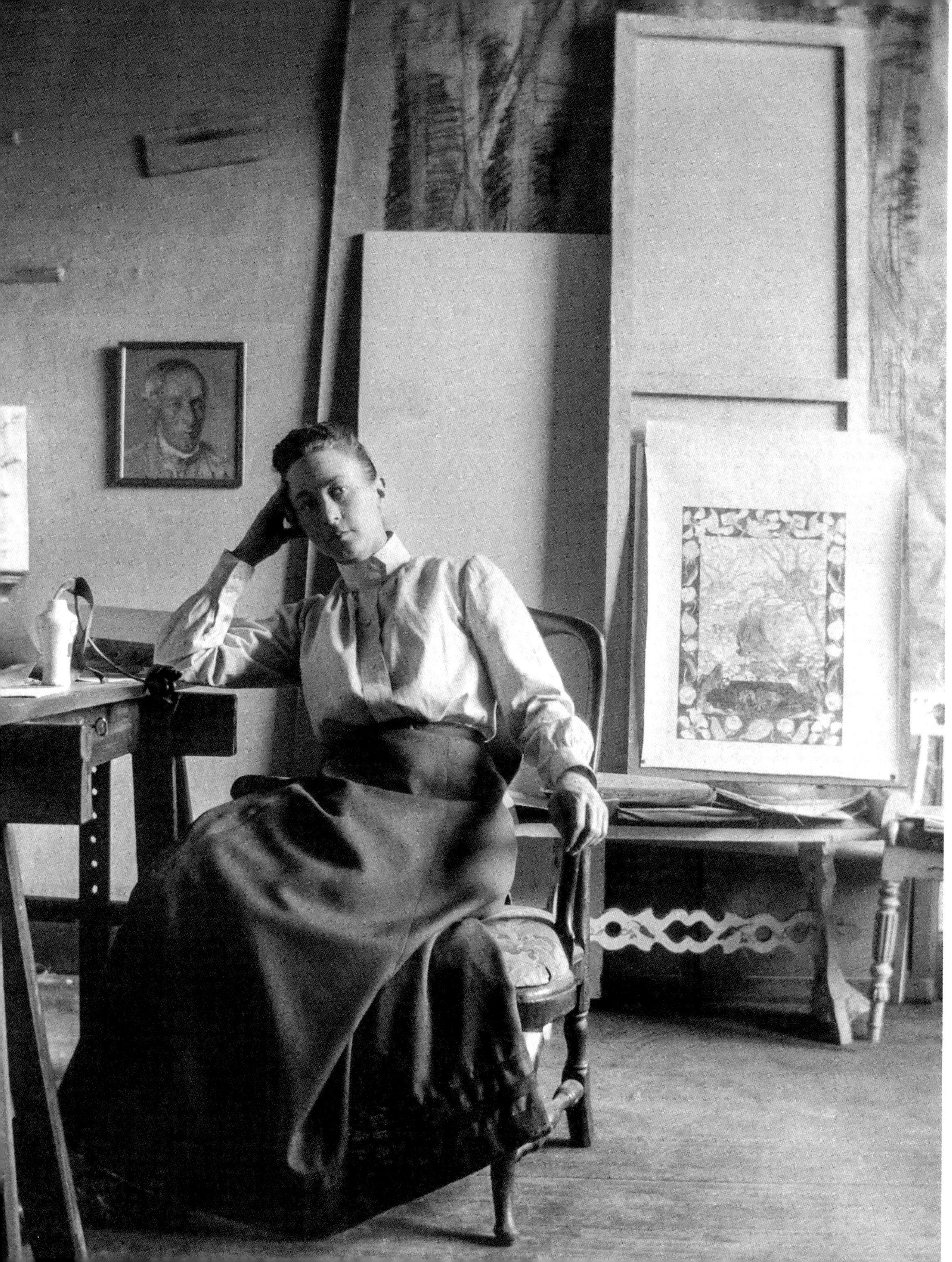

Hilma af Klint
1862–1944
Life and Work

1862 Born October 26 in Karlberg Palace, Solna, near Stockholm, Sweden. Her father, Victor af Klint, directs a military academy for officers in Stockholm. Her mother, Mathilda Sonntag, hailed from Finland.

1879 Completes secondary school. Matriculates at the Technical School (*Tekniska Skolan*) and studies classical portraiture. Meets Anna Cassel who also studies there, and becomes a lifelong friend, lover, and collaborator. Supplements her instruction with additional art classes at Kerstin Cardon's art school. Participates in her first séances, probably known to her through painter, photographer, and spiritualist Bertha Valerius, who receives messages from unseen spirits.

1880 Af Klint's younger sister Hermina dies unexpectedly.

1882–87 Studies at the Royal Academy of Fine Arts, Stockholm, and develops the naturalistic style of painting taught there. Graduates with honors in 1887. Receives a 100-crown award in her final year for working from the human model at the Academy.

1891 Channels spiritual messages herself for the first time. The location of her studio in the 1890s is not known.

1896 Joins the Edelweiss Society, a spiritual group dedicated to simplicity, purity, and love that synthesized Christianity and Judaism with a belief in reincarnation. The group records visions and messages received during mediumistic encounters. During a séance, the spiritual subgroup The Five (De Fem) is founded—members are af Klint, Sigrid Hedman, Anna Cassel, Cornelia Cederberg, and Mathilda Nilsson. The group records meetings in notebooks through text and automatic drawings. These automatic pencil drawings include motifs that would occur in her later work.

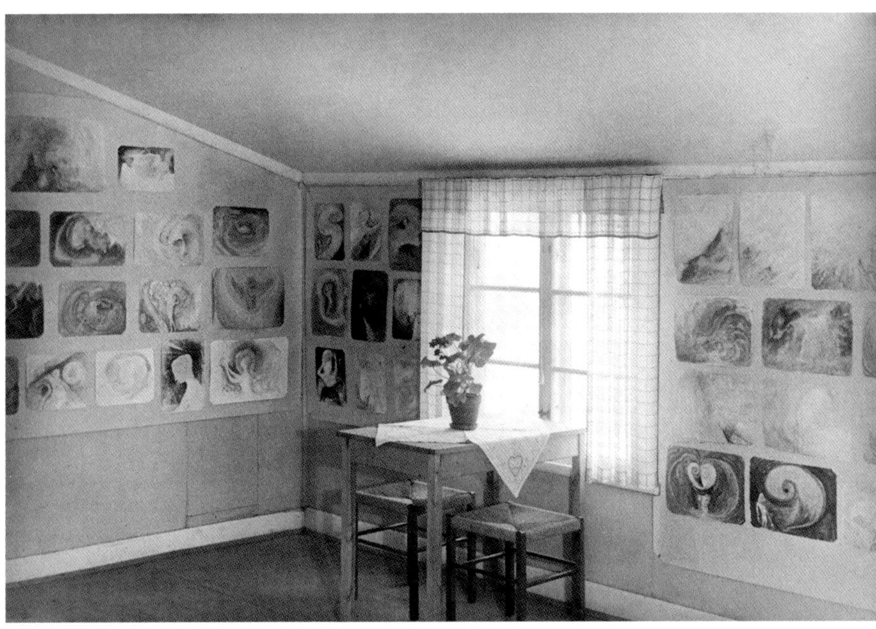

1898 Af Klint's father dies.

1899 Moves to live with her mother at Brahegatan 52, Stockholm.

1900–01 Af Klint and Cassel illustrate a technical book on horse surgery written by John Vennerholm, director of the Veterinary Institute in Stockholm.

1902 Becomes a vegetarian.

1902–08 Rents a shared studio at Hamngatan 9, in Stockholm's arts district. She is included in group exhibitions mostly organized by the Swedish General Art Association. Supports herself in part with paintings of landscapes and commissioned portraits. Travels to Germany, Norway, the Netherlands, Belgium, and Italy.

1904 Senses herself in touch with a spiritual being named Ananda, who predicts she will create "astral paintings" that proclaim a new philosophy of life. Becomes a member of the Theosophical Society.

1906 Receives a message from another spiritual being, Amaliel, who commissions work from her. Begins the first series of "The Paintings for the Temple," known as "The WU/Rose Series, Group 1" or "Primordial Chaos," working together with Anna Cassel.

OPPOSITE
Hilma af Klint in her studio. Stockholm, *c.* 1895

ABOVE
Hilma af Klint's studio at Furuheim. Munsö, *c.* 1931

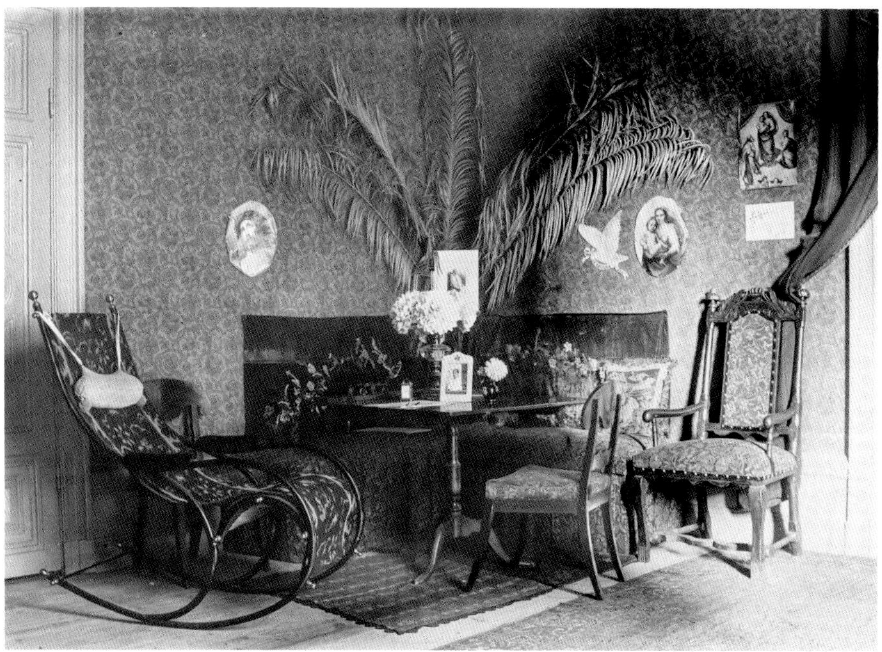

1907 The spiritual commission continues with the series "Eros," "The Large Figure Paintings," and "The Ten Largest." Moves to a new shared studio space in Hamngatan 5, Stockholm, above the popular Blanch's Café and the Swedish General Art Association. Perceiving the sexual references in her work, her studio mates call her new work "unsuitable." Af Klint receives a spiritual message that she will become the leader of The Five.

1908 The Five dissolves as a group. Another constellation of 13 women come together over time. Af Klint continues with "The Paintings for the Temple"; three more series come into being. By April, 111 paintings have been completed. Her mother loses her sight, and af Klint relinquishes her studio. She starts to develop an interest in the writings of Rudolf Steiner.

1908–12 Stops work on "The Paintings for the Temple"; among other duties, she cares for her mother.

1910 In early January, Steiner lectures in Stockholm, and af Klint probably shows him the thus far accomplished "Paintings for the Temple." Joins the Association of Swedish Women Artists, a new organization of about 40 female artists, and becomes their secretary for a year. Executes at least two paid portrait commissions. Continues to paint and draw naturalistically, and submits one painting to a group show in Norrköping, Sweden.

1912 Returns to work on "Paintings for the Temple." Attends a meeting of the Theosopical Society in Norrköping to hear lectures by Steiner. Steiner founds the Anthroposophical Society, having left the Theosophical Society.

1913 Begins to move to a lake house on the island of Munsö in Lake Mälaren. Paints the series "US" and starts on the series "Tree of Knowledge" (finished 1915). Shows 17 spiritual paintings in a theosophical exhibition in Stockholm.

1914–15 Shows a non-spiritual, naturalistic painting in the Baltic Exhibition, Malmö. The First World War breaks out in 1914. In reaction to this, af Klint begins the series "The Swan," then the series "The Dove," followed by "Altarpieces." Now complete, "The Paintings for the Temple" totals 193 artworks.

1916 Wassily Kandinsky exhibits paintings in Stockholm. Af Klint paints her series "Parsifal."

1917 A new studio building on island of Munsö is finished, financed largely by a loan from Cassel. "The Atom" series is started. Af Klint dictates *Studies of the Life of the Soul*, over 2,000 pages about her spiritual beliefs and her ideas about gender fluidity.

1918 The First World War ends. Af Klint moves her mother and her mother's nurse, Thomasine Andersson, to Munsö. Andersson becomes the artist's partner until Andersson's death in 1940.

1919 Creates the "Dornach Nature Studies." Begins her nature study *Flowers, Mosses, Lichens*, with translation into German by Andersson. To effectively present the spiritual paintings to Steiner and others, from 1919 she and Andersson begin work to reproduce "The Paintings for the Temple" in "The Blue Books," which contain accurate watercolor miniatures of the works paired with black-and-white photographs of each painting.

1920 Her mother dies. Creates "Series II" about world religions. First trip to Dornach, Switzerland, together with Andersson, to visit Steiner's Goetheanum. Becomes a member of Steiner's Anthroposophical Society. Over the next 10 years she and Andersson make numerous trips to Dornach.

1920–22 Develops a wet-on-wet watercolor painting style, and uses this almost exclusively thereafter. Studies Goethe's *Theory of Colours* (1810), edited by Steiner.

1922 The Goetheanum burns down while she and Thomasine Andersson are in Dornach.

1924 Writes to Steiner asking where her paintings could be of use. Reports in notes that Steiner advises her not to destroy the paintings.

1925 Steiner dies.

1926 Moves to Uppsala with Andersson and begins editing her old notebooks as well as those of The Five. Anna Cassel helps with the editing.

1927–28 Travels to Amsterdam and London. Concerned with her legacy, she donates her notebook *Flowers, Mosses, Lichens* and her series "Tree of Knowledge" to the newly built Goetheanum in Dornach. Several works from "The Paintings for the Temple" are exhibited in London at the World Conference on Spiritual Science, organized by the English branch of the Anthroposophical Society.

1931 Develops sketches for a spiral-shaped temple structure.

1932 Marks many notebooks with "+ x" to indicate that they cannot be viewed until 20 years after her death. Develops ideas about building "a museum to show what lies behind forces of matter."

1934 Moves to Lund with Andersson.

1937 Speaks at the Anthroposophical Society in Stockholm. Cassel dies.

1938 Af Klimt's nephew Erik af Klint visits her; she shows and explains her works to him in her Munsö studio, including "Paintings for the Temple."

1940 Andersson dies.

1944 Moves in with her cousin Hedvig in a suburb of Stockholm. Dies on October 21 after being hit by a streetcar. Erik af Klint inherits her artwork and notebooks.

ABOVE
Séance room used by The Five, Stockholm, *c.* 1890

Endnotes

1 Biographical facts about Hilma af Klint's life were taken from Åke Fant, *Hilma af Klint: Occult Painter and Abstract Pioneer*, Stockholm 2021, originally published in 1989, and from the first full biography of the artist, Julia Voss, *Hilma af Klint: A Biography*, Chicago 2022. Voss accepts af Klint's transcendental experiences as authentic and sensitively integrates her notebooks with her work.
2 Voss, *Hilma af Klint* as note 1, 26.
3 Ibid., 34.
4 Ibid., 35.
5 Stephen Kern, *Abstraction, Technology, Androgyny, Nihilism*, in: *Hilma af Klint: The Art of Seeing the Invisible*, edited by Louise Belfrage and Kurt Almqvist, Stockholm 2020, 30 ff and 40 ff.
6 Iris Müller-Westermann, *Hilma af Klint in Her Time and Ours*, in: ibid., 158.
7 The city phone directory for Stockholm registered her profession as "artist." Ibid.
8 Voss, *Hilma af Klint* as note 1, 66.
9 Kurt Almqvist and Daniel Birnbaum, *Foreword*, in: *Hilma af Klint: Catalogue Raisonné, Volume I, Spiritualistic Drawings 1896–1905*, edited by Kurt Almquist and Daniel Birnbaum, Stockholm 2021, 7.
10 Voss, *Hilma af Klint* as note 1, 102 ff.
11 See Johan af Klint and Julia Voss, *The Library of Hilma af Klint*, in ibid., 323.
12 Illustrated in *Anna Cassel: The Saga of the Rose*, edited by Kurt Almquist and Daniel Birnbaum, Stockholm 2023, 111 ff.
13 Fant, *Hilma af Klint* as note 1, 23.
14 Hilma af Klint, notebook, 1/1/1906, HaK 555, p8, quoted in: *Hilma af Klint: Notes and Methods*, edited by Christine Burgin, with texts by Iris Müller-Westermann and Johan af Klint, and translations by Kerstin Lind Bonnier, Elizabeth Clark Wessel, and Anne Posten, Chicago 2018, 8. Although written in 1906, the statement is phrased retrospectively, possibly due to the fact that af Klint recopied and edited her notebooks at a later date.
15 Hedvig Martin, *Who Created The Paintings for the Temple?*, in: *Anna Cassel: The Saga of the Rose*, edited by Kurt Almqvist and Daniel Birnbaum, Stockhom 2023, 157–61.
16 Helena P. Blavatsky, *The Secret Doctrine*, London 1893.
17 Cited in Julia Voss, *Hilma af Klint: A Biography*, Chicago 2022, 134.
18 See ibid.
19 Hilma af Klint, notebook unknown to the author. This passage is widely quoted in the literature on af Klint.
20 Hilma af Klint, notebook 431, cited in *Letters and Words Pertaining to Works by Hilma af Klint*, in: *Hilma af Klint: Notes and Methods* as note 1, 246.
21 See *Hilma af Klint: Notes and Methods*, as note 1.
22 HaK 556, 380. Cited in Voss, *Hilma af Klint* as note 7, 148.
23 Helena P. Blavatsky, *Sunrise: Thoughts on Ormuzd and Ahriman*, 1891.
24 The first radio transmission in Stockholm did not take place until 1924, when a high mass from Saint James's Church was transmitted. Radio's first use in Stockholm therefore served a spiritual need.
25 See Voss, *Hilma af Klint* as note 7, 142, 149–50.
26 Ibid., 146.
27 Rudolf Steiner, *Theosophy and Rosicrucianism*, lecture delivered in Kassel, June 16, 1907.
28 This line may also be intended to read as the letter "W." Af Klint attributed eight different possible interpretive meanings to this letter in her glossary of letters and words from her paintings. See *Hilma af Klint: Notes and Methods*, as note 1, 283.
29 For a theosophical discussion of the chakras, see Charles W. Leadbeater, *The Chakras*, Wheaton, 1927. Although first published in 1927, Leadbeater's book reflects previous theosophical publications and a longstanding familiarity with ancient Indian philosophy. In the first chapter, he states that a clairvoyant person perceives the chakra as a saucer-like depression or vortex on the surface of the "etheric double," slightly beyond the outline of the "dense body."
30 See Voss, *Hilma af Klint* as note 7, 152.
31 See ibid., 155.
32 Rudolf Steiner, "The Three Paths of the Soul to Christ," lecture delivered in Stockholm, April 16, 1912.
33 Annie Besant, *Occult Chemistry: A Series of Clairvoyant Observations on the Chemical Elements*, London 1919.
34 See Tracey Bashkoff, *Parallel Visionaries: Hilla Rebay and Hilma af Klint*, in: *Hilma af Klint: Visionary*, Stockholm 2020, 42.
35 See Linda Dalrymple Henderson, *Hilma af Klint and the Invisible in Her Occult and Scientific Context*, in ibid., pp. 71–91, especially 79.
36 Af Klint, text written on the back of *Tree of Knowledge No. 2*, quoted in: Åke Fant, *Hilma af Klint: Occult Painter and Abstract Pioneer*, Stockholm 2021, 64–65.
37 Susan L. Aberth, *At the Theological Crossroads: Hilma af Klint's Tree of Knowledge*, in: *Hilma af Klint: Tree of Knowledge*, New York 2023, 90.
38 Jakob Boehme, preface to *Aurora* (1612).
39 See Voss, Sigrid Lancén notebook, cited in Julia Voss. *Hilma af Klint: A Biography*, Chicago 2022, 190.
40 Ibid., 164, notebook HaK 557, 4, 27.
41 Voss, *Hilma af Klint* as note 9, 194, notebook HaK 1164, 47.
42 Voss, *Hilma af Klint* as note 9, 189–90.
43 Notebook, HaK 1164, 59. See Voss, *Hilma af Klint* as note 9, 191.
44 Voss, *Hilma af Klint* as note 9, 212.
45 William Glassley explains his encounter with af Klint's work in a conversation with her biographer Julia Voss. See *Crystal Visions: Julia Voss and William Glassley in Conversation*, in *Hilma af Klint: Tree of Knowledge* as note 6, 100–07.
46 Ibid.,101–02.
47 Voss, *Hilma af Klint* as note 9, 104.
48 Britt Lundgren, *Action at a Distance. Did Physicist Thomas Young's 1807 Lectures Inspire Some of the Earliest Examples of Abstract Art?, Leonardo* 58, no.2 (2025), 206–13.
49 See Julia Voss. *Hilma af Klint: A Biography*, Chicago 2022, 206.
50 Blaise Cendrars, *La Prose du Transsibérien et de la Petite Jehanne de France,* English translation with French original and art by Sonia Delaunay-Terk.
51 Rudolf Steiner. "Parsifal," lecture delivered in Landin, July 29, 1906.
52 See Briony Fer, *Hilma af Klint: The Outsider Inside Herself*, in: *Hilma af Klint: Seeing is Believing*, Stockholm 2020, 105–13.
53 For Goethe's first illustrative table, see Rupprecht Matthaei, *Goethes Farbenlehre*, Ravensburg 1971, 94.
54 On the financing of the studio, see Voss, *Hilma af Klint* as note 1, 213.
55 The Hilma af Klint Foundation has dedicated an entire volume to *The Blue Blooks* in the catalogue raisoneé of her work. See *Hilma af Klint: Catalogue Raisonné, The Blue Books (1906–1915)*, edited by Kurt Almquist and Daniel Birnbaum, Stockholm 2020.
56 Rudolf Steiner, "Nature and Spirit Beings – Their Effects in our Visible World: Part II, IV. Group Souls of Animals, Plants, and Minerals II," lecture delivered in Heidelberg, February 2, 1908.
57 HaK 579, pp. 84–85, cited in Voss, *Hilma af Klint* as note 1, 227.
58 See *Hilma af Klint, Catalogue Raisonné, Volume 7: Landscapes, Portraits and Miscellaneous Works (1886–1940)*, edited by Kurt Almquist and Daniel Birnbaum, Stockholm 2022, 240 ff.
59 See Voss, *Hilma af Klint* as note 1, 204.
60 Sixten Ringbom, *Überwindung des Sichtbaren: die Generation der Abstrakten Pioniere*, in: *Das Geistige in der Kunst – Abstrakte Malerei 1890–1985*, edited by Maurice Tuchman and Judi Freeman, Urachhaus 1988, p. 144 (German translation of 1986 catalogue).

Photo credits

Works by Hilma af Klint courtesy of the Hilma af Klint Foundation, photos: Moderna Museet, Stockholm. All other photos: Crouch Rare Books, London: 11; © Photo R.M.N. Musée d'Orsay, Paris: 17; The National Gallery of Art, Washington, D.C.: 75; The Museum of Modern Art, New York/Scala, Florence: 84.

The author

Janis Mink studied art history at Smith College and the University of Hamburg. She works as an adjunct professor, writer, and curator.

FRONT COVER
The Swan, The SUW Series, Group IX, Part I: No. 12, 1915
Oil on canvas, 151.5 x 151 cm (59¾ x 59½ in.)
Stockholm, Hilma af Klint Foundation, HaK 160

PAGE 2
Hilma af Klint, *c.* 1910.

PAGE 4
The Dove, The UW Series, Group IX, Part II: No. 2, 1915
Oil on canvas, 155.5 x 115.5 cm (61¼ x 45½ in.)
Stockholm, Hilma af Klint Foundation, HaK 174

BACK COVER
Hilma af Klint in her studio. Stockholm, *c.* 1895

Imprint

EACH AND EVERY TASCHEN BOOK PLANTS A SEED!
Each year, we offset our annual carbon emissions with carbon credits at the Instituto Terra, a reforestation program in Minas Gerais, Brazil, founded by Lélia and Sebastião Salgado. To find out more about this ecological partnership, please check: www.taschen.com/institutoterra.
Inspiration: unlimited.
Carbon footprint: (almost) zero.

Want to see more? Visit taschen.com to view our current publications, browse our latest magazine, and subscribe to our newsletter.

Hohenzollernring 53, D–50672 Köln
www.taschen.com

Project Editor: Claire Brandon, Madrid
Design: Andy Disl, Los Angeles;
Merrit Schomakers, Cologne
Production: Marion Boschka, Cologne

Printed in Bosnia-Herzegovina
ISBN 978-3-8365-9903-0